THE HANSARD SOCIETY SERIES
IN PARLIAMENTARY GOVERNMENT

Volume V

POLITICAL PARTIES AND THE PARTY SYSTEM IN BRITAIN

A Symposium
edited by
SYDNEY D. BAILEY

Frederick A. Praeger
NEW YORK

First published in the United States of America
in 1952 by Frederick A. Praeger, Inc., Publishers,
105 West 40th Street, New York 18, N.Y.

Published in London by the Hansard Society, a
non-party, non-profit educational service for
promoting knowledge of and interest in parliamentary government.

All rights reserved

Library of Congress Catalog Card Number 52-7494

BOOKS THAT MATTER

PRINTED IN GREAT BRITAIN BY
CHISWICK PRESS, NEW SOUTHGATE, LONDON, N.11

CONTENTS

	Page
INTRODUCTION by Sydney D. Bailey	v

i. THE EVOLUTION OF PARTIES AND THE PARTY SYSTEM

BEFORE 1600 by S. B. Chrimes	1
THE SEVENTEENTH CENTURY by Hugh Ross Williamson	13
THE EIGHTEENTH CENTURY by Professor W. L. Burn	18
THE NINETEENTH CENTURY by Professor John A. Hawgood	26
THE TWENTIETH CENTURY by D. C. Somervell	35

ii. THE PARTIES

THE CONSERVATIVE PARTY

HISTORY by Sir Charles Petrie, Bt.	42
PHILOSOPHY AND PRINCIPLES by Kenneth Pickthorn, M.P.	49

THE LABOUR PARTY

HISTORY by Professor G. D. H. Cole	59
PHILOSOPHY AND PRINCIPLES by Francis Williams	70

THE LIBERAL PARTY

HISTORY by the Rt. Hon. Sir Henry Slesser	77
PHILOSOPHY AND PRINCIPLES by Dingle Foot	85

THE MINOR PARTIES
    Anon 92

THE INDEPENDENT IN POLITICS
    By Stephen King-Hall 101

iii. SOME PROBLEMS OF THE PARTY SYSTEM

PARTY ORGANIZATION
    By R. T. McKenzie 114

A NOTE ON PARTY FINANCE
    By R. T. McKenzie 134

THE FORMULATION OF PARTY POLICY
    By H. G. Nicholas 140

PARTIES AND THE PEOPLE'S MANDATE
    By Cecil S. Emden 152

THE PERSONNEL OF THE PARTIES
    By J. F. S. Ross 168

THE PARTY SYSTEM IN LOCAL GOVERNMENT
    By J. H. Warren 177

REFLECTIONS ON THE PARTY SYSTEM
    By Sir Ernest Barker 193

THE BRITISH PARTY SYSTEM: A SELECT BIBLIOGRAPHY
    Compiled by Sydney D. Bailey 203

INDEX 208

INTRODUCTION

THIS book describes the evolution of the British party system, discusses the basic philosophy and political principles of the three main parties, and examines some of the problems to which the system gives rise.

The party system is often praised, occasionally denounced, but rarely described or explained. Yet Disraeli declared that without party, parliamentary government is impossible. Nevertheless there are those in our own day, as there were in Disraeli's, who assert that the party system is unnecessary and even dangerous.

What is the case against the party system? Four different arguments may be used, though they cannot all be valid.

1. That the division of the nation into two nearly equal parts makes stable government impossible because each general election is likely to produce a change of government.

2. That the plight of the nation is such that salvation can only be found in remedies so unpalatable that no party alone could advocate them without courting disaster at the polls.

3. That there are no real differences between the parties; that the British parties are, as an eminent journalist described American parties to Bryce, identical bottles with different labels denoting the liquid inside, all empty; that the party system divides the nation when the nation ought to be—and but for the machinations of party bureaucrats would soon become—united.

4. That the differences between the parties are comparatively insignificant; that the country would be best governed if the best men, irrespective of party, sank their differences and united for the general good.

The first argument is comparatively new; it applied especially to the conditions which existed after the general elections of 1950 and 1951. Small majorities are not new to British political life, but in the days when an adverse vote in the House of Commons did not necessarily cause the downfall of the Government, a bare majority in the Commons—or even a minority—was no barrier to effective and stable government. But today, with virtually universal suffrage, with general acceptance of the idea that a Government which is defeated in the House of Commons on an issue of major importance should resign, and with the increasingly rigid organization of parties, the fact that nine out of ten voters support (in almost equal proportions) the two major parties creates new problems. The introduction of proportional representation might provide a partial remedy by reducing the representation of the major parties in the House of Commons, but, for whatever reason, public opinion does not at the moment favour any change in the method of voting. It is, in any case, doubtful whether proportional representation would necessarily provide a more stable system than exists at present, since a multi-party system is no guarantee of stability. The average life of French Governments since the war has been about four months.[1]

It is, moreover, open to question whether continuity of administration[2] is essential. Ministers carry a heavy load of responsibility and often have too much work to do. They are so busy taking decisions that they have little time in which to think. A spell of Opposition gives a man the opportunity of seeing the tasks of government in perspective. And it should not be forgotten how greatly our literature has been enriched by the writings of politicians during enforced leisure between periods of office.

The second argument—that no party alone dare admit that the nation is in indifferent health, or prescribe the remedies needed—is also comparatively new, though it may persist for some time to come. This is not the place to discuss current economic and social problems, but it is proper to record that there is nothing in the party system *per se* which prevents a party from advocating unpopular measures. And it should be added that a party leader who conceals from the nation its true plight does not escape judgment at the bar of

[1] The case for proportional representation is not, of course, that it guarantees stability of government.

[2] Continuity of administration is to be distinguished from continuity of policy; in the field of foreign affairs, for example, the latter is usually regarded as desirable.

history: the circumstances of Stanley Baldwin's "appalling frankness" (page 166) will be remembered long after the positive achievements of the Baldwin Government are forgotten.

The third argument is that there are no essential differences between the parties. This is denied, at least in public, by the leaders of the three main parties but finds favour among a respectable body of enlightened opinion and (though for different reasons) in Marxist circles. Is it true that there are no essential differences between the parties? It is not for the Hansard Society to try to answer the question. This book, and especially Section II, provides certain data which may help the reader to reach a conclusion.

The fourth argument is that though there are differences, they are unimportant, and that it is the patriotic duty of the parties to moderate their programmes in a search for unanimity. Lord Elton put this point of view forcibly in an important debate in the House of Lords in 1950. He argued that there was "a great solid mass of central opinion" which could agree on a short-term political programme. This argument is not a plea for the merging of parties; it apparently rests on the assumption that multi-party co-operation, such as characterizes the French Republic, for example, is preferable to single-party government, such as there has been in the United Kingdom since 1945. The validity of this argument can only be judged against the background of British history; when were parties first formed, what functions were they intended to exercise, and why were they first defended?

* * *

Political parties in Britain were first defended by Edmund Burke. "Party", he wrote, "is a body of men united, for promoting by their joint endeavours the national interest, upon some particular principle in which they are all agreed." Before Burke's time it was fashionable to denounce such arrangements as subversive. So long as government was the task of the king and his friends at court, to be opposed to the acts of the government was to be opposed to the king, and it was no doubt difficult to distinguish between the king as a person and the monarchy as an institution. This attitude reached its logical conclusion in the Civil War. The majority of the parliamentary leaders did not see how they could oppose Charles I without opposing the monarchical system;

so having beheaded Charles, they abolished kingship, declaring it to be "unnecessary, burdensome, and dangerous".

The events of the succeeding decades showed that it is individuals rather than offices that are potentially dangerous. And the accidental circumstances attendant on the fact that a German Elector became King of England in 1714 led to the transformation of the executive government from a heterogeneous body of office-holders dependent on royal favour into a homogeneous committee dependent on parliamentary support. The discovery that the king could reign without ruling, that government could be carried on in the king's name and yet be responsive to the sentiments of the nation's assembly, made it possible for men to criticize the acts of the government of the day without criticizing the institutions of government.

For half a century after the accession of George I in 1714 the Whigs consolidated their hold on the machinery of government. They used methods which in our day would be considered corrupt. Many men bought their way into Parliament[1]; those who could not afford to purchase or rent a seat sought the sponsorship of some territorial magnate. Palmerston was first elected to the House of Commons for the pocket borough of Newport whose owner, Sir Leonard Holmes, had stipulated that the candidate should "never, even for the election, set foot in the place." Dr. T. H. B. Oldfield, writing in 1816, estimated that of 658 Members of Parliament, 487 were returned by nomination of patrons and only 171 represented independent constituencies.

Because getting elected to Parliament was an expensive business, Members sought sinecures, pensions, and other means of meeting their expenses from public funds. Horace Walpole writes that in 1762 "a shop was publicly opened at the Pay Office, whither the members flocked, and received

---

[1] Governor Thomas Pitt, whose high-minded advice to his son is quoted on page 108, owned the pocket borough of Old Sarum where, at the beginning of the nineteenth century, seven electors returned two Members to Westminster. The story behind the acquisition of Old Sarum by the Pitt family is of some interest. Thomas Pitt, an East India merchant, acquired a large diamond in Madras in 1701 for £16,000. This diamond he smuggled home, and in 1717 sold it to the Regent of France for £135,000. With the proceeds of the transaction he purchased Old Sarum which thereafter returned to the House of Commons a succession of Pitts—among them the first Earl of Chatham.

the wages of their venality in bank bills ... £25,000 as Martin, Secretary of the Treasury, afterwards owned, were issued in one morning."

The Tories denounced this elaborate system of rewards. It was partly, no doubt, that some of them disliked corruption as such; but there were many whose objection sprang from their disappointment at being excluded from the fruits of the system. Moreover, the idea of organized opposition to the government of the day was becoming less disreputable, and by 1770 it only needed a Burke to defend what the Tories had been doing for a generation or more.

Burke argued that to combine to capture the government was not subversive or dishonourable. "When bad men combine, the good must associate; else they will fall, one by one, an unpitied sacrifice...." It was no good, wrote Burke, for those who controlled the machinery of government to claim that they were the only loyal subjects of the king. Their conduct was just as much a conspiracy as was the conduct of their rivals. It was perfectly legitimate, thought Burke, for political parties to compete within the parliamentary arena for the control of the king's government.

It was not a great step to the idea that those who opposed the government in power performed a useful function. John Cam Hobhouse's casual use of the phrase "His Majesty's Opposition" during an unimportant debate in 1826 created a happy tradition.

A new problem arose with the passing of the Reform Acts of the nineteenth century. The electorate increased tenfold: politics had once been primarily a matter for the well-born and the well-to-do, but after 1832 hundreds of thousands of working-men received the privilege of voting. Many of them no doubt followed the practice of the Honiton elector who told Lord Cochrane that he always voted for "Mr. Most". But the growth of the electorate made bribery more expensive. Moreover, bribery itself was deplored by enlightened opinion and made difficult by a series of legislative enactments.

The nation-wide organization of political parties during the last third of the nineteenth century can be seen as a respectable successor to the older system of bribing voters. Formerly the candidate had sought the suffrage of a small electorate by offering to those who voted for him immediate and tangible evidence of his gratitude; now he had to create a local organization to advocate a political programme which, he hoped, would attract more electors than any rival programme. The new system demanded that Members of Parliament should do more than act as the nation's watch-dogs. The struggle to capture the king's government was no longer fought at Westminster alone but also in the constituencies. Thus began the transition to what Commander King-Hall refers to as "belly politics" (page 113).

The result has been that electors have become less and less interested in the personality of the candidate and more and more interested in the programme of the party. The parties have become more highly organized and more strictly disciplined, and dissent may now be punished by expulsion. Burke's definition of party as a body of men promoting the national interest upon some agreed principle is nicely phrased; but it would, perhaps, be truer to say that party is a body of men seeking to capture the queen's government. Burke, indeed, says as much in another place. The first principle of party, he writes, is "to put the men who hold their opinions into such a condition as may enable them to carry their common plans into execution. . . ."

D. C. Somervell and Sir Ernest Barker liken the party system to a game (pages 38 and 197), and D. C. Somervell suggests that this is what makes politics attractive and interesting.[1] Walter Bagehot defended the idea of constitutional monarchy for the same reason. But party politics can only be interesting so long as the players abide by the rules and trust the umpires. If the stronger side changed the rules to suit their own convenience and replaced the umpires with their own partisans, the game would become dull.

One party in the House of Commons—the Irish Nationalists—decided that their grievances would never be satisfied if they played the game according to the recognized rules. They therefore tried to prevent the game being played at all, and the rest of the players were driven to changing the rules. Even though the changes would probably have come in any case, they can hardly be said to have advanced the cause of Irish Nationalism. It is, moreover, instructive to note how difficult it is to advance sectional interests in the parliamentary arena.

[1] It is not without significance that Members of Parliament refer to their own party as "our side" and their opponents as "the other side".

Burke defines party as a body of men promoting the national interest. When he stood for election in Bristol in 1774, he emphasized that a Member of Parliament does not represent local purposes or prejudices but the general good of the whole nation. The trouble is that those who advocate local purposes or prejudices usually convince themselves that they are acting in the national interests. Indeed, many people believe that their own party invariably acts in the national interests whereas their opponents wish to divide the nation by partisan measures. This raises a difficult problem. There comes a point when opposition degenerates into faction. George Tierney used to say that the duty of an Opposition is to oppose. But Opposition, to be effective, must be kept within bounds. An Opposition usually thinks of itself as the next government, and a wise Opposition keeps its activities within those limits which it hopes its own opponents will respect when the tables are turned.

Is it true that the party system is unnatural and artificial, that the national interests would be well served if the best men, irrespective of party, united to form the government? In the course of the debate on this subject in the House of Lords in 1950, Lord Samuel said that to adopt this idea "would mean the withdrawal of the Government from the control of the electorate". If there were no competing parties, he said, differences of opinion would be settled by secret bargaining rather than by open debate. "These systems degenerate into struggles between personalities. There are no stable, recognized policies resting on definite principles." Disraeli made much the same point in his Manchester speech in 1872. "I look upon parliamentary government as the noblest government in the world, and certainly as the one most suited to England. But without the discipline of political connection, animated by the principle of private honour, I feel certain that a popular assembly would sink before the power or the corruption of a Minister."

The fact is that in a democratic society, opposition is constantly generated. D. C. Somervell shows (page 41) how the National Government formed in 1931 soon collected an Opposition and was so little "National" in 1940 that a National Government under Mr. Churchill had to be formed to replace it; and the author of the article on the Minor Parties suggests that the need to criticize the war policy of

Mr. Churchill's National Government led in its turn to the formation of the Common Wealth Party. Opposition will either be expressed openly and constitutionally or secretly and subversively. The purpose of "Her Majesty's Opposition" is to provide a channel of discontent which is respectable.

Furthermore, opposition and criticism keep the political Ministers and, what is perhaps as important, the officials whose activities they direct, on their toes. The tendency of power to corrupt is balanced by the checks of informed and responsible criticism.

Criticism is good for a government; it is also good for an Opposition. A major weakness of the form of colonial government in which the official members are in a majority in the Executive and unofficial members in a majority in the Legislature is that the unofficial members have the opportunity of criticizing without the responsibility of governing. Criticism is likely to be useful if it comes from those who may be called upon to translate their criticisms into action; and a party which is in the wilderness too long tends to criticize irresponsibly.

In the final analysis the party system is inevitable in a democratic society because men disagree about political objectives and political methods. The system has developed and changed in response to new ideas about how men may govern themselves. The system is not fixed and static. It will no doubt continue to change as men discover more about the art and science of government. Parties, like other human institutions, are no better and no worse than the men and women who compose them. There is nothing sacred or immutable about the system. It is merely a convenient device to enable the majority to have their way and the minority to have their say. The secret of making the system work is to know when to put it into cold storage.

* * *

It should be emphasized that the authors alone are responsible for the papers in this book: the Hansard Society is a non-party organization and expresses no opinion on matters of political controversy.

SYDNEY D. BAILEY.

1 March, 1952

THE EVOLUTION OF PARTIES AND THE PARTY SYSTEM

I. Before 1600 by S. B. Chrimes.
II. The Seventeenth Century by Hugh Ross Williamson.
III. The Eighteenth Century by Professor W. L. Burn.
IV. The Nineteenth Century by Professor John A. Hawgood.
V. The Twentieth Century by D. C. Somervell.

I. BEFORE 1600
by S. B. Chrimes

PARTIES within the State existed long before Parliament in the modern sense had come into being, but they were not political parties as we understand them; they were not organized groups of politicians contending with each other for the power and spoils of office, proclaiming rival policies and programmes and appealing for the votes of a democratic electorate. None of these things existed until quite modern or even recent times. Nevertheless the struggles for power in the later mediaeval and early modern era were real, and at times violent, and sometimes resulted in a genuine shift of the balance of political power, and were necessary preludes to more modern developments.

All such struggles were conducted by a faction, or a group, or in some instances perhaps by something like a "party", the members of which were temporarily held together by family ties, by calculation of interests and the spurs of ambition, rather than by any close adherence to a particular set of political ideas or even political programmes, although such common bonds were by no means absent as early as the middle of the thirteenth century. The essential characteristic of all such associations was opposition to the king's government, manifested in one way or another, carried to one degree or another, and usually with some specific objective or another in view. The "parties" to all such struggles, in short, were the king and his officials and supporters—the "court party"—on the one hand, and a group of lay and often also ecclesiastical magnates—a "baronial" opposition—on the other. The purpose of all such oppositions was to influence the policy of the king's government, usually with a view to procuring some specific reforms in law or government, especially local government, regarded either as indispensable to the interests of the opponents themselves or of the social classes to which they belonged, or more vaguely to the interest of the community of the realm in general. Sometimes the opposition would go so far as to usurp to itself the executive power of the king and in effect "to put the kingship into commission" without however at any time (before 1649) purposing to abolish the monarchy as such. Baronial oppositions of this kind were manifested from time to time in the period of which we are speaking—several times before the days of representative Parliaments. But although, as we shall see, the Commons played some part in these occasions of political crisis from the latter years of the fourteenth century, the initiative was not theirs much before the seventeenth century, and until the sixteenth century their part was seldom much more than that of pawns in the contests between Crown and magnates, except perhaps on occasions when the Crown itself was in especial need of financial aid, and was prepared to purchase it by paying heed to proposals that might be put forward by the Commons in parliament. The oppositions of which we need to take account in this period were not primarily parliamentary in character, and indeed could not have been. For the representative parliaments were not in origin any more than royal expedients to assist in government at such times and for such purposes as suited the Crown; they were comparatively infrequent and invariably of short duration, dependent for summons and dissolution entirely upon the Crown's discretion. Parliaments of this sort could not readily become the breeding ground of sustained opposition, and although important precedents were set and some successes gained by the Commons in the parliaments of the fourteenth and fifteenth centuries, they were no more than precedents or ephemeral successes. The struggles, as we have said, were essentially between the king and magnates, leading to substantial baronial gains in the late fourteenth and the fifteenth centuries, but ending, and finally so far as baronial opposition was concerned, with the resounding triumph of the monarchy under the Tudors in the sixteenth century.

It is not possible to understand why these things should have been so, unless we firmly grasp the fact that, from time immemorial, what we call "executive power" was wholly vested in the king, and the king alone. Fundamentally, the whole of our constitutional history consists in the eventual modification of this principle, first by the participation of other persons or bodies in the exercise of executive power, later by its transference away from the king himself to Ministers who at first were wholly responsible to him alone, but who later became responsible to others than the king himself, whether Parliament or the electorate. Today executive power remains legally vested in the Crown, but its exercise in practice is almost wholly confined to the Ministers of the Crown, who are legally responsible for their actions according to law, and politically responsible through parliament to the electorate.

When William the Conqueror in 1066 acquired the kingdom of England, he inherited the traditions and usages of the Anglo-Saxon kingship built up and enshrined in the custom of five hundred years. The Anglo-Saxon kings, imbued with the moral duties of defending the people and of enforcing the law which was the custom of the people, were the sole repositories of what we call executive power. The administrative agents and agencies which they created, mostly out of the domestic officers and organs of their own household, comprised all that there was in the way of central government. By custom they acted often with the advice of the "wise men", whose sanction gave weight and an element of national assent to their decisions in major affairs, but they themselves alone possessed executive power, the due and proper exercise of which was their moral duty and legal prerogative.

The monarchy of the Normans was a continuation of the Anglo-Saxon, with the addition of the principles, rights and duties implicit in the overlordship of a feudalized Society. After the Conquest, and for several hundred years thereafter, the monarchs were in a dual position; they were national kings as inheritors of the Anglo-Saxon traditions, and also heads of the feudal hierarchy. Apart from the resistance, passive or otherwise, of the natives, the opposition which the Normans met was feudal rather than political—contention over questions of feudal rights rather than over the exercise of executive powers, and as such, outside the scope of the present discussion. But all through the Norman period (except perhaps for the reign of Stephen) and above all in the time of the first Angevin, Henry II, the monarchy was steadily developing its agencies and instruments of administration, and building up the means for more effective and indeed more ruthless and efficient exercise of executive power, with a consequential expansion of the reality of royal government. The abuses to which a more powerful central administration could lend itself were the principal internal cause of the baronial rebellion under King John which led to the wresting from him of *Magna Carta* in 1215. In a sense, no doubt, the barons of Runnymede constituted "an opposition party". But at best they were a minority party whom military circumstances for the moment favoured; their aims were largely, though by no means exclusively, feudal in character, and legalistic not political in their bearings. They aimed at imposing a number of definitions of legal rights upon the king, and only in the specified respects did they propose to limit his discretion. The "Committee" of twenty-five barons set up was merely to coerce the king, if need be, and to compel him to uphold the terms of the Charter, not to deprive him of executive power, which remained legally as free as it had ever been by custom, except in the specified respects.

The long minority of Henry III (1216-1232) gave the

baronage an experience of responsibility for the carrying on of the government which undoubtedly was to be of great importance for the future. In effect and in modern terms, the "opposition became the government" for a number of years, and it is probably true to say that the conception of government was never to be quite the same again as it had been in the past. Henry III, when he assumed the prerogatives of the Crown, could and did fully revive the Angevin conception of royal government, and he himself exercised the executive powers of the Crown, and re-invigorated all the administrative agencies based partly on the household and partly on organizations that had grown out of it. But after some years he was confronted with a genuine and formidable political opposition which forced him for a time to modify radically the governmental scheme, and indeed to comply with demands which, in effect though not in theory, involved the transference of executive powers to a baronial council and administrative officers responsible to it. The Provisions of Oxford of 1258 resulted for a few years in a régime in which the supreme executive rested not in the king's court, but in a baronial council of fifteen, and a régime in which the king reigned while the council ruled. It remains uncertain whether the baronage envisaged this arrangement as possibly permanent or only as temporary, but during the eighteen months during which it lasted, it was certainly a radical, even a revolutionary, expedient, and in some ways perhaps represented the high-water mark of mediaeval opposition to the Crown, and is curiously anticipatory of far more modern developments. But it did not, and in the general prevailing circumstances and ideas, probably could not, last. The imposition by force of arms of a similar régime by Simon de Montfort and his supporters a few years later soon ended with military defeat, and before the end of his long and eventful reign, Henry III was once more fully restored to the free exercise of his prerogatives and executive power, and to such freedom Edward I succeeded in 1272. The immense resilience of the monarchy's administrative machinery, the ancient traditions and firmly rooted conception of the monarchical principle, were all too strong to yield more than temporarily to the baronial opposition, which indeed showed no sign of seeking to supersede the monarchy as such. With the succession to the monarchy of so able and masterful a personality as Edward I, no more was heard for the time being of baronial councils or of attempts to usurp executive powers.

Opposition to some aspects of Edward I's government, however, arose and was directed not to the form of the government but to its financial exactions. The grave embarrassment confronting Edward I in financing his strenuous military undertakings in Scotland, Wales, and France, led him to arbitrary and high-handed methods of raising money which evoked demands for the confirmation of the Charters in 1297, and involved the imposition of some additional legal restrictions on the Crown in the fiscal sphere. Finance was to prove ultimately to be the Achilles heel of the mediaeval monarchy, and in the long run—in the seventeenth century—was to be the means whereby the opposition—by then the Commons in parliament—was to force modifications in the monarchical principle.

It was not however until a few years after the accession of Edward II that the Crown was forced to accept for a second time the ministrations of a baronial council acting in its name. It was a council to make ordinances for reform, and its participants are consequently known as the Lords Ordainers; and of the many ordinances promulgated by them in 1311 and the following years, the most important sought to procure the appointment of the principal administrative officers by advice and assent of the baronage and *in* (not of course *by*) parliament, and to procure the removal of "evil" councillors from the king's entourage. The opposition to the Crown put forward by the Lords Ordainers was formidable, and the support it received from the enormously powerful but not very astute Thomas, Earl of Lancaster, and his adherents, has given rise to the conception of a "Lancastrian party" and of a Lancastrian "programme". There is some justification for these conceptions, provided they are understood with the mediaeval limitations. The later dukes of Lancaster, John of Gaunt, the son of Edward III, and his son Henry Bolingbroke, were not indeed descendants of Thomas, but in so far as we can legitimately speak of a "Lancastrian" party in late mediaeval politics, it means the baronial party which sought, from time to time, to share in the exercise of the royal executive power by procuring an effective participation in the king's council. But the failure of the Lords Ordainers in their struggle to maintain themselves against Edward II, and the resources of the court and its adherents showed that this objective could not be secured without the goodwill or at least acquiescence of the king himself. In his hour of triumph, Edward II was able to procure what was in effect, and indeed in intention, a statutory declaration that it was illegal to impose restrictions on the free exercise of the royal prerogatives except by an act made by the king himself and with the assent of the magnates and the commons in parliament (Statute of York, 1322). The deposition of Edward II in 1327 was the result merely of faction, and not the consequence of a "baronial opposition".

When in due course Edward III was in a position to exercise the royal powers, the form of government remained substantially the same as it had been at the end of Edward II's reign, with the king able to choose his councillors and officers freely as he thought fit. It was essentially Edward III's policy of war with France that produced circumstances destined to modify the position. The enormous cost of the prolonged military campaigns of the earlier phases of the Hundred Years' War put a strain upon the king's administration greater than it could bear and gave to renewed and in some degree a new kind of opposition, leverage which in some measure did result in modifying the principle of personal government by the king. As early as 1340–41 a severe political crisis arose which obliged the king to modify his conception of the administration, and in a lesser degree similar consequences ensued in 1371. By 1376, the centre of opposition—ostensibly at least—came to be in the Commons in parliament, which for the first time so far as we know played what may have been a leading, and was certainly a substantial part, in opposing the government in the sense with which we are concerned here. How far the initiative in the Good Parliament in 1376 was really taken by the Commons and how far it was inspired by magnate interests, is too difficult a matter to discuss here, and the trend rather than the achievement of the opposition on this occasion was significant. The principal concrete demands made were for a reconstruction of the king's council, and for the king's agreement that he would do nothing important without its advice; an attack on one or two ministers by the device later known as "impeachment"—collective accusation by the Commons and presentment for trial by the Lords—was to be important as a precedent for the future and carried implications as to the responsibility of ministers which were far from being worked out as yet. The demand for a "continual council", *i.e.* a council which should be continually in attendance upon the king, the members of which should at least be announced in parliament, and in some of whom at least parliament should have confidence, had been made; and this kind of demand, which, because it did not in itself encroach upon the royal prerogatives, could be conceded without flirting with "revolution", was to appear from time to time, and may be regarded as the hall-mark of late mediaeval or "Lancastrian" constitutionalism. The essential issue had come to be whether the king should be entirely free in his choice of councillors and ministers, or whether he must modify, and if so, how far he must modify, his freedom of choice to suit the wishes of the magnates or even the Commons in parliament. This was by now the burning question in politics, for whosoever could control the council could largely control the administration as a whole. During the last century of the mediaeval period this theme recurred again and again, and the degree of personal government and the degree of conciliar government in operation at any given time varied greatly according to circumstances. In the last years of Edward III, the king himself, aged and increasingly infirm, largely retired from active administration, and acquiesced in an increase in conciliar government, which inevitably continued far into the minority of Richard II. The struggles of Richard II to free himself from the heavy incubus of his ambitious uncles entrenched in the council gave rise to the practical supersession of the kingship by the Lords Appellent in 1386–89. The bitterness of these struggles brought violence far beyond anything experienced in the time of Edward III. For a few years after 1389 stability was secured, with a due recognition of the royal prerogatives and co-operation between the king and a small council which itself undertook most of the administrative work. This stability however was eventually upset by what may be called a "monarchical *coup d'état*", which left Richard II, for what was to prove the last year or two of his reign, in a position of untrammelled freedom. The deposition of Richard II in 1399 at the hands of his cousin Henry Bolingbroke of Lancaster was not a direct outcome of this royalist reaction, nor due to more than an unexpectedly successful rebellion headed by an aggrieved individual. Richard II's regime, however, quickly collapsed and Henry secured the crown itself.

The Lancastrian interest had now come to the throne itself, and although Henry IV soon secured a parliamentary declaration that his regality was no less than that of his predecessors the kings of England, circumstances in the first half of the fifteenth century favoured the growth of conciliar ideas of government. Henry IV could not rid himself of his magnate supporters who expected to share in power and spoils, nor, in the increasingly deplorable conditions of his finances, could he ignore renewed demands by the Commons for a council in which they might have confidence. The Articles for the Council forced upon the king in 1406 went far to "institutionalize" the council, and show a clear intention of making the government more definitely conciliar in form. The more popular reign of Henry V suspended rivalries for power, but his long absences in the pursuit of military conquests in France inevitably left the Council at home to carry on government in his name, and added still further to the financial difficulties and the growing debt of the dynasty. His premature death in 1422 gave to the country the long minority of Henry VI, and to an aristocratic Council its longest spell of practically unlimited executive power on behalf of the Crown. It brought also in its train the end of mediaeval "conciliar government". The personal rivalries of councillors, the fundamental difficulty of instilling vigour into the administration without the monarch himself, the hopeless financial embarrassments, and other circumstances led to the breakdown of the aristocratic Council. From 1437, Henry VI and a new court party revived a substantial degree of personal curial government, and the old Council was to pass away. The issues that remained were personal and dynastic rather than political, but when in 1461 the Yorkist Edward IV replaced Henry VI, the problem was essentially how to restore and revive the personal initiative of the sovereign. Both Edward IV and Richard III in some measure succeeded in this aim, and went far to point the way to a revival which, however, it was left to the Tudors to complete.

The old feudal, baronial, or aristocratic opposition was dead by the time the Tudor dynasty became firmly established and for long there was nothing to take its place. The rebellions centring around the pretenders to the throne under Henry VII achieved no results, and Henry VIII was the first king for a hundred years to succeed with an undisputed title. The measures of Henry VII to revive and expand the executive powers of the Crown and to rehabilitate the royal finances were largely successful. The struggle of the Crown and the baronage for control of the executive had ended in the overwhelming triumph of the Crown; no more is heard of proposals to put the kingship into commission or to impose continual councils upon the sovereign. The Tudors throughout their period enjoyed unfettered prerogatives and free initiative and choice of councillors and officials. They maintained this position by allowing the officers of the household, except for the king's secretary, to sink back into domestic activities, whilst at the same time evolving a small but powerful administrative council (the Privy Council from 1540) to which the great "public" officers, the Chancellor, Treasurer, and Keeper of the Privy Seal, and others of the Council selected freely by the Crown, played a great part in government, always, however, under the supreme direction of the sovereign. The old issues were thus shelved, and new ones were slow to emerge, and when they did, the arena and the causes were quite different from what they had been in the past. The arena was to be parliament and especially the Commons in parliament, and the causes were primarily religious in character.

The political importance of parliament and of the Commons in parliament was enormously enhanced by Henry VIII's decision to encompass his ecclesiastical reformation by means of parliamentary enactment. King-in-parliament legislated away the powers within the realm of the mediaeval papacy. The Commons were called upon to co-operate with the king's government in working this greatest of revolutions, and emerged from it with greatly enhanced power and prestige. The ecclesiastical reformation itself met with singularly little opposition, and although some of Henry VIII's proposals met with stiff criticism and resistance in the Commons, it can hardly be said that parliamentary parties were engendered by Catholic and Protestant differences under any of the Tudors. The weight of the successive governments, whether Catholic under Henry VIII and Mary, or Protestant under Edward VI and Elizabeth, was too great to permit of the formation of anything like a formed parliamentary opposition on such lines.

The party split, when it came, was not between Catholic and Protestant, but between Protestants, between moderate and more extreme Protestants, between episcopalian Anglicans and nonconforming Puritans.

Once the Elizabethan church settlement had been made (not without the application of much pressure from the Puritan interest or party) it was inevitable that supporters of the Church as by law established should, broadly speaking, support the Queen's government, whilst advocates of further and more "puritanical" religious reform should, broadly speaking, criticize and in some measure oppose that government. Many circumstances, however, tended to delay or soften the impact of opposition. The menace of foreign invasions, the immense popularity and political astuteness of the Queen, and the great ability of many of her principal secretaries of state and privy councillors, and not least the deeply rooted tradition of the executive discretion of the Crown, all served to minimize the force of political opposition. But, more and more, the duties of the Queen's officers and councillors came to include those of expounding the government's policies in the Commons, of forestalling criticisms, and of restraining debate. For by now the Commons were much more capable of developing opposition to the government than in the past; most of its members were drawn from the ranks of the country gentry, well-educated, experienced in local government, very prone to independence of thought and action, not easily overawed or placated. As yet, however, all the trump cards were in the hands of the Queen's government; it was strong enough to make concessions from time to time; it need not and did not summon Parliaments very often nor keep them in being for very long at a time; it had extensive means of influencing their attitudes when assembled. Hence nothing like the modern "parties" emerged in the Tudor period. The conditions precedent to such developments had perhaps been set, but it needed the far more extreme differences of opinion manifested during the first forty years of the seventeenth century to produce parties which were, indeed, so fundamentally divided as to take their contests out of the parliamentary arena into the battlefields of the Civil War. But when that time came, there were still essentially only two parties, as in the old days—the Crown and its supporters, and the opposition. The idea that two or more political parties might contend with each other for power in the name of a Crown above all of them, and the leaders of one of them become Her Majesty's Government, was not and could not have been an idea readily acceptable to those born into the English tradition. On the other hand, to those alone could such an idea have ever occurred.

* * *

II. THE SEVENTEENTH CENTURY
by Hugh Ross Williamson

" '1680, origin of the Whig Party' seems almost as fixed a point as '1066, Norman Conquest'," one historian has written. This may stand as an epitome of the paradox of parties in the seventeenth century; for in one sense, the great party struggles were over before the party system emerged. The main lines of three centuries of debate had been laid down—paradoxically, again, not in Parliament but at Putney—before English monarchy died on 30th January, 1649.

Certainly, if one wished to select a date for the birth of the two great parties, 8th February, 1641, would be the safest choice; for that was the first day on which, in Gardiner's words, "two parties stood opposed to one another in the House of Commons, not merely on some incidental question, but on a great principle of action which constituted a permanent bond between those who took one side or the other." And the fact that the division took place on a religious issue—in this case, the continuance of episcopacy—merely emphasizes the other great paradox: that, in the formative years, the party division was primarily religious.

It is, of course, both possible and popular to interpret this phenomenon in terms of prevalent economic rationalizations; or even to make the equivocal identification of theology with ideology to bring it easily within the orbit of modern thought; but this would show a misunderstanding of history in two ways. It would ignore the issues which the actors in the events themselves considered important; and it would omit the main problem which faced the century in politics as a whole—to find a workable substitute for the theoretical theocracy which had been shattered by the Reformation; to restore some kind of Divine Right which was not a temporal tyranny.

This problem was faced by the one great political thinker of the century, Hobbes, who both saw that "the deepest question for the State is its relation to religion" and solved it by giving Divine Right to his Leviathan; and it was fought out with swords and words by the Elect who tried to carry democracy to a point which has not yet been reached, but which was set, in their minds, in a new theocracy.

Needless to say, the religious issue was inextricably bound up with many others. Also, there were a considerable number, from Pym to Shaftesbury, who used the issue for coldly political ends; and more whose adherence to religion was nominal but whose interest in property was real. Yet essentially the emergence of parties in the seventeenth century was a continuance of the Reformation experiment, in the realm of theological debate. The Divine Right of Kings itself was the answer to the Divine Right of the successor of St. Peter, speaking for the whole Church; (as Jeremy Taylor put it at the Restoration, "obedience to Princes is the glory of the Protestant religion"); but the implications of such a right proved incalculable. In secular politics, if these alone had been involved, a constitutional answer might have been found without war—for the constitutional struggle, as such, was simply a further stage of evolution of what had gone before. The necessity of a check on a tyrannical and capricious executive was recognized on all sides. Here Falkland agreed with Fiennes, Clarendon with Cromwell. The early Stuart parliamentary struggles were indistinguishable in form from those of the late Tudor days. Parties, such as in embryo they were, were still as they had been—the supporters and nominees of the Crown and the small but growing core of the opposition. Politically speaking, it was the disastrous incompetence of Buckingham, controlling Royal policy in the 'twenties, which precipitated a crisis which, but for him, need never have been; and even as late as 1640 an evolutionary instead of a revolutionary answer could still have been found had it not been for the religious question.

But what Parliament could not control—at least on any theory which commanded general assent—was the other aspect of Divine Right: the Crown (in the personal sense of the King) functioning through the Bishops. Here, not only in theory but in practice, was an instrument of absolutism which could not be touched except by a new theology.

Charles I could be prevented from implementing his policies through Buckingham and the Houses of Parliament; he could not be prevented from doing so through Laud and the Court of High Commission. That was the crux which the extreme Puritans saw more clearly and approached more logically than anyone else. In the last analysis, Divine Right—in the sense of ultimate and unquestioned power, answerable only to itself—resided in the people, who, through their elected representatives, must appoint not only civil but also ecclesiastical dignitaries. This was the issue which led to the birth of modern parties.

By the February of 1641, Lords and Commons had both passed the Triennial Bill; in the Commons both sides were in agreement about the limitation of royal power implied by this action. Then, on the question of the abolition of episcopacy, the split came and, after a prolonged debate, the matter was carried to a division. Hereafter "those who had taken their sides on this 8th February were found agreeing or differing on all other points as they had agreed or differed then . . . . The supporters of episcopacy would gradually become supporters of the independent authority of the Crown. . . . Those on the other hand who wished to be quit of bishops, lest in retaining them in the Church they should be retaining influences bitterly hostile to the parliamentary system which they wished to found, would only be confirmed in their distrust of a king to whom the bishops looked for support and did not look in vain."

The final conversion of the Episcopalian party into the Royalist party was accomplished by November, 1641, and after the final debate on the Grand Remonstrance by candlelight on 22nd November—passed by a majority of 11—the motion for adjournment found the opposing sides facing each other in the House itself with drawn swords in their hands.

The appeal to arms, transferred in actuality to a wider arena, proved a forcing house for theories. In action all, from now until 1660, is empirical. The religious issue takes on a different aspect, for episcopacy is, in fact, abolished and the Church of England proscribed and persecuted until the

Restoration. The constitutional issue is debated interminably; but the stark fact is military dictatorship. Parliament is purged by the Army and then, when it has done the Army's will, turned out by the Army, with no dog to bark at its going.

Of these years, the most important debate is, as has been said, not in Parliament but in the Council of the Army at Putney in October, 1648—important because it adumbrated all future party lines and was a discussion, mainly between Members of Parliament (who also happened to be officers), at a point where the Council held supreme power and was forced to attempt some theoretical justification for a non-communist solution. The subject of the debate was the *Agreement of the People* which proposed that the size of constituencies should be based on their population, that there should be universal manhood suffrage, that Parliament, consisting of one chamber, should be elected biennially, and that sovereign power resided in these representatives of the nation except in four matters, two referring to the particular circumstances of the wars and the other two being matters of religion and genuine equality before the law.

Here were the extremists arguing for the abolition of a vote based on property because "the poorest he that is in England hath a life to live as the greatest he"; the defenders of property laying down the principle that no one should have a vote who had not a permanent fixed interest in the kingdom; some urging a policy by which all property and titles would be abolished; others (including Cromwell) fearing that manhood suffrage tended to anarchy.

If the honours of the debate may be said to have gone to the extremists, it was in practice Cromwell and the conservatives who won the day, and who, for the next decade, ruled in the spirit of Divine Right by the power of the sword.

With the Restoration, the development from 1641 was continued. Theories and experiments were abandoned. The Royalist-Episcopalian party was so overwhelmingly triumphant that the situation might seem a parallel rather to the less obstreperous Parliaments of Elizabeth than to any previous Stuart situation; and, though the Opposition came again into being by the attempt of the victors (through the Corporation Act) to exclude its opponents from the municipal corporations who returned the great majority of Members to the Commons, Parliament remained a homogeneous body until the fall of Clarendon initiated a new party struggle for power.

Yet once more, the critical issue was religion. It is true that, to some extent, Harrington's prophecy "let the King return and call a Parliament of the greatest Cavaliers, so they be men of estate, in seven years they will all turn Commonwealth men" had been virtually vindicated; but, since men on all sides were men of property, this was not so much a new alignment as a repetition of the old. 1661 carried on from 1641 and pointed towards 1688. The parliamentary manoeuvrings of Charles II, with his own "party" in the Commons, was a successful version of his father's policy, with the difference that everyone now admitted the role of Parliament. But when the religious question appeared again as practical politics—whether or not there should be a Roman Catholic King of England to succeed Charles—the division differed and sharpened as it had done in 1641. On the one hand were the exclusionists, who claimed Parliament's right to limit, if not control, the power of the Crown even in the matter of hereditary right and who were prepared to tolerate everyone but Catholics; on the other, the supporters of the prerogative. Gardiner's estimate of the meaning of the 1641 division has already been quoted; one may give here the words of another historian, Professor G. N. Clark, on the 1680 alignment, because the similarity of analysis points the similarity of the situation. The two parties "were competitors for office and power, so that their principles were then and always subject to the constant transforming pressure of personal and tactical interests. In relation to some questions they were still imperfectly defined: the parties were not yet irrevocably ranged against one another on foreign or economic issues, but during the period of the struggle over the succession these came gradually forward until all were interlocked and a decision over one often carried with it the decision of the rest."

And, as in the 'forties, so in the 'eighties, the issue was

carried to war—none the less desperate because the Whig triumph in the Revolution of 1688 was bloodless. With this triumph, the stage was set at last for the appearance of the parties in their modern sense. It did not happen in the seventeenth century itself. The grouping was still, in William III's reign, between "court" and "country"; there was no "opposition." Both Whig and Tory had accepted the new settlement and the Tories, at that point, had no political theories to oppose to the victorious Whigs. The character of the last twelve years of the century (and, indeed, the first fourteen of the eighteenth until the Stuart dynasty was ended) was one of exploring the party idea, not exercising party government. Twice in the century, the fanaticism of religious convictions had led to civil strife; during the century, the doctrine of sovereignty had been debated from every angle and pushed to the furthest extremes. Divine Right had at last disappeared. Both Puritans and Catholics, who despite their mortal antagonism in other matters were united in their opposition to Erastianism, had been defeated. Episcopacy had been vindicated, but, since the King himself was now subordinated to Parliament in fact, if not in theory, it would give no further trouble to any but theologians. And with the end of Divine Right came the true beginning of parties. The political issue became paramount as the religious disappeared and its basis was convenience, not conviction. What had still to be decided was how the tamed inheritors of the rival fanaticisms should conduct themselves in a peaceful contention for the control of Parliament. The seventeenth century had given them a myth and a martyrology and the names of two gangs of ruffians, Whig and Tory. Thus equipped, they awaited the urbane century.

* * *

III. THE EIGHTEENTH CENTURY
by Professor W. L. Burn

If one seeks it in a country town nowadays, it is not difficult to discover at least the skeleton of party organization, the bones if not the flesh and blood. One will be directed to the agent; probably his office is in the telephone directory. If he is forthcoming he will speak about his organization in the constituency, his Chairman, the members of his Executive Committee and his Financial and General Purposes Sub-Committee and his "workers" generally. He may even be lured into confidences about the Association's Funds and how they are raised, and relations with the Central Office or Transport House. Outside, or in a public-house, it is not an impossible task to find a friendly elector who will provide something in the nature of an analysis of his political beliefs and affiliations. He may be a bigoted partisan, who is prepared to vote for his party through thick and thin; he may say "I admit our lot have made mistakes but I still prefer them to the other side"; or, again, he may argue that the mistakes have been too many and that he intends to vote for "the other side" next time. But whatever he says it will be almost certain that he accepts the necessity for the highly organized party system of which the agent is the symbol.

Now, let the reader suppose that he had gone to make similar enquiries in the same town (then a two-member constituency) in 1752. The task of finding anyone who openly held himself out as a political agent would have been only a little less difficult than that of finding a telephone. If he had been able to overcome the suspicion with which he would be initially greeted, he might find some attorney or land agent with all the political threads in his hands. But there would be no talk of Associations or Committees and certainly no talk of finance. At most, the attorney might admit that he managed Lord So-and-So's affairs and that Lord So-and-So usually consulted him on political questions. "Then you would say, Mr. Smith, that this town is predominantly Whig, under Lord So-and-So's influence?" "Yes, I would say that. We stand for Protestantism and the Hanoverian Succession, Sir." "But you have a few Tories, I expect. Are they Catholics and Jacobites?" "Oh, no, but it wouldn't do to have the Tories in." "Well, how do you account for the fact that Lord So-and-So, who calls himself a Whig, and your two members, who call themselves Whigs, are in opposition to the Whig government?" "Account for it, sir? Why shouldn't they be? Surely a man like Lord So-and-So isn't to be tied hand-and-foot to any government? We like to see our members showing their independence". "But I doubt whether your Central Office likes it as much". "Our Central Office, sir! What the devil do you mean?" After that the enquiry would probably have had to be continued elsewhere.

Suppose that an intelligent elector had been questioned on the party system. The odds are a hundred to one that he would have damned it right and left. "Party, sir? Party means one thing, faction. It's just a contrivance to share out the jobs and the pensions. It stops a man thinking for himself. Didn't you ever read what Bolingbroke said about parties? I know he was a dangerous man in some ways but he was right there. Parties would be the ruin of this country". And so on. After that the reader would be glad to escape from his confusion by returning to the twentieth century and the neat division between Whigs and Tories which he could find in the older text-books.

But the intelligent elector would have been right on one thing: the informed, and for that matter the uninformed, opinion of the country was opposed to a party system and would have regarded the existence of organized parties as we know them as being almost tantamount to treasonable conspiracy. When Bolingbroke attacked parties he was not saying anything new; he was only repeating a commonplace. Halifax, "the Trimmer", had said much the same thing in the previous century. To write of a statesman that he gave up to a party "what was meant for mankind" signified regret at a deforming narrowing of interests and deflection of talents. George III had no need to defend his attitude towards parties because, in principle, they had almost no defenders until Burke.

The doctrine that Burke eventually propounded was new and its acceptance meant a fundamental change in constitutional theory and practice. The theory was, as it still is, that Ministers were the King's Ministers, that every man who held a public office, great or small, was a servant of the Crown. This applied as much to what we would nowadays call politicians as to what we would call civil servants. It was almost an obligation to accept office under the Crown if it was offered; it was unconventional, at least, to say, "I will only accept office on such-and-such conditions".

It will be obvious that such a theory of the Constitution left no room for parties as we know them. A twentieth-century party has committed itself on many fundamental issues, however vaguely and reluctantly, before it secures office. No doubt it finds tactical reasons from time to time for not implementing this or that part of its programme, but its leaders cannot stand up and deny their faith as a condition of being appointed to office. They represent, however indirectly, a particular political philosophy and they are expected to stand up for that philosophy, whether in office or in opposition. The highly-organized modern party and the highly-drilled modern politician are, consequently, not very flexible animals. When they try to perform some radical manoeuvre they are apt to come to grief, as the Liberals did in 1886 and the Conservatives in 1905. A politician today could not change his mind on a major question so easily as the elder Pitt changed his on the use of British troops on the Continent or remain in office after he had been defeated on a major issue, as the younger Pitt was defeated on parliamentary reform.

It would be amusing to construct an imaginary interview between George III and a twentieth-century political leader with hopes of the premiership. One can imagine the politician's confusion as he was forced to give up one position after another. "You're not making this a *sine qua non*, Mr. Smith, I hope? You're not making it a condition that I shall admit Mr. Jones to office? And there must be no nonsense about excluding my old friend Mr. Robinson . . .". But, in fact, the basis for such an interview does not exist. The eighteenth-century politician was not merely well aware that he could not force a list of his colleagues on the Crown or get *carte blanche* for his political programme: he had no such complete list of colleagues to suggest and no such programme to put forward. Had he ventured at a general election to present to the electors a vast programme under heads and sub-heads, he would have invited political ruin. No doubt he had certain plans in mind; no doubt he knew, up to a point, how far these plans were acceptable to a dozen other important politicians; but there was no party programme to which he and the other party leaders were bound and which, if he took office, he would be obliged to carry out. And it is as difficult for a party to flourish without a programme of some sort as it is for a novel to sell without a name.

Theory and practice, of course, were not the same thing and even the theory that all holders of national office were the servants of the Crown was not the end of the matter. They were, no doubt, but they were also in some measure the servants of Parliament which could refuse to pass the legislation they wanted, or refuse supplies or, as a last resort, impeach them. Consequently, the Crown's choice of possible Ministers was not illimitable. The government of the country must be carried on and if it could only be carried on by Ministers acceptable to Parliament and especially to the House of Commons, then Ministers must be found with that qualification. What made Lord North so useful to George III was that until shortly before 1782 he did possess that qualification.

The House of Commons, then, had to be managed. How could it be managed without party organization? In one or two respects the task of management was easier in the eighteenth century than it is today and therefore a less elaborate organization sufficed. If there was no government party, there was no opposition party; there was no organized and coherent "shadow cabinet" waiting to take over. Most of the county members were independents who regarded their function as that of jurors; they had no intention of taking office and would have been repudiated by their electors if they had. They were, on the whole, rather more likely to support the government than not. Then, again, the eighteenth-century House of Commons did not witness such continuous fighting between the government and its opponents as we assume to be natural today. There were a few big field days from time to time when the great oratorical guns were fired but there was nothing like the perpetual skirmishing which in itself demands something in the nature of a permanent cadre. And, finally, there were in the middle of the eighteenth century few issues sufficiently acute and fundamental for the nation at large to take permanent sides upon. There was one, or, rather, there had been: Hanoverians or Stuarts. It had resulted in the people called Tories being excluded, not from Parliament or local government, but from national office. The Whig propaganda which represented them as politically unreliable was effective enough to relegate them for half a century to the position of political backwoodsmen. But parties could not continue to exist indefinitely, even in an embryonic state, on the basis of one issue and that one increasingly unreal.

What was needed to create permanent, coherent parties was new issues of first-class importance. They came, in the form of the Wilkes agitation, the movement for economical and parliamentary reform, the American War and, above all, the French Revolution. By the first decade of the nineteenth century there were two sufficiently distinct bodies of political doctrine. The Tories, by and large, stood for the maintenance of the national institutions, the monarchy, the established Churches, Parliament as it was constituted; the Whigs for institutional reform. Both parties accepted the new *laissez-faire* philosophy but the Whigs accepted it more eagerly than the Tories and tended to draw an increasing amount of strength from the great release of intellectual and physical energy which marked the age.

Even so, these two opposing doctrines were not organized as we today understand party organization. "Party" was no longer such a term of reproach as it had been in the eighteenth century but it was still more accurate to speak of groups of or nuclei of political power than of parties. In the eighteenth century these nuclei consisted of certain forces which attracted political power as a magnet attracts iron filings. There was the Crown; there was the government of the day with its "treasury boroughs"; there were the borough-owners such as the Pelham-Holles connection and the Lowthers; there were the West Indian and the East Indian interests, and so on.

Men who sought an active career in politics as distinct from the semi-passive role of the county member would be drawn within the orbit of one or other of these groups, and from a combination or alliance of some of these groups a government would be formed. If, as happened in the earlier part of the reign of George III, the Crown chose to act independently and to challenge the vested interests of the great Whig borough-owners its actions were bound to lead, as they did, to resentment and confusion.

There was one more thing to be considered, public opinion. Today, public opinion has so many channels for expression that it is fairly easy for the government to see the direction in which it is moving. The comparative paucity of such channels in the eighteenth century has allowed the erroneous conclusion to be drawn that public opinion was not a force in politics. No contemporary who had seen the Gordon Riots or was acquainted with the brutality of the eighteenth century mob and the exiguousness of the means for maintaining law and order would have agreed. Public opinion existed and counted. But it gave very little in the way of a day-to-day lead to the government. It was, rather, in the nature of a minefield through which the government could walk, at the risk of being blown up.

By the beginning of the nineteenth century a change in the composition of political forces was apparent. It was true that the realities of political power were still to be found, not under the names of Whigs and Tories but under the names of Pittites, Addingtonites, Canningites, Grenvillites, and so forth. It was also true that very little in the way of political organization, as distinct from the political side of social organization, existed in the constituencies except for Pitt Clubs and Fox Clubs. A superficial observer might have found the political scene little different in 1815 from what it had been in 1785.

Nevertheless, there were real and important differences. We have noticed one, the emergence of two sufficiently distinct sets of doctrine. Another was the declining power of the Crown. A third was the growth, aided by more rapid transport and the growth of towns, of organized public opinion. Politics were still dominated by personal and local considerations and the Reform movement of 1830-32 can best be understood as a coincidence of a great number of local movements which might quite easily have taken a different political colour. But the *raison d'être* of the party system was coming to be understood, and in 1845-46 it was to be the main accusation against Peel that he had betrayed his party.

In the light of this, eighteenth century political organization becomes clearer. Such an accusation could not have been made convincingly against a politician in 1746. He might have been accused of betraying his friends or even the nation at large; but he could not betray a party because there were no parties (as distinct from groups) to betray. If he were so challenged he could reply, with the assurance of public support, that he would be bound by no such factional interests.

The development of the party system as we understand it was a much slower process than is often realized, and if we look at eighteenth century political organization with an eye for Central Offices and Annual Conferences and Constituency Associations we shall see neither them nor anything else. Then, political and social power were almost indistinguishable and the ordinary social organization supplied much of what we look for in party organization today. But there is one warning to be given. The elements of political power are not the same thing as the structure of political organization. To put this in a more positive way, a man who commands the allegiance of strong economic interests will always be able to exercise more political power than would fall to his share if such power were divided on an egalitarian basis. This is equally true whether he is an eighteenth century duke or a twentieth century trade union leader. In the relatively simple structure of the eighteenth century he could exercise his political power directly without the necessity for a party system either to assist or disguise his activities. Today the relations between political power and political organization are far more difficult to discern.

* * *

IV. THE NINETEENTH CENTURY
By Professor JOHN A. HAWGOOD

When the nineteenth century began William Pitt the Younger, Prime Minister after seventeen years of continuous office, still did not have an organized political party behind him, and he was still, strictly speaking, neither a Whig nor a Tory. His antecedents and his upbringing were Whig, and his illustrious father, Chatham, fought as a Whig and died a Whig—if a very independent one. But, by the year 1800, the Younger Pitt had sponsored or approved many purely Tory measures, and the Whig leadership was now indisputably in the hands of Charles James Fox, whose unholy alliance with his former arch-enemy Lord North had shocked King Goerge III into calling to the helm of State in the year 1783 this young and almost untried second son of Chatham.

Pitt, who had a personal following of barely fifty Members (compared with the 150 at least who followed Fox) when the French Revolution broke out in 1789, has still by 1800 not so completely come to dominate the Tories, with whom he had worked so closely during the subsequent decade, that he could succeed in carrying them with him in his policy of Roman Catholic Emancipation (which he desired to implement when the Union with Ireland came into force); and, faced also with the stubborn opposition of the King, he was forced to resign in 1801. He had been the first complete Prime Minister in a strictly modern sense, and the parliamentary executive had, as an institution, made great strides during his period of office; but as a party leader he was still in the eighteenth century tradition. Though the Whig oligarchy was dead, the organized political party as the nineteenth century came to understand it did not yet exist. Pitt's ministry was a personal *tour de force* perhaps unmatched in British history, but to party and to strict party allegiance it owed little, and to the history of parties it contributed almost nothing.

With the disappearance of Pitt (after his short-lived second Ministry in 1804-6) and the final flash in the pan of Fox (in the even shorter Ministry-of-all-the-Talents in 1807), a long period of Tory reaction set in, broken only by the death of Lord Liverpool in 1827. Liverpool had led his party, with skill but without distinction, mainly from behind, and his lieutenants—Castlereagh, Canning, Peel and Huskisson, Sidmouth, Eldon, and others—tended to be much more active and more in the public eye, though not always more able, than ever he was himself. The fear of Jacobinism, and the ever-present danger until 1815 of the power of Napoleonic France, sufficed to make a policy of domestic reaction almost the line of least resistance. The old Whiggism was dead and the "New Whigs" of the Burkian philosophy had been scared over to the Tories by and with Burke himself in the 1790's, while the radicalism associated with the movement for parliamentary reform was only just again effectively raising its head by the middle 1820's, after its repression during the Revolutionary and Napoleonic Wars.

Until the first Reform Act of 1832 was passed, conditions did not exist for the emergence of a modern party system. Even William Ewart Gladstone first entered parliament (in 1832) as member for the pocket-borough of a noble lord, and Benjamin Disraeli, lacking such influential connections, only succeeded in becoming an M.P. at the fifth attempt, in 1837. So confused and easy to cross were the party lines of even the 1830's that Gladstone began his parliamentary career as "the rising hope of the stern unbending Tories" and Disraeli's first inclinations were Radical rather than either Whig or Tory. The majority of Members of Parliament, even after 1832, continued to take their orders from the influential individuals or groups controlling their constituencies rather than from party leaders in Westminster. The lines of Tory *versus* Whig-Radical were so loosely drawn during that decade that Members could stray from the one fold to the other and back again with impunity, unpursued (though not always unremarked) by their parliamentary leaders. So badly organized were the Whigs, back in office after nearly two generations in the wilderness, and so unamenable to discipline were their new Radical allies, that their irresistible majority of 370 in 1832 had sunk (despite the great legislative achievements of the first and second reformed Parliaments) to 112 by 1835 and to only 18 by 1837. The easy-going Melbourne succeeded Grey as Prime Minister in 1834 without appreciably tightening up discipline, and Peel, who became the undisputed parliamentary leader of the Tories in 1830, following the deaths of Liverpool, Canning and Huskisson (and the growing political morbidity of the Iron Duke) succeeded in pulling his party together after the humiliation of 1832, by, first of all, the astute—though premature—challenge of the Tamworth Manifesto of 1834 (which gave it a new and more forward-looking policy); and, secondly, by reorganizing its somewhat sketchy structure and machinery in Parliament as well as in the constituencies.

Peel swept into power in 1841 with a useful working majority of 76, and his five years as Prime Minister (despite its end in the temporary disintegration of his party over the Corn Law issue in 1846) was one of the most brilliant and successful administrations, Whig or Tory, Liberal or Conservative, of the nineteenth century. In legislative achievement it compares with the first and second reformed Parliaments of the previous decade, and in the power and significance of its debates with the great first Gladstone administration of 1868-74, and the great last Disraeli government of 1874-80. During Peel's administration the modern Conservative Party may be said to have been born (the name "Conservative" had been coming gradually into use to rival, though not yet to supplant, the term "Tory", for a decade or more), though its organization and discipline were still too weak and still too much based on "personal loyalties" in 1846 to resist the profound shock of his decision to repeal the Corn Laws. Embracing a policy advocated by the arch opponents of the Tory landowners (the manufacturers of the hated "Manchester School") Peel placed the courage of his convictions so far above considerations of party cohesion that, not only was he himself driven into political exile, but his so-recently rejuvenated party was split from top to bottom (much more fundamentally than when he and Wellington had accepted Roman Catholic Emancipation in 1829) and had to wait another full generation (until 1874) before it could heal its wounds sufficiently to secure a working parliamentary majority—for the Derby-Disraeli "stop-gap" ministries were (except in 1852, when the majority was 20) minority governments holding office precariously, briefly and (at least as far as Derby was concerned) almost reluctantly.

Yet Peel was a great Prime Minister, and his conception of a party policy and a party organization (though performance may have fallen short of theory) was far removed from eighteenth century ways. He was the political mentor of that great parliamentarian Gladstone (who followed him out of office as a "Peelite" in 1846 and thus took his first step across the floor of the House toward Liberalism) and the grindstone upon which the parliamentary claws of another great leader and debater, Benjamin Disraeli, were so cruelly sharpened after Disraeli and the other Tory protectionists had broken with their leader and Prime Minister. The Peel administration of 1841-46 deserves the closest study by all who are interested in the history of political parties and their leaders in Britain. It forms the chief watershed of the century between old and new ideas and practices.

The Whigs (for it is still premature to call them Liberals) were not ready to reap the full fruits of the Tory split of 1846, for their party organization—though strengthened by the experience and the new leadership brought to them by the spectacularly successful anti-Corn Law League—was little better than it had been in the middle thirties, and many of their left-wing allies of those days had drifted away into the ranks of the Chartists, or had at least lost their enthusiasm for a party now deliberately standing "pat" in domestic affairs under the influence of Lord John Russell and, above all, of Lord Palmerston. It was unfortunate for the party in those middle years of the century that it had as its outstanding parliamentary leader a man who had neither sympathy for, nor belief in, the tightly-drawn two-party system that had begun to emerge in nineteenth century England. Temperamentally and politically Palmerston preferred the eighteenth century system of groups and influence and of personal prestige and initiative. He was an unreconstructed Whig of the old school and proud of it. He was cheerfully prepared to preside over a government of discordant elements, which he could charm, browbeat, or blackmail if need be, into temporary harmony, and to face a parliament from which a majority had to be won afresh by front bench eloquence, by backstairs intrigue and by nicely-timed appeals to popular prejudice and enthusiasm, almost every time he placed a measure or a policy before its members.

It is not exactly true that the floodgates of parliamentary reform were held closed by Palmerston and Palmerston alone until his death in 1865, but while he remained in office the Whig Party could not be modernized into the new Liberal Party it was to become under Gladstone's leadership. Both parties seemed prepared to maintain a tacit truce under the spell of Palmerston, and their leaders were more than willing to enter into coalitions and arrangements with their political opponents. The period from 1846 to 1866, though one of great material prosperity and achievement for Britain, both at home and abroad, was not a very memorable era in either parliamentary or in party history, compared with the period immediately preceding it (1830-46) and the one immediately succeeding it (1867-1885). It is singularly uninspiring from that point of view—even if from no other. Indeed, with regard to this period of precarious majorities (18 for the Liberals in 1847 and 20 for the Conservatives in 1852), of unstable governments and of changing party allegiances, acute observers have noted that a marked tendency seemed to be developing at this time toward a system of many parties and of *bloc* governments in Britain, such as became general about this time on the European Continent and was to remain a permanent feature of political life in neighbouring France.

Why was it that this period of blurred party lines and loose allegiances was succeeded by what has rightly come to be regarded as the classic era of the two-party system, during which

"Every little boy and gal
  Who is born into this realm alive
Is either a little Liber-al
  Or else a little Conservat-ive"?

Had W. S. Gilbert been writing the libretto of *Iolanthe* either before the year 1868 or after the year 1885 he could hardly have put such a cocksure statement into the mouth of Private Willis of the Grenadier Guards, but in the year 1882—if a blind eye be turned toward the Irish Nationalists—it was by no means beyond the limit of poetic licence to make such a claim. Gladstone had brought his fellow Peelites into the Whig fold and then had created a new Liberal Party; Disraeli had made a new Conservative Party out of the Protectionist rump of the old Tory Party; the Radical Party which had tended to maintain a separate existence and leadership—though in the country rather than in Parliament—from about 1825 to 1865, now (at the death of Palmerston and on the disappearance of his old Whiggery) felt it possible to merge and identify itself almost completely with the Liberals, though at times (as in 1857) it also flirted with the Conservative Party too; Chartism was dead and the Labour Party not yet born; that stormy petrel, Joseph Chamberlain, was still "radicalizing" the Liberal Party from within and had not yet left it, as he did with his fellow "Liberal Unionists" in 1886.

The reviving Conservative Party was aware of its continued weakness in the middle years of the century, and both in 1860 and again early in 1865 indicated that it was not yet prepared to take office; but at Palmerston's death Disraeli observed that "The truce of parties is over!" and saw that it was to the advantage of the Conservatives to form yet one more administration without a majority (in 1867), with the Liberals in temporary confusion through the Adullamite secession of the forty Members who had refused to support Russell's reform bill of 1866 and had thus ensured its defeat,

Disraeli's Parliamentary Reform act of 1867 has been variously interpreted and often misinterpreted. To him it was primarily yet another move in the game of party politics. Its advantage to his own party was not immediate, for he was only able to get it through parliament by buying radical support (notably of John Stuart Mill and his group) by means of concessions which helped to lose him the general election of 1868. He had to wait until 1874, when he had the satisfaction of seeing a clear Conservative majority—the first since 1841—elected to Parliament under the new franchise of 1867. He had indeed "dished" the Whigs, but Gladstone's six-year premiership of 1868 to 1874 had made the dish far less unpalatable to them than if Disraeli had come immediately into power in 1868.

The great merit of the Reform Act of 1867 from the party politician's point of view—and none of the party leaders in 1866 and 1867 actively desired a further measure of democracy—was that it helped to restore the clear-cut two party system in the country and in Parliament and ended the dangerous drift toward a system of groups. Gladstone's majority in 1868 was 116 and Disraeli's in 1874 was 98, both without counting the uncertain and fickle support of any group not definitely forming a wing of his own Party. Even after 1880 Gladstone's majority in his second (and much more harassed) administration was 115, of which the new and less reliable element of the Irish Home Rulers amounted to barely one half. The reform of the franchise of 1867 undoubtedly played a great, if perhaps unexpected, part in producing nearly two decades (1868-1885) of orderly two party government.

Oddly enough, though the two party system was in this period more clear-cut than ever before, the ideological difference between the two opposing parties was less, and certainly less than it was ever again to be up to the present day. Never in British party history has the identification of programmes and ideologies come closer to the (admittedly still more close) identification which existed in the great Democratic and Republican parties in the U.S.A. by the first half of the twentieth century. The Conservative reform act of 1867 was more radical than the Liberal reform bill of 1866; there were no fundamental differences between the two Parties and only parliamentary skirmishes over details with regard to the Education act of 1870, the Trade Union act of 1871, the Conspiracy act of 1875, the Employers' Liability act of 1880, and to many other important measures. During these years a progressive Liberal had much more in common with a Conservative "reformer" than he had either with an old type Whig or Tory—a number of whom still existed in the Parliaments of the seventies and eighties.

It was, of course, a calm before the storm. Disraeli had modernized and reorganized the Conservative Party, but it remained for Lord Randolph Churchill to attempt, after Disraeli's death, to radicalize it as well. Joseph Chamberlain's effort to radicalize Gladstone's Liberal Party while its leader was still alive and in office would undoubtedly have persisted through the eighties as well as the seventies had not Chamberlain broken with that party over the Home Rule issue in 1885 and gone over (leaving some of his radicalism behind him) to the Conservatives. From 1885 onward the party stability of the period 1868-85 no longer existed. The Liberal Party—which had enjoyed during those years nearly twice as many years of office as the Conservative—was the first to break up. After the election of 1885 Gladstone had to depend upon the undependable Parnellite Home Rulers and a number of disgruntled Radicals for his majority in Parliament (now, even with their votes, sunk to a mere 86) and the Nonconformist vote was no longer, since its revolt against clause 25 of Forster's Education Act of 1870, so solidly Liberal as it once had been. In the crisis of 1886 Gladstone found that he could no longer hold the loyalty of both wings of his Party at the same time, and his Home Rule bill drove the Liberal "Unionists" into the opposition lobby. Without them he was lost and a handsome Conservative majority of 114 (including 74 Liberal-Unionists) emerged from the General Election of 1886. Before this majority the Gladstonian Liberals (even supported by the Parnellite Nationalists) were powerless, and it was not until twenty years later that the Liberal party was to come back into power again with a working majority—for his miserable nominal majority (of 40) of the election of 1892 gave Gladstone only two years and Rosebery a year of frustrated office without power, until the Conservatives swept into power again in 1895, to enjoy another ten years of rule, with the resounding majority of 152. It was then that their turn to be split by internal dissention came—Joseph Chamberlain was again the villain of the piece, surely the only man in

British history possessing the doubtful distinction of having split *both* the great parliamentary parties—and they were scattered, electorally speaking, to the four winds, at the end of 1905. But that story belongs to another century.

In the year 1900 Lord Salisbury, a peer of the realm (and the last to hold that office), was Prime Minister, whereas in 1800 the commoner William Pitt had been in power; but in every other respect the parliamentary and party system had developed almost out of recognition during the nineteenth century. A tightly-drawn party discipline now controlled the members of both great Parties; rigorous new rules of procedure put limits both of time and in scope upon debates; local associations adopted candidates (thus ensuring in most cases a wide measure of popular selection) and also watched closely how their Members voted and behaved in Parliament; pressure groups, making use of the techniques developed by such organizations as the Anti-Corn Law League of the 1840s and the National Education League of the seventies, and, working both inside and outside Parliament and the political parties, forced policies upon governments and their leaders or "sold" these policies to the country at large. Both great Parties were committed to the "collectivist" trend and to ever-widening measures of social welfare and reform. Third parties had risen, played their part and disappeared, but the two-party system, and not a system of groups or coalitions, was now recognized as the norm. A Prime Minister was now invariably the recognized and responsible leader of the strongest party in the House of Commons, or at least of a party capable of gaining and holding the confidence of a majority in the House. These developments owed much to the great parliamentarians and Prime Ministers of the century —and to Peel, Gladstone and Disraeli above all. The debacle of the Conservatives in 1905 and the even greater debacle of the Liberals in and after 1922 were due to new causes arising out of new circumstances, as was also the rise after 1900 of a new Labour Party which, in its time, was to usurp the place once held in the two-party system by the Liberals.

* * *

V. THE TWENTIETH CENTURY
By D. C. Somervell

If one enquired how many parties there were in the House of Commons at the opening of the twentieth century a precisian might answer "four", but one of these, the Irish Nationalist Party, was there with only one object, to secure the establishment of an Irish parliament and thereby its own departure from Westminster. Its success entailed its disappearance. Another, the Liberal-Unionist Party, which had split with Gladstone fifteen years before, had already become amalgamated for all practical purposes with the Conservatives, like the National Liberals of today, and its leaders were in the Conservative, or Unionist, cabinet. So there remain the Liberal and Conservative parties, but beside them a discerning eye, aided by a microscope, might have discerned an embryo, conceived but as yet unborn. It was not yet born for it was not yet apparent in the House but it had been conceived, on the very day of the relief of Ladysmith, which attracted far more notice, 28th February, 1900. A Conference had appointed a Committee and the Committee had appointed a Secretary. His name was James Ramsay MacDonald.

The main subject of this paper must clearly be to explain why the Labour Party came into existence, why it prospered, and why it was the Liberal Party and not the Conservative Party that it displaced.

The Labour Party like the rest of us is the offspring of two parents. Indeed the parents are still alive and occasionally venture to have ideas of their own about the conduct of their offspring. The lady's name is Socialism; the gentleman signs himself T.U.C. which stands for Trades Union Congress. The lady had charm though some thought her a bit flighty. The gentleman was very respectable and he had the cash. In retrospect their union seems inevitable, but nothing in history is inevitable and they were acquainted for many years before either felt that sort of interest in the other.

The socialism that we are concerned with, modern British socialism, was a reaction against the bad times of the later seventies and the eighties, which pricked the bubble of Victorian optimism. It was not in the main a working-class movement; it appealed to middle class intellectuals and even higher than that. Eton was conspicuously represented. Its main springs were logic and philanthropy, the head and the heart, not the empty belly. Hyndman with his top hat and a volume of Marx in his pocket; Morris with one foot in the middle ages and the other in the handicrafts; the encyclopedic intelligence of Webb; the scintillating fun of Shaw; most important of all perhaps Charles Booth, a successful capitalist who never called himself a socialist but devoted his fortune to a statistical survey of the awful facts of London poverty: these are the typical figures. None of them displayed any particular interest in the Trade Unions, and why should they?

The gentleman was about ten years older than the lady. The T.U.C. had been established in 1868 to organize the demand for certain specific improvements in the legal status of trade unions. These had been secured, and thereafter the T.U.C. lapsed into quiescence. The unions of those days were small organizations of skilled craftsmen, an aristocracy of labour intent on the preservation of their exclusiveness. Twice in the eighties the T.U.C. rejected motions in favour of manhood suffrage.

And then quite suddenly the pair were brought together. A great movement for the democratization of trade unionism sprang emotionally from the dock strike of 1889, led by the engineers Burns and Mann. Then the Scot Keir Hardie, a miner and a socialist, started his movement for the establishment of an independent labour party. There had been a few working class M.P.s since 1874 but they accepted the Liberal whip. Hardie wanted his party to be independent and expressly socialist. Rejected by the T.U.C. he went ahead under his own steam and was elected in 1892. He lost his seat in 1895 but not his cause. The T.U.C. was stirred, and so we come to the "conception" of 1900 when a Conference of delegates from the T.U.C. and three socialist societies appointed a Labour Representation Committee with MacDonald as its secretary. He was a Keir Hardie man but it is to be observed that the prospectus, if we may so call it, of the Committee avoided all mention of socialism. That would have frightened more than it attracted.

The unborn infant was fortunate in its six pre-natal years, for the famous Taff Vale judgement, which the Conservative Government refrained from reversing by legislation, gave the trade unions a really juicy grievance. Never was there an election in which a "swing to the left" was more certain than that of 1906. Side by side with an enormous Liberal majority there appeared a Parliamentary Labour Party of some fifty[1] members. The proud parents had hardly dared to hope for such a bouncing boy.

The most conspicuous result was a gingering up, a socializing, of Liberal policy. The old Gladstonians who led the party probably did not much like it. They were Victorian traditionalists, but there was a young Welshman among them who was neither Victorian nor traditional. The Lloyd-Georgian epic ensued: the People's Budget, Limehouse, Land campaign, "rare and refreshing fruit", "ninepence for fourpence", foundations of the Welfare State. Lloyd George sensed a cut-throat competition between the Liberal and Labour Parties for the position of "party of progress" in the new century. He might have gone over to Labour himself, for his ideas were certainly nearer to those of Snowden than those of Asquith, but he staked his money on the Liberal horse and, having done so, mounted it and dug his spurs into the disconcerted animal. In 1914 it was far from clear which horse would win in what was likely to prove a long race.

Then came the first war. Labour members were divided on this issue. Several of the leading socialists were pacifists whereas the T.U.C. men were solidly patriotic and supplied undistinguished members to the coalition governments. On the other side the Liberal "wizard" soared aloft as the national leader loyally surrounded by titled Conservatives whom a few years earlier he had lampooned as "prancing proconsuls".

[1] Twenty-nine elected candidates had been sponsored by the Labour Representation Committee, and twenty-four others (miners' representatives and "Lib-Labs") from the first collaborated with and ultimately amalgamated with the twenty-nine in a single Labour Party.

Then came the post-war. An enthusiastic electorate renewed Lloyd George's lease of power, whereas Labour remained, in spite of a new constitution, at a mere fifty—and what a fifty! The big brains all lost their seats and a squad of inarticulate trade-unionists entrusted their leadership to—have you ever heard of him?—Willie Adamson. It looked as if the Liberal horse was winning, and yet. . . .

Before we complete this sentence we might tackle some rather wider questions. And first, why this game of musical chairs with three parties and only two chairs? Why not three chairs, or enough chairs for all comers? The answer is that the House of Commons used to sit in the choir of a desecrated chapel, St. Stephen's, where the seating was, as in all such chapels, *decani* and *cantoris*, the dean's side and the precentor's side. When this chapel was burnt down in 1834 the new chamber was constructed on the same pattern, and the process has just been repeated. This makes for the establishment of two *sides*, those for the government and those against it. No doubt there will be a wide diversity of views among the members, but in practice each *side* will be held together by its "for-ness" and its "against-ness" and will tend to become a single party, the "ins" or the "outs". There is a good deal to be said for this arrangement. It makes parliamentary politics more like cricket; that is to say it makes it attractive and interesting, and when politics is not interesting democracy is a sham.

And now for another question. Granted that there were only two chairs and three parties wanting to sit on them, why was it that the Conservatives had as it were a safe seat? The answer was given long ago by the Sentinel in *Iolanthe* when he said that everyone was born either a Liberal or a Conservative. By this he meant that everyone has a natural attachment either to ideals or to institutions. The Conservative is an institutionist and descends from Burke. Liberals and Socialists are both of them idealists and descend from Rousseau—a disreputable ancestor but it can't be helped. Of course boldly-venturing Conservatives may be prepared to deal drastically with their institutions and stodgy-minded

Liberals or trade union bosses paying lip-service to socialism may be very shy of their ideals. So some Conservatives are for practical purposes much more progressive reformers than some Liberal and Labour men. But the psychological distinction remains between those who want to stay here and improve it and those who want to get away from here because it will be better somewhere else. That is what the Sentinel meant to say.

Of course the party called Conservative *might* have lost its chair. In that case the party called Liberal would have become, in the technical terminology of the Sentinel, Conservative. Such things have happened in other countries.

What, then, ruined the Liberal party? The answer is obvious: the career of Lloyd George. Up to the war and through the first half of it he had been content to serve with the Old Gladstonians, standing to them much as, a little earlier, Joseph Chamberlain on the other side had stood to the House of Cecil. At the end of 1916, with mainly Conservative support, he drove the Old Gladstonians from office and became Prime Minister. Henceforth there were two sorts of Liberals, Independent Asquithian opposition Liberals and Coalition Lloyd-Georgian government Liberals and of course they hated each other like brothers.

What did Lloyd George, and Churchill, the closest of his Liberal associates, intend? Historical precedents suggested that the marriage of 1916 would prove a permanent union and that they would prove the dynamic figures of post-war Conservatism. One of them, in the long run, actually did so. Thus Burke and his group had infused new vigour into the Toryism of the 1790s; thus the Peelites had fused with and invigorated the Whigs; thus the Liberal-Unionists had fused with and invigorated the post-Disraelian Conservatives. All this would have happened if things had gone well in the first post-war years. But they didn't. It seems odd today that anyone should expect anything to go well after so shattering a victory, but we did expect it and we did not get it; and we blamed Lloyd George.

At this point a new figure became suddenly discernible: Stanley Baldwin. Baldwin attached great importance to the

Conservative Party. He considered—and who will disagree with him?—that Lloyd George was not a Conservative and that a Lloyd-Georgified Conservative Party was a contradiction in terms and an organized hypocrisy. He decided to see if he could pull it down. L.G. was much surprised. "What? little Baldwin? the Board of Trade man?" said the Welsh Goliath when he heard what manner of David was coming out against him. But David always beats Goliath, and Baldwin carried his motion, against nearly all the bigwigs of his own Party, that the Conservative Party would fight the next election as a separate Party under their own leader.

In the election that followed (1922) the Conservatives won, in round numbers, 350 seats, the two rival Liberal parties 60 apiece, and Labour 140. That meant several things. For one thing it meant that the Conservatives, extricated in the nick of time from their Lloyd-Georgian entanglement, were to be the predominant political party for the next twenty-three years. Secondly it meant that Labour leapt ahead of Liberal and became His Majesty's Opposition with its leader the next tenant of 10 Downing Street, a tenancy which came sooner than anyone had foreseen. The bouncing boy of 1906 took over the government of the country when not yet out of his teens. No wonder his first efforts proved a trifle crude.

As for the Liberals they secured 157 seats in the election of 1923 when circumstances specially favoured them, but they were still forty behind Labour and thereafter their descent was steep and irreparable. This was partly because they had become the "third" party, which is not what the electorate wants, and partly because they continued to be divided. The old Lloyd-Georgian feud faded with the passage of time, but a middle party is inevitably pulled apart by the fact that its members differ as to which of the other parties is the lesser evil and one cannot vote against both at once.

The Labour Party came a cropper in 1931 and its Prime Minister with three of his senior colleagues "ratted to the wicked Tories". Labour played a poor part in the years before the second war, which is the reason why its spokesmen have never since stopped accusing the Conservatives of having done the same. The foundations of the Labour recovery were laid when Churchill gave its new leaders key positions in his National government. It is with the 1945 election rather than with that of 1923 that the new party really reached years of discretion.

We have mentioned three coalitions or "National" governments; that of Lloyd George 1916-22, the MacDonald-Baldwin affair 1931-40, and Churchill 1940-45. If we add the Asquith coalition of 1915 it will be seen that they cover nearly half our period. Some people say, why have this party system, these organized and artificial antagonisms, at all? Surely there is, in this country at least, a vast preponderance of agreement on a middle way. Surely the two front benches are more nearly in agreement with each other "off the record" than either is with the wild men among its followers. Why not have a stable central government all the time with the Blimps left out at one end and the Reds left out at the other?

There are two general objections to this. One is that if the same gang of Moderates were in office all the time they would soon die of it. We get efficient service in office only so long as the office holder is refreshed by periodic draughts of opposition. Perhaps there is an answer to that, but there is no answer to this one. Under the system proposed there would be nothing to vote about in a general election. However dismally the Moderates performed they would always get in again. The poor Blimps and the Poor Reds would never have a chance. Or would they? Beware of a system in which the alternative to a, or rather the, parliamentary party is an anti-parliamentary party, Fascist or Communist.

The trouble about National governments is that, except in war time, they are not National. An opposition soon collects itself. The MacDonald-Baldwin combination was a case in point. In many respects an excellent government (though few seem now aware of this) it quickly became so little National that, when war came, a National government had to be created to replace it. The party system is rather a joke, but it is a very English joke and we must make the best of it.

THE CONSERVATIVE PARTY

I. History by Sir Charles Petrie, Bt.

II. Philosophy and Principles by Kenneth Pickthorn, M.P.

I. HISTORY
By Sir Charles Petrie, Bt.

THE first difficulty which faces the historian of the Conservative Party is to know where to begin. He can go back to the seventeenth century and seek its origins in the Civil War, or in the struggles over the Exclusion Bill in the reign of Charles II; if he feels this is too remote he can trace its rise from the decline of Jacobitism, and the consequent acceptance by the Tories of the Revolution Settlement and the House of Hanover; lastly, he can commence his study with Disraeli, who gave the party its modern form, and during whose life much of its existing machinery was devised.

The choice is certainly not an easy one, but the arguments for the earlier, rather than for the later, dates are strong. The Conservative, whatever he may happen to have called himself, has always been a profound believer in the statement of Sir Walter Raleigh that "the councils to which Time is not called, Time will not ratify". Time has always meant much to him, so when he thinks about the matter he tends to feel that he is the co-religionist of those who upheld the cause of Church and King three centuries ago; perhaps, then, it is not too farfetched to say that the Conservative Party was born when Charles I raised his standard at Nottingham on 22nd August, 1642. Certainly the inspiration of Charles I, particularly on the religious side, is stronger in the party today than it has been for many a long year.

In its great days Toryism has always opened its doors wide, sometimes too wide; it is in its periods of weakness that it becomes exclusive. Under Charles II it was the national party, and it loyally supported that monarch in his efforts to make the interests of the nation as a whole prevail over those of the factions as represented by the early Whigs. For some years all went well, and then the party of Church and King found itself, or thought it found itself, called upon to choose between Church and King. It could not make up its mind, and although it represented the majority of the nation it allowed power to pass into the hands of the Whig oligarchs who had no doubt at all about what they wanted. The end came when the House of Hanover succeeded peacefully to the throne, and the Tories split into factions which ranged from those who accepted the new dynasty to Jacobites who saw no hope save in the successful application of physical force. No leader appeared who could unite these discordant groups, and the consequence was that for two generations the Whigs ruled the country.

All this time, however, the Tory strength, particularly in the rural areas, was unimpaired, and when, during the latter part of the eighteenth century, the Whigs began to split into factions, Toryism soon showed signs of a revival. It was in many ways a different Toryism from that of Stuart times; there was more insistence on loyalty to the Constitution and to the throne as an institution than to the monarch personally, and very little was now heard about the Church. This tendency was reinforced by the advent of the French Revolution, which further weakened the Whigs by causing a considerable number of them to join their old opponents. Above all, the Tories found a leader in the younger Pitt, and under him and his successors they were, with one brief interval, in power for forty-seven years.

The party was held together from 1812 to 1827 by the most under-rated of British Prime Ministers, the second Earl of Liverpool, who presided over the most brilliant Cabinet in the country's history, the only other in any way comparable with it being that of Mr. Asquith before the First World War. For some years before Liverpool's retirement, however, it had become obvious that the Tory Party was divided into two main sections—the progressives who followed Canning, and the reactionaries who looked to Wellington. What would have happened had Canning lived the normal span it is impossible to say, but he died after his hundred days as Prime Minister, and the party split as it had done at the death of Anne. Canning's disciples, of whom one of the most notable was Gladstone, eventually drifted into Liberalism, and the Wellington faction drifted on to the rocks. From 1830 to 1874 the Tories were rarely in office, and only once in power.

Not for the last time defeat caused the party to think of an allegedly more popular name, and the designation "Conservative" was first suggested by John Wilson Croker in the *Quarterly* in January, 1833, as more appropriate than "Tory", since it implied that the essential characteristic of the party was to maintain and preserve existing institutions. The idea gradually won favour, and it was as a Conservative that Sir Robert Peel held office from 1842 until the party split again four years later over the question of Protection. The word Tory, however, was never completely abandoned, and it has regained favour in many quarters since the Second World War.

Modern Conservatism really dates from Disraeli, whose great achievement was to combine the ideals of the Toryism of Stuart days with the needs of an industrial age. Its aims, he declared, were "the preservation of our institutions, the maintenance of our empire, and the amelioration of the condition of the people", while abroad its policy was one of "Peace with Honour". These principles may be said to have formed the basis of Disraeli's own last administration (1874-1880), and they were faithfully observed by his successor, the third Marquess of Salisbury, who led the party for twenty-one years after Disraeli's death in 1881. The late Lord Henry Bentinck well said of Lord Salisbury's leadership that "the people gave its confidence (with a three years' break) from 1886 to 1900 with a remarkable constancy to the Tory party, because the party gave sufficient evidence of its honesty in the cause of the commonweal" and "it was not until the death of Lord Salisbury that its popularity began to wane."

This is profoundly true, but there were all the same forces at work which have had a great influence upon the subsequent history of the Conservative Party. During the closing decades of the nineteenth century the Liberal Party under the influence of Mr. Gladstone, himself in origin a Tory of the Canning school, as we have seen, began to shake itself free of Whig control, and the Whig magnates thereupon began to secede to the Conservatives. Unhappily for the domestic peace of the British isles, this development coincided with one of the recurring crises in Irish affairs, and as the Whig magnates were acred up to the eyes with Irish land they swung their new-found Conservative friends into opposition to Irish national aspirations. In short, the heirs of the Cavaliers adopted the policy of the Roundheads. Lord Henry Bentinck was right in his belief that the Whig influence, which was definitely sectional, did not begin to be dominant until after Lord Salisbury's death, though even before that it had been sufficiently strong to embitter permanently the relations between England and Ireland. Thereafter it was disastrous, and the Conservative Party became increasingly Whiggish in its approach to every problem that presented itself, with the not unnatural result that it lost three General Elections in succession. Whiggery had never enjoyed popular support, and when the extension of the franchise rendered popular support a necessity, Whiggery became a definite liability.

The opening years of the present century witnessed the growth of another influence in Conservative counsels, namely that of finance and industry, which had hitherto been chiefly ranged under the Liberal banner. It is, for instance, often forgotten that for many years the City of London was a Liberal stronghold. The advent of Big Business was to prove a very mixed blessing to the Conservative Party, for the Tories of the past, men like Shaftesbury, Richard Oastler, and J. R. Stephens, had always been the champions of the small man, with the result that the working-classes had never identified the party with the "bosses"; even in the great Conservative *debâcle* of 1906 such constituencies as Hoxton and Stepney returned Conservative Members to Westminster.

Nor was this all, for wealth is always timid at heart, and it infected its new allies with its own timidity. Having no principles of their own, many of the industrial and financial magnates endeavoured to persuade the Conservative leaders to compromise on theirs.

It was during these years that the question of the name of the party was raised once more. Those Liberals who, with Joseph Chamberlain, had broken with Gladstone over the question of Home Rule, called themselves Liberal-Unionists; for many years they retained their own organization both in Parliament and out of it, but in 1912 they amalgamated with the Conservative Party which henceforth was officially designated the Conservative and Unionist Party. Indeed, for a period after the First World War there was a tendency for the word "Conservative" to be replaced by "Unionist", but lately, as has already been mentioned, there has been a reaction in favour of "Tory". Nevertheless, in Scotland, Northern Ireland, and in parts of the Midlands, it is usual for Conservatives to call themselves Unionists.

By the time of the resignation of Lord Salisbury in 1902 the Conservative Party was thus already a good deal of a coalition, and it would have required a statesman of the first rank to hold it together. Possibly Joseph Chamberlain might have done so—though this is by no means certain—but he was never given the chance. Arthur Balfour and Bonar Law struggled in vain against the centrifugal forces, with the result that the years 1902-1914 are among the most inglorious in the party's history. Divided on the question of tariffs it went down to disaster at the General Election of 1906; then, after a brief revival of popularity, it allowed its opponents to go to the country on the cry of Peers *versus* People, with the result that two more General Elections were lost in succession; the lesson of these misfortunes went unappreciated, and the leaders of the party alternated between opposition to Home Rule and advocacy of Tariff Reform as their primary objective.

The outbreak of the First World War restored the prestige of the Conservative Party in the eyes of the country. The dignified and patriotic attitude of Mr. Bonar Law and his colleagues during its early days made a profound impression upon their fellow-countrymen, and their previous inconsistencies were forgotten. Then it was remembered that the party had always stood for effective armaments, and people began to ask where Great Britain would have been but for the pressure of the Conservative Opposition upon the Liberal Government in favour of a strong navy. As the war progressed Conservative stock continued to rise, and in 1916 the Liberal Party broke, for ever, on the resignation of Mr. Asquith. Mr. Lloyd George, who succeeded him, was entirely dependent upon Conservative support, and his leading Ministers, with the exception of Mr. Winston Churchill, were Conservatives. So, when the war finished in 1918, the electorate did what it was to do again twenty-seven years later; that is to say, it voted down the party which had been in power when the conflict began, and put the Opposition of pre-war days in its place.

In this connection it is not without interest to note that for many years the new electorate, based upon adult suffrage, was extremely loyal to the Conservative Party which it supported from 1918 to 1945 with only two short breaks: indeed, but for the Second World War and its repercussions, at least one more General Election might have been won by the Conservatives before their time came to go into Opposition once more.

It must be admitted that to some extent the party was aided by the fact that Liberalism was in a state of disintegration, and Socialism was hardly regarded yet as an alternative government. Nevertheless the Conservative Party owed its long tenure of power more to its own achievements than to the demerits of its opponents. No one could justly accuse it of being a mere capitalist conspiracy or of indifference to social reform while Neville Chamberlain was at the Ministry of Health, and whatever his later faults Stanley Baldwin at this stage of his career held the scales pretty evenly between the various sections of the party. The widespread depreciation, even vilification, of him during the Second World War cannot obscure the fact that for several years he was one of the most popular Prime Ministers this country has ever known: particularly was this so with the women, and there was a time when it was as dangerous to criticize him in female society as to tell an improper story in a Victorian drawing room. During the later twenties it is no exaggeration to say that the strength of the Conservative Party was the strength of Stanley Baldwin.

When he first came into office in 1923 his avowed object was to allow tempers to cool after the bitterness of the immediate post-war years, and his policy in his first two administrations went a long way towards healing this particular sore. Where he made the error which was to cost the country dear was in assuming that the circumstances of the thirties were the same as those of the twenties. On the earlier occasion the most pressing problems were domestic, where appeasement was not only practicable but desirable, and, if possible, sleeping dogs should be allowed to lie; on the later occasion they were foreign, and although Hitler was certainly the dog to lie, he was not the one who could be induced to sleep.

At this time, too, the Conservative Party was subject to internal dissensions, first of all on the subject of India, and then, when Mr. Neville Chamberlain had become Prime Minister, over the attitude to be adopted towards the Axis Powers. On both occasions Mr. Winston Churchill was found in opposition to the official policy, and his later success during the war redounded to his personal credit rather than to that of the party. On the other hand, what might have been a split of the first magnitude was avoided when Mr. Churchill succeeded Mr. Chamberlain in May, 1940. Both men acted in a manner above reproach. The new Prime Minister's immediate request to his predecessor to serve under him, and the other's ready agreement to do so, will be remembered when much else regarding that particular change of government is forgotten. A different approach might well have had the same unhappy consequences for Conservatism as the substitution of Mr. Lloyd George for Mr. Asquith had for Liberalism in the First World War.

For reasons which do not concern us here, but which chiefly arose from the desire for a change and partly also from the obsolescence of the Conservative machine, the electorate decisively rejected the Conservative Party at the General Election of 1945, which may be said to have been the fourth serious reverse in its history, the others being in 1714, 1830, and 1906. Defeat drove the party to look to its organization and its programme, and the consequence was that when the next appeal to the country took place in February, 1950, it was found that Conservatism and Socialism had the support of the voters in almost equal proportions.

What lesson, then, has the past of the Conservative Party for its future? Surely it is that the party is today a coalition of those who hold various, and sometimes conflicting, points of view, and its success or failure depends upon a leader who takes care that no section of the party is allowed to become too powerful, but that all are subordinated to the good of the nation as a whole, which it is the duty of Conservatism to foster.

★ ★ ★

II. PHILOSOPHY AND PRINCIPLES
by Kenneth Pickthorn, M.P.

Party names are more often hypnotic than illuminating. They implant an excess of assumptions, often unconscious and still more often unexamined, about the virtues of the parties most agreeably labelled and, by contrast, often even more effectively, about the vices of their opposites.

That the Liberals care more than other men for Liberty, and Socialists for Fellowship, that Radicals are uncommonly Profound, are extremely debatable propositions. It is still more doubtful whether opponents of the Liberal Party are in general enemies of freedom, whether anti-Socialists are haters and destroyers of comradeship, whether to speak up against Radicalism is to proclaim yourself superficial.

To take such implications of the names for granted is often the result of their unquestioned use, as it was sometimes the object of their choice. "Labour" has been, and is, the principal asset of the Socialist Party in Britain.

In this sweepstake, or conspiracy, "Conservative" is not on the face of it a winning ticket. A man who says that he wants to conserve is apt to be suspected of being specially interested to conserve something of his own. It is true that, apart from all questions of distribution and of separable interests, what each generation has to conserve is immensely more valuable both to society and to each member of it than what any one generation can hope to create. But it is the sort of truth which is often not noticed, and which when it is acknowledged is often written off as so much in the nature of things as not to require attention.

It would be much better if political parties, like patent medicines and made-up sauces, had to advertise proper or made-up names, rather than take leave to appropriate, as titles, words with an unlimited use and value. Whig and Tory, Bolshevist, Fascist—such words have no ready-made content of their own; whatever value they have is put into them by the parties which bear them, not exploited by parties which they carry.

Conservative is certainly not a magic title or word of power, like Tom Tit Tot or Sesame. But it is a family name to be reasonably proud of, and it does, not unfairly, attempt to indicate the principles for which the Party stands.

A Conservative is a man who believes that in politics the onus of proof is on the proposer of change, that the umpire when in doubt should give it for the batsman. There will be few to go so far as the royal duke who is supposed to have said that "any change at any time for any purpose is highly to be deprecated"; and not many to set their standards of proof so high as to make Change feel herself put out of court and therefore absolved from rules and ready to appeal to arms or barricades or bombs. But there will be many who do not doubt that always, in politics, Change must make her case before receiving a welcome; I believe that in England this has always been the general view.

The Conservative might be characterized more alluringly,

but I believe that this is the simplest and most essential characteristic, and therefore the fairest to start from. Probably almost every one who makes this approach to politics (or any other, for that matter) starts from temperament rather than logic; marks of the Conservative temperament are devotion to place, country, family, institution, rather than to notions or fashions, capacity rather for affection and fidelity than for philanthropy and apprehension, power for adapting means to long-desired ends rather than for thinking out new purposes.

There are no politics without some force, and the less force needed, the better. The Left are apt to have a curious prudishness about force; they tend to decry any consciousness of the necessity of force as cynical; they like to assume that in internal affairs any use of force by a Government not wholly of their alliance is wicked; wickeder still, the use of force in any war which they cannot harness to their party postulates. This is all the more remarkable since the common Leftish idiosyncrasy is an over-valuing of politics, that is, of state force; and, particularly, it is the more remarkable since Socialism is in essence the subjection of all economic relations, and, in effect, the subjection of everything else, to the constraint of the central power; and particularly remarkable again, since all schemes for a world order are in essence the entrusting of force to an authority which does not arise from a genuine and living consent.

Order can be maintained most easily and with the least coercion among men who have most in common. Not necessarily in common property (about which something will be said later) but in common memories, sentiments, aversions, hopes, and principles. In a family, not merely the ideal family but the average family, there is less compulsion than in any other society. The virtues of that association cannot be indefinitely expanded by taking thought. But much of them can be cherished and increased where there has existed for generations a population closely related by race, speaking the same language, starting most discussions from identical assumptions, not needing much to fear forcible interference from outside, occupying the whole of a compact and clearly marked territory. Among civilized states we have been almost uniquely fortunate in occupying an island. It was a great blessing also that when the three portions of that island came to be united it was first the smallest which gave a dynasty to the largest, and then the next smallest which gave a dynasty to the whole. The fourth part of the kingdom, the other island, approached union not by supplying a dynasty but by suffering domination, and largely for that reason the joining has never been a real and effective union.

But, to take Great Britain at any rate, a large, spirited, and active population has been governed with the maximum of consent and the minimum of violence, and with almost constant and quite unprecedented increase of wealth. This has been done not by democracy, a word difficult to define and until recently always in our politics a term of reproach. Nor have Liberty and Power been reconciled and multiplied by any standardized efficiency, but by the habit of tradition and discussion, by the cherishing of liberties, even sometimes beyond the point where they were clearly founded in reason or respectable for their utility, and by the keeping of administration subordinate to rule of thumb about what is practical and tolerable: in short, the achievement comes from the extension, less than half-conscious, and the more stubborn for that, of family feeling.

Not that English government and politics have always been rosy and tender; there can be scarcely a village in England where someone does not remember what his grandfather told him about the harshness of the game laws (even if he does not think them harsh still) or about the sufferings of nonconformists; but still, for very long, in England, interests have been less ferocious and vicissitudes less violent, force both more concentrated and less busy, than elsewhere. One of the main reasons has been a sense of community all the more difficult to break or divert because it rests not on any deeply-thought history or hotly-felt legend, but on an inability to forget that the dead are the great majority and posterity probably a greater still, that a man may well fight for the customs his father valued unless he be shown very clear reason why he should let them go.

The sense of solidarity in time as well as space, of a continuity between generations which neither begins nor ceases, is one of the things which preserve Conservatives from excesses of individualism, from the delusion that all social and political problems are reducible to units of independent self-subsistent individuals each by himself acting for himself. Probably most men, and certainly the great majority of women, act in the main during most of their lives not at all by themselves and not principally for themselves but (to take the simplest of their associations) mostly with, and still more for, their families.

If there is to be any discussion, any government by consent, a high degree of community of fundamental sentiment there must be. The Conservative believes that this can be got with more reality and less selfishness, more spontaneity and less aggressiveness, on a basis of tolerant and receptive nationality than on any other basis, than on the basis, for instance, of class or race or "ideology". All those bases have their own vices, and no virtues not shared by a nationality like ours, with its ancient and continuous kindliness and co-operation, its unbroken and unended chain of linked kinships, its universally-shared community of language, literature, law, manners, and principles.

Accordingly, Conservatives feel no need of making excuse for the national basis of their politics. They do not blush to recognize that politics imply essentially the use of force, that even between Englishmen good feeling is not always (nor likely for generations to be) enough, that good laws sometimes need physical compulsion. So they are not shocked (however regretful) to think that, between nations also, force must be occasionally necessary.

From the most tiresome and dangerous errors in this connection Conservatives have some safeguard in their habit of thinking in terms of people and not of abstractions. They have less excuse than others if they forget that it is only a sort of shorthand to say that France made war on Germany or Italy on Ethiopia, if they forget that it is the men managing the government of a state who make war and peace.

Certainly Conservatives are not likely, in any future with

which we need be concerned, to wish to be driven into any war of which they are not persuaded that it is defensive. Their highest duty (apart from the direct relation of each one's soul to God) is to defend this country, this empire of which the essence is communication, and to defend also every promise made in the name of this country or empire in pursuance of that defence: obligations to a League of Nations or any other international entity are promises of such a nature, and the only complete and ideal defence is general peace based on universal agreement universally trusted.

Towards that ideal our clearest duty is the choosing of governors who will not say more than they mean nor promise more than they reasonably think our State can perform. The last thing we should tolerate from them would be that they should make use of the power they owe to us for the purpose of imposing on foreigners their notions of morality, or even of the proper relations between foreigners; no Conservative statesman is likely to say, "We have to exercise British moral leadership for the regeneration of the World, and, when we have got Europe tidied up, then America will come in". No British statesman should feel himself authorized to spend British blood for the promotion of something superior to British interests. If a man doubts that British interests can be defended without prejudice to the highest concerns, British government is not his affair.

Not merely is it not immoral for the foreign policy of the British Government to be concerned with British interests, but it would be immoral and impertinent and foolish (and to all foreigners incredible) that it should be concerned with anything else. Only, it should be directed by honest men honestly concerned with honest interests.

No British Government in the recent past has required much virtue, and none is likely in any foreseeable period to require much virtue, to resist temptation to aggressive war. Recently other temptations have been more serious: the temptation, for instance, to defeatism, to say that the next war would be the end of civilization, or that with the development of aviation Britain had ceased to be defensible, or that gas, or atoms, had made war too horrible for British soldiers, or at least for British electors, to face.

Conservatives, less inclined than other men to regard civilization as new-made or freshly thought or suddenly perfectible, may be the more sceptical of its being catastrophically ended; being less ashamed to think the defence of Britain the greatest of political goods, they may have more faith that it will stand; never having believed that the valid objection to war is its hardship, they are the less easily terrorized by the assumption that its hardship is increasing. And these habits of mind are good, for peace has never come from fears and despair, least of all from defeatism among the victorious and the possessing. Nor may we forget that our country still bears the responsibility of victory and of possession.

Governments exist for more than the maintenance of domestic order, sometimes involving the use of force, and the preservation of subjects' interests abroad, sometimes involving the waging of war.

Though the Conservative is less apt than his opponent to assume that politics are the supreme concern, that is not because he thinks them the mere shadow of economics. We are running a very difficult experiment, trying to manage the most large and complicated of societies while we agree to allow each other all the possible differences of opinion on all the most fundamental questions. We are thus experimenting in a world where perhaps foreign politics are more violent and casual and the economic process more changing and unpredictable than ever before; where, at any rate, almost everyone thinks so.

A man's external activities and their motives may be classified into moral, political, and economic. These terms do not correspond to tangible entities: no man, and hardly any act, is only moral or only political or only economic. And secondly, though these categories *cannot* be divided, they *must* not be confounded: any moralist should be suspected if he demands political or economic action to enforce his views, any politician who in his political activities poses as a moralist, any economist who speaks as one having political or moral authority.

One of the most tiresome and persistent of modern heresies has been the assumption that economics is the real dog and politics no more than the way its tail is wagged. This assumption ought to be challenged, for in its implications and in its exploiters there are many inconsistencies. If there is nothing in politics but the forms taken by economic factors, what are the motives of the people who tell us so? What reason is there why any of us should think about politics at all, or feel any interest but what is material and selfish? If all politics resolve themselves, under a sufficiently close analysis, into economics, how can one possibly account for Bolshevism or for Fascism?

Almost all our ancestors for a very long time, and till a very recent period, were quite certain that upon property reposed not only all hope of prosperity but also all assurance of liberty. They were so sure of this that on the axiom of every Englishman's inherited right to the law's protection of his goods they founded arguments for his right to dispose of his own person, to freedom of movement, personal liberty.

This deducing of liberty from property may seem to many nowadays like hanging a house from its roof. But those who think that there can be no liberty without economic revolution, who want to abolish property in order to multiply freedom, may reasonably be reminded that historically almost all they revere as a striving for liberties was a striving also for property. They may be reminded also that no one has yet explained how, when Government owns and manages all material goods, the Individual will retain any freedom of movement and discussion.

At any rate, they will not be able to deny that Property exists. We do not start in a level empty field: even were we sure that there would be less poverty if there were no property, we should still be very far from knowing that Property had best be abolished tomorrow, or even that our policy ought to be dominated by a resolve for its ultimate abolition. Many things that ought never to have been done ought not now to be undone, and no institution that has been for centuries an essential part of human life ought to be speedily annihilated; no institution that has been for so long a time as property so great a part of human life can be destroyed in one generation without the certainty of destroying for that generation much more happiness than there could be any certainty of creating; no one can set out to destroy such an institution in the course of several generations without a strong probability that his intentions will be reversed by his successors, long before they have been fulfilled.

The Conservative will approach property as a conception which has been useful for centuries, which is almost indispensable to our thinking now, which has been and is abused, which has been and must be continually modified, which is in no particular above question, but whose total destruction must cause misery, and might cause little else.

The principal object of politics is the preservation of order; secondly, what is partly another way of saying the same thing, the exclusive exercise of force by sovereignty is justified only by the consequent diminution of the total play of force in human conduct; it is death and damnation to assume that a policy is justified by the mere preservation of *any* order, by being a police.

It is certain that an order in which there is not an evident and continual desire for improvement will be beset by a continually increasing need of force. In the sense which this implies we may all be progressives; we had better distrust profoundly those who are progressives in the sense of assuming that the stream of human history flows upwards as naturally as water flows downward. Still more profoundly may we distrust those preposterous pirouetting Progressives for whom history is like a ship automatically producing out of its own nature an infinity of self-propelling perpetual motion, a ship which has hitherto been always travelling on wicked courses conned by pirates and privateers, and which after all this erring and transgression is somehow now at a point where it needs only a thrust of doctrine to reach its terminus, to arrive at the harbour where it should be.

We will not forget that politics involve force, but we will not believe that, if only we, our party, could have enough force for just long enough to impose some cure-all regimen, then everything would come right for good. We will not be laughed or hectored out of loyalty to our nation or our tradition, though we will allow ourselves, on proper occasion, to be argued or experimented out of excessive subservience to them. We will not believe that every political question is reducible to economics or soluble by mere conscious moral rectitude, nor that every economic yearning can be satisfied by political action, nor that positive moral values are the direct objectives, and results, of political and economic force.

We will not assume that the State is superior to all the people in it and all the relations between them, nor that it can always infallibly find more skilful and altruistic managers of things, and of their production and distribution, than were ever found before.

Certainly we will not assume that what those who want the maximum of change say against existing arrangements is always exact. Against the assumption that there can be no personal or political freedom without economic equality, we will contrast the memory that for centuries Englishmen felt themselves freer than other men, and that there has been no liberty except where there has been property.

We believe that no great long-lived institution can be wholly destroyed or very swiftly transformed without the infliction on one generation of more unhappiness than any one's vision into the future can justify.

No less firmly, we believe that nothing human can long endure without the desire and the effort to improve; when men improve themselves, if only by keenly feeling that they need improvement, then the State is most improved. When men are much concerned to improve each other, and each man assumes that he would be good enough, if only the State would enforce virtue and tax-paying on some other men, then the State is most in danger, and men still more.[1]

---

[1] This paper reproduces some of the arguments and language used in my pamphlet *Principles and Prejudice*, which was published in 1943.

THE LABOUR PARTY

I. History by Professor G. D. H. Cole

II. Philosophy and Principles by Francis Williams

I. HISTORY
by Professor G. D. H. Cole

THE British Labour Party did not take its present name until 1906, when it first appeared as a substantial party in the House of Commons, having won thirty seats. It had been founded six years earlier, as the Labour Representation Committee (L.R.C.), and was the direct descendant of Keir Hardie's Independent Labour Party (I.L.P.), which had been established in 1893. The I.L.P., out of which the Labour Party grew, was the immediate outcome of the spread of the New Unionism, ushered in by the great London strikes of gasworkers and dockers in 1889. The New Unionism brought large numbers of less-skilled workers into the Trade Union movement and led to big changes in trade union policy; and the Reform Acts of 1884 and 1885 were also favourable to the growth of the working-class movement because they extended the franchise to large numbers of the less-skilled. These workers, and the new leaders who represented them, wanted improved conditions and greater security: the slogans of the New Unionists and of the I.L.P. were the legal eight hours day, the legal minimum wage, and the Right to Work. The I.L.P. gave its allegiance to Socialism, which had previously been represented in Great Britain by the Marxist Social Democratic Federation; but the new Socialism it stood for was evolutionary and undogmatic, and its immediate concern was with getting social reforms. Its leaders were much influenced by the Fabian Society—*Fabian Essays* had been published under Bernard Shaw's editorship in 1889, and Sidney Webb and others were pouring out Fabian tracts full of information about riches and poverty and of practical proposals for reform.

The I.L.P., under Hardie's guidance, set to work to persuade the Trade Unions to support independent working-class political action. It was no new thing for the Trade Unions to take part in politics—the miners and a number of others had been doing so ever since the Reform Act of 1867 had enfranchised a section of the workers in the towns. But the Trade Unionists returned to Parliament had attached themselves to the Liberal Party, from which the New Unionists and the I.L.P. called on the Unions to break away.

Seven years of I.L.P. propaganda induced a number of Trade Unions to join with the Socialists in 1900 in setting up the Labour Representation Committee. The Co-operative movement was invited to join them, but only one local Co-operative Society came in. The main body of the Co-operative movement did not turn to politics until 1917, when resentment at unfair treatment in connection with wartime rationing and at the imposition of Excess Profits Duty on the Societies led to the establishment of the Co-operative Party, which has always acted in close electoral and parliamentary alliance with Labour.

At first the L.R.C. grew but slowly. But the Taff Vale Judgment of 1901, which in effect made strikes almost impracticable by threatening the Unions with actions for damages caused by them to employers, brought many more Unions in, and greatly increased the political keenness of nearly all. Joseph Chamberlain's tariff crusade of 1903 drove the L.R.C. to form a common front with the Liberals; and in the General Election of 1906, which brought overwhelming victory to them, the Labour Party won nearly all its thirty seats with Liberal support.

The appearance of the Labour Party in Parliament with a substantial following took most people by surprise, and led for a short time to an exaggerated estimate of its influence. Aided by the many Liberals who had given election pledges to vote for the undoing of the Taff Vale Judgment, the Labour Party was able to insist on complete reversal by the Trade Disputes

Act of 1906; and it also succeeded in putting on the statute book the first Act authorizing the feeding of children at school. But it was soon struck a heavy blow by a further legal decision in the House of Lords: the Osborne Judgment of 1909 declared all political action by Trade Unions to be unlawful, and thereby knocked away the financial foundations of the party. Thus handicapped, it was able to do no more in the two General Elections of 1910, arising out of the struggle with the House of Lords over Lloyd George's 1909 Budget, than defend its existing seats and contest a very few others. It just about held its own, coming out bigger only because the Miners' Federation, whose M.P.s had sat as Liberals up to 1909, had joined it in that year.

From 1910 to 1914 the Labour Party was the prisoner of the Liberals, who depended on it and on the Irish Nationalists for their continuance in office. Labour was held to the Liberals, first during the struggle that ended in the Parliament Act of 1911 and thereafter during the Irish crisis, by its support of Home Rule. Until 1913, when a new Trade Union Act authorized political expenditure by Trade Unions under conditions, it was also badly hampered by the Osborne Judgment. It lost ground in the country, and was vigorously challenged from the left by a new generation of Trade Unionists influenced by the ideas of Direct Action preached by Syndicalists and Industrial Unionists.

It was still in these difficulties when war broke out in 1914. The majority of the Party, after working for peace up to the invasion of Belgium, thereafter supported the war effort; but the I.L.P., which had continued as a separate body within the federal structure of the Labour Party, took an anti-war line, headed by Philip Snowden and Ramsay MacDonald. (Keir Hardie was ill, and died in 1915). Largely because of the efforts of Arthur Henderson, then Secretary, who became leader in succession to MacDonald in 1914, the I.L.P. was not thrust out of the Party, despite its dissident line; but up to 1918 it acted virtually as an independent group. The Labour Party was given a minor representation in the first Coalition under Asquith, and a much larger one in the Lloyd

George Coalition formed late in 1916. It remained in the Coalition until war ended; but its leader, Henderson, was expelled from the War Cabinet in 1917 because of his advocacy of the Stockholm Peace Conference. Thereafter, Henderson set about a complete reorganization of the Party, which was completed in 1918, when the Party Conference endorsed its first explicitly Socialist programme—*Labour and the New Social Order*. This, drafted mainly by Sidney Webb, was an essentially Fabian document, committing the Labour Party to Socialism as a goal, but also to a gradualist and strictly constitutional approach to it by the methods of parliamentary democracy.

Up to 1918, the Labour Party had no organization at all in the majority of constituencies. It had never fought more than a small minority of seats, and had made no claim to be more than a third party in the State. Nor had it any individual membership: it was a loose federation of Trade Unions and Socialist societies, with the latter acting as the agencies for recruiting individual supporters. Henderson set to work to seize the opportunity presented by the break-up of the Liberal Party into rival factions by creating a local Labour Party in almost every constituency and getting ready to fight every possible seat at the first post-war election.

The Labour Party left the Coalition as soon as the war ended, and was plunged straight into the Election of 1918. Confronted with Lloyd George's "coupon" candidates, it fared badly in comparison with its pretensions, but even so increased its seats from thirty-nine in 1914 to fifty-seven. It soon made big further advances—to 142 at the Election of 1922, and to 191 a year later. At this point, early in 1924, Ramsay MacDonald formed the first Labour Government. Being in a minority, the Government depended on Liberal support. It lasted less than a year, and had no opportunity for large achievements, though it managed to pass some good social legislation—especially the Wheatley Housing Act and an Act improving the position of the unemployed by making extended benefits for those who were long out of work a statutory right. The Government, however, got into a tangle over British relations with Russia and over the handling of

Communism at home and abroad. The Liberals turned against it, and it fell. In the ensuing Election it was heavily defeated, largely because of MacDonald's mis-handling of the Zinoviev Red Letter episode. Its seats fell to 152.

Back in opposition, the Labour Party had to face the problems arising out of the General Strike of 1926, which was followed by the Trade Unions Act of 1927. From 1913 the Party had been financed largely by means of a levy on the members of Trade Unions which had decided by ballot to raise a Political Fund. Anyone who objected to paying this levy could contract-out by signing a special form; but few did so, though in practice a good many failed to pay. The Act of 1927, besides outlawing general and most forms of sympathetic strikes, altered this procedure to contracting-in, so that the levy could be collected only from those who signed forms declaring their willingness to pay. Party membership fell sharply from $3\frac{1}{4}$ millions to $2\frac{1}{4}$; but the economic setback was positively favourable to the Party's political appeal, and at the Election of 1929 its poll rose to nearly $8\frac{1}{2}$ millions, as against $5\frac{1}{2}$ in 1924, and the seats won from 152 to 288. This made Labour for the first time the largest Party in Parliament; and MacDonald formed his second Government, again depending on Liberal support.

The second Labour Government lasted for two years. It was in difficulties almost from the beginning, in face of mounting unemployment, with which it made no serious attempt to deal; and during its second year of office it had to meet the full impact of the world economic crisis, which upset the balance of payments as more and more countries cut down their buying and dumped their surplus products on the British market, which almost alone remained open. There were serious strains inside the Government and the Party, and these finally reached breaking point. MacDonald, Snowden and J. H. Thomas, with a handful of supporters, seceded and formed a National Labour Party; and MacDonald, discarding most of his colleagues, became the Prime Minister in a "National" Government which went to the country with a demand for a "doctor's mandate" to deal with the crisis.

With all the other parties combined against it, the Labour Party was crushingly defeated, its vote falling to not much more than 6½ millions, and its seats from 288 to 46—a mere handful.

This defeat left the Parliamentary Party impotent in the House of Commons, and shifted the centre of activity to the Party outside Parliament. The I.L.P., which had been working inside the Labour Party for a programme of "Socialism in Our Time", had quarrelled with it before the Government's fall and did not become reconciled when MacDonald and his group seceded. A handful of I.L.P. candidates fought as a separate group in the Election of 1931; and soon afterwards the I.L.P. disaffiliated from the Party. This led to a split in its ranks: a section which wished to remain in the Labour Party joined hands with certain other groups to form a Socialist League, which, under the leadership of Sir Stafford Cripps, pressed for a left-wing policy. The Party Executive, under pressure from this and other groups, set out to reformulate its policy in a series of reports which were debated and endorsed at Party Conferences during the next few years. These reports of the early 1930's actually formed the basis for a large part of the Labour Government's measures after 1945.

The world crisis, meanwhile, carried Fascism into power in Germany, and as the European situation worsened, the centre of Party interest shifted from home to foreign affairs. The Labour Party had strong pacific, though not pacifist, traditions; and from 1932, when Henderson resigned the leadership in order to continue to devote his full attention to the Disarmament Conference, it was led by George Lansbury, the only front-rank leader to escape electoral defeat in 1931. Lansbury was an actual pacifist; and the Party as a whole was in a dilemma because, on the one hand, it wanted to oppose Fascism, but on the other hand it was reluctant to support re-armament under Conservative control. It therefore took refuge in ambiguities. Presently, the menacing development of Fascism and the growth of Trade Union feeling against Lansbury's leadership enforced his resignation, and Clement Attlee succeeded him in the autumn of 1935.

At the Election of December 1935 the Labour Party's vote rose to 8½ millions—about the same as in 1929—and it won 152 seats—fewer than in 1924. This result left it still in a weak position in the House of Commons during the critical years before the second world war. The continued growth of the Nazi danger and the open intervention of the Germans and Italians in the Spanish Civil War led to demands for the formation of a Popular Front against Fascism, on the model of the Popular Fronts in France and Spain. The Communists were active in this movement, which was supported by the Socialist League and other Labour "leftists" and by a number of Liberals and Independents. But the Labour Party Executive, deeply hostile to both Communists and Liberals, would have none of it, and presently Sir Stafford Cripps, Aneurin Bevan, and other protagonists were expelled from the Party, after the Socialist League had dissolved itself in order to avoid expulsion. There was, however, no real split, the Trade Unions and the bulk of the individual members being determined not to divide the Party. In the Munich crisis of 1938 the Party leadership favoured going to the help of the Czechs, and this attitude did much to rally its supporters. When war came in 1939 practically the whole movement was united in support of the struggle against Fascism, only the I.L.P.—and of course the Communists after an initial hesitation—taking an anti-war line.

In the dark days of 1940, during and after Dunkirk, the Labour Party supported Winston Churchill against Neville Chamberlain; and from then until 1945 its leaders were holding key posts in the Churchill Coalition Government. Attlee became Deputy Prime Minister and Ernest Bevin Minister of Labour: other important positions were held by Herbert Morrison, Arthur Greenwood, Hugh Dalton and, later, Sir Stafford Cripps, who did not, however, rejoin the Party until 1945. The part played by these and other leaders during the war greatly strengthened the Party's hold on the electorate, and also made its mark on the reconstruction policy laid down by the Government for the period after the war. Meanwhile, the electoral truce proclaimed for the duration of hostilities led to some restiveness among Party members; and a new Party, Common Wealth, founded by the former Liberal, Sir Richard Acland, with a Socialist programme, stepped into the breach to fight by-elections and attracted a substantial following. This following melted away when the truce ended, and Acland himself soon afterwards joined the Labour Party.

Most people, including most Labour supporters, were surprised by the sweeping victory won by the Labour Party in the Election of 1945, at which it secured 394 seats and a large majority over all other parties combined, though it fell short of a clear majority of the total votes cast. The victory was due largely to the great swing of votes among the salaried classes and among service men, as well as to the better support given by the wage-earners. The third Labour Government, led by Clement Attlee, found itself free, unlike its predecessors, to carry through an advanced policy, including considerable measures of nationalization as well as far-reaching measures of social welfare and drastic taxation of the higher incomes. Labour had gone into the Election with an ambitious, but limited and definite, programme which it pledged itself, given a majority, to carry out in full; and by 1950 it had actually done practically all it had promised, except that the nationalization of the steel industry, though enacted, was not yet in force on account of delays caused by the opposition of the House of Lords. The industries and services transferred to public ownership included the Bank of England (but not the other banks), coal mining, electricity and gas supply, civil aviation, and the main agencies of internal transport; and the retention of war controls under emergency powers carried with it a considerable power to influence the policies and investment programmes of industries remaining in private hands. The educational system had already been marked down for reorganization on a more democratic basis under the Butler Act of 1944; but the other social services mostly remained to be dealt with, and the Labour Government carried out the essential principles of the Beveridge and other wartime reports, and went in some respects beyond them, by setting up the new comprehensive National Insurance and Assistance and Industrial Injuries schemes and the all-in National Health Service. It also carried out its pledges to pursue economic and financial policies ensuring full employment, and embarked on an extensive housing programme.

Up to 1950, the Labour Party remained without serious internal dissensions over home policy, though there was a fair amount of dissatisfaction with the administration of the nationalized industries. On foreign policy it was less united, though Ernest Bevin, Foreign Secretary since 1945, was always able to rout his critics at Party meetings and conferences. The main criticisms were that the Party and the Government did much too little in and after 1945 to give support to the continental Socialist Parties or to the revival of Socialism in Germany, and that, in following its consistent line of hostility to Communism, it was in danger of becoming the ally of anti-Socialist forces in both America and Europe. Bevin's policy in Palestine and the Middle East was also sharply attacked from the left. On the other hand, the granting of complete freedom to India, Pakistan, Ceylon, and Burma was generally acclaimed; and the critics recognized that the Government was doing its best to work out a positive programme of reform and development in the colonies.

Despite notable achievements, by 1950 the Labour Party had seriously lost ground with the electorate. Especially, much of its middle-class support had fallen away, largely because of growing dislike of the controls and rationing of which world shortage and acute balance of payments difficulties made it impossible to get rid without giving up the policy of Fair Shares to which the Government was pledged. In the Election of 1950 the Labour Party just retained a clear majority of seats; but it came back to office in no position to carry out any programme involving a considerable amount of controversial legislation. This did not much worry some of its leaders, who thought that a period of consolidation was needed for digesting the legislative changes already made. Indeed, the programme on which the Party fought the Election of 1950 was unambitious in comparison with that of the previous five years, and showed signs of doubt about the desirable lines of further advance.

By 1950 the Party's position had also been further complicated by the unfavourable developments in international affairs. Marshall Aid from the United States, which had been a very important factor in West European, including British, economic recovery, had also been partly responsible for growing tension between the Soviet Union and the West; and from 1947 there had been both an increasing rigidification of policy behind the Iron Curtain and a mounting anti-Communist frenzy in the United States. In 1950 the Korean invasion rapidly intensified these tendencies and led, under American pressure, to the adoption of massive programmes of European rearmament which could not be put into effect without greatly slowing down economic recovery or without adverse reactions on the standard of living. Differences came to a head over the Budget of 1951, and resulted in the resignation of three members of the Government—Aneurin Bevan, Harold Wilson, and John Freeman. A group led by these three published in July, 1951, a statement strongly critical of the policy of intensive re-armament, as more calculated to weaken than to strengthen the West because of the economic effects. But Bevan and his group, though highly critical of the Government, did not wish to do anything to prejudice its retention of office and continued to support it in parliamentary divisions.

Meanwhile rising prices, caused mainly by the impact of huge American purchases in the world market, were undermining the policy of "wage-restraint" which the Trade Unions had followed throughout the post-war years for fear of provoking uncontrollable inflation; and criticism of the over-centralization and bureaucratic administration of the nationalized industries was also gaining ground. A keen sense of loyalty, however, combined with a fear of the effects of a return to Conservative Government and a strong dislike of playing into the Communists' hands, kept the critics from pushing their differences to the point of breaking up the Government, which despite its very narrow majority continued to weather one parliamentary crisis after another. In the late summer of 1951 Clement Attlee decided to dissolve Parliament. During the ensuing election campaign the Labour Party steadily regained ground, but not quite enough to prevent electoral defeat, though it actually polled more votes than the Conservatives and their allies. The differences within the party were temporarily buried: the leading Bevanites all secured re-election to Parliament—as they had done to the party executive at the National Conference held just before it. The strength of the support for Aneurin Bevan came out plainly both at the Conference and in the election; and the Bevanites made no secret of their intention to continue pressing their policy when the election was over.

This necessarily summary record of the essential facts about the Labour Party's history will have brought out the point that it has followed throughout an essentially constitutional and gradualist policy. Until 1918 it was not even explicitly Socialist; and from that time on its successive programmes have been variations on a common theme of evolutionary, democratic Socialism, with measures of social welfare taking precedence over any far-reaching attack on the basic structure of society. After 1945 it carried out considerable schemes of socialization; but it made no attempt at any general overthrow of private enterprise, and, after it had fulfilled its nationalization pledges, it seemed more and more disposed to contemplate the continuance of a "mixed economy" for a considerable time to come, and to rely mainly on the cumulative effects of progressive taxation and educational and social reform to modify the class-structure gradually in the direction of greater social equality. Economically, it was influenced greatly by Keynes; and in its desire to come to terms with progressive American opinion, it veered away from the older conceptions of Socialism towards an attitude more nearly akin to that of the New Deal. These tendencies it shared with other Western Socialist Parties, partly out of common hostility to Communism and partly because experience of office and of the conditions of office in a world of deep insecurity impelled its leaders towards a higher estimation of the advantages of Western democracy as it is, and a greater fear of taking any action that might threaten its foundations or lead to a withdrawal of American support.

* * *

II. PHILOSOPHY AND PRINCIPLES
by Francis Williams

It is inevitable that the fact that the Labour Party first achieved power as a Government with a parliamentary majority at the end of a war which had left the nation economically weaker than at any time in its history should to some extent have blurred and obscured the true pattern of British Socialist philosophy.

Much that the Labour Government did during its six-and-a-half years of administration sprang directly, of course, from the basic principles which inspire the British Labour movement. But much else represented a pragmatic and administrative response to urgent current problems: a pattern dictated by a siege economy rather than a specifically Socialist one.

Thus much of the system of food rationing, of control over the price and distribution of many consumer goods and of raw materials, as also the power—never in fact used—to direct labour, which have characterized in many people's minds Socialist philosophy fall, in fact, within this second and, let us hope, transitory category. They have represented a response to immediate and passing problems, although they may prove to be of stubborn duration, rather than the expression of permanent Socialist beliefs—although the choice of the methods used to meet such problems was, of course, coloured by the Socialist approach.

It is necessary to make this distinction at the outset of this article. Without it, it is not possible to isolate what is impermanent and based to a large extent on an empirical response to current circumstance from what is properly to be regarded as an expression of basic philosophy.

Like all political systems Socialism is a means to an end,

not an end in itself. The specifically British brand of Socialism from which the Labour Party historically derives and from which it takes its political and economic colour is based on an ethical conception about the nature of man. This is the belief that man is a moral being moved, or capable of being moved, by ideals and aspirations ultimately more satisfying than the materialist conceptions which govern in varying degree both the other great political creeds of the modern world—Communism and Capitalism.

Even when it outgrows its more ruthless manifestations and becomes benevolent and paternal, Capitalism is—as are the political systems of Conservatism and Liberalism which rest on it—rooted in the belief that the acquisitive instinct is the primary (although not of course the only) instinct upon which civilized communities must depend for their development.

Marxist Communism is rooted in the belief that, as Engels stated, the stage of economic development reached by society *alone* determines its form, its political pattern, and its culture.

Socialism rejects the doctrine of economic man whether it is presented in Capitalist or Communist terms.

It is based instead on the belief that although economic forces are, of course, important, a good society is possible only if it is recognized that the most fundamental need of man's moral nature is to combine and co-operate. In terms of practical politics this involves the assumption that incentives other than those of material personal interest can best provide the motive power for economic and social advance, that human beings will work most fruitfully together and give of their best if they feel themselves members of a social partnership of whose purpose they approve, and if they feel that there is a positive value in cooperation and human fellowship.

It is from this moral belief that the social, economic and political principles distinctive to the Labour Party have derived. Indeed it is true to say, as one of the most devoted apostles and architects of British Socialism in the early years of the Labour Party, Bruce Glasier, wrote: "It is from the prophets, apostles and saints, the religious mystics and heretics, rather than from statesmen, economists and political reformers, that the Socialist movement derives its examples and ideals."

But since a political Party is by its nature devoted to the attainment of a system of social living in harmony with the philosophy it holds to be good, it must obviously translate its ideals into principles capable of providing a guide to practical social acts.

It is to a reinterpretation—or rather, as most Socialists would say, to a natural development of—the principles of political democracy as so finely expressed, for example, in the American Declaration of Independence, that the Labour Party looks for this guidance.

> "We hold these truths to be self evident, that all men are created equal, that they are endowed by their creator with certain inalienable Rights, that among these are Life, Liberty and the pursuit of Happiness. That to secure these rights Governments are instituted among Men deriving their just powers from the consent of the governed...."

How are these principles to be applied in the modern world? The Labour Party would hold that they are only capable of full application within a society as aware of the need for economic democracy as it is of the need for political democracy, as convinced of the value of social equality as it is of the value of political equality.

The insistence of Socialists upon the need for economic planning of national wealth and resources does not derive primarily from an economic thesis: the argument of efficiency although important is secondary. What is at issue is not simply the case for one technical system as opposed to another in dealing with the creation and distribution of wealth and resources in modern industrial society. The issue, as the Socialist sees it, is that which has troubled men and women ever since they first began to live in communities: the issue of how to tame power.

Political democracy was an attempt to tame political

power by taking it out of the hands of groups who had acquired it by inheritance, by force or by wealth, and to spread it over the whole community. It involved the recognition—not easy even to many men of goodwill at the time—that however much men and women may differ in their individual talents and abilities they must properly be regarded as equals in their membership of a common society. But it failed of its full purpose, Socialists believe, because it left untamed and insufficiently subject to the community mandate, concentrations of economic power exercising an authority over fields of public policy and public well-being far more extensive than that exercised by the legislature in most of its legislation; one, moreover, much more decisive in many important respects than is the political authority in determining the shape of men's lives and the material framework of the society within which they exercise the freedoms acquired under political democracy.

Communism, recognizing the need to tame economic power, has taken it out of the hands of the monarchical, aristocratic or oligarchic groups which formerly possessed it, and has placed it in the hands of the State. But because of its preoccupation with the economic motive in society it has, in doing so, replaced one tyranny by another and has concentrated both economic and political power in the hands of a small group not subject to the controls which political democracy provides.

Thus both systems have failed to tame power and establish a social framework in which man can fully live up to his potentialities of freedom because each has chopped off only one of the heads of a two-headed giant.

It is the Socialist thesis that true freedom for the individual is only possible if both are chopped off: if the democratic control of political policy is extended to include the democratic control of economic power by the State as the agent of the community and if the concentration of economic power in the hands of the political executive thus involved is constantly curbed and tamed by the positive processes of political democracy.

It does not follow from this, in the modern Labour Party view, that all the means of production and distribution must be owned by the community. What does follow, however, is that the basic sources of economic power, and those industries which are primary in the sense that the policies followed by their managements, the level of efficiency they reach, and the control they exercise over supplies of raw materials or services all largely determine the national economic pattern and establish the real level of activity at which secondary industries can operate, ought to be communally owned and operated with the public interest as their governing purpose.

The Labour Party does not accept the capitalist assumption that the automatic controls of the price system can of themselves secure the public good. It believes that the whole weight of experience as manifested in past social insecurity, in periodic large-scale unemployment, in the misuse and dissipation of national resources and in gross inequality proves the contrary. And it believes that in a system in which such things happen, it is impossible for most ordinary men and women to benefit to the full extent from the freedoms political democracy exists to promote.

Nor does it believe that the sector of the national economy lying outside these primary sources of economic power, the section, that is, in which the incentives of private ownership and management can well remain since they are capable of giving variety and flexibility to the economic life of the community without endangering the communal control of basic economic power, should operate solely under the stimulus—often of necessity socially irresponsible—of private profit. I say of necessity often socially irresponsible. I am aware that in doing so I may seem unjust to many public-spirited owners and managers of private enterprises. But the existence of such men neither does nor can alter the fact that where a private corporation is primarily governed in its operations by the test of its ability to serve and promote the interests and profit of its shareholders—and such a test is a quite legitimate one within the framework of the profit system—there can be no guarantee that the interests of the whole community will be served other than accidentally or intermittently.

It is therefore, in the view of the Labour Party, right that the Government, as the agent of the whole community in such matters, should have the authority to require that all those operating in the private enterprise sector of the national economy shall be subject to such general control as appears to be in the community interest at any time. This means in practice the exercise by the Administration of such financial and physical controls and planning authority as will secure a balanced industrial economy judged by the standard of national need without limiting unnecessarily the individual initiative of those concerned in a vast number of manufacturing and productive purposes.

It is true that such a system requires of all those participating in it responses different in degree and in kind from those called for in a society whose economic life is based primarily on the potency of material rewards. That such rewards are potent the Socialist would not deny. But he holds, it is indeed a cardinal part of the moral philosophy which I have referred to as the mainspring of Socialist principles, that other incentives are no less potent, that men and women obtain reward from the exercise of their abilities in ways which they know to be of value to their fellows and find satisfaction in a society which they believe to be good.

It is not a principle of the Labour Party that a good society involves absolute equality of material reward. It believes on the contrary that since men's satisfactions no less than their abilities and energies vary, exceptional rewards are justifiable for exceptional effort or exceptional responsibility or exceptional talent. It does however hold two things. First that rewards ought always to be related to what men do, not to what they have inherited; to social usefulnesses not to possessions. Second that they ought not to be of such a nature as to create or permit gross social inequalities.

This insistence on the importance of a more egalitarian society which has been demonstrated very strongly during the period a Labour Government has been in power derives in part from the social reform struggle to which Labour has been deeply committed throughout the life of the Labour Party—the struggle to improve the condition of the poorest sections of the community, to remove the fear of insecurity, and to increase the share of the national wealth going to productive workers which has equally been reflected in the whole programme of the Welfare State.

But it derives also from the central philosophy of Socialism as a moral creed—the belief in the moral nature of man which has, as its counterpart, that emphasis on the uniqueness of the human personality and the value of the individual which is as essential a part of the Christian ethic as it is of the democratic philosophy. Holding these beliefs the Socialist holds also that a society in which men and women are divided by social and economic inequalities and in which human intercourse is made more difficult by the existence of great privilege is a bad society, because it is one that runs counter to the deepest human values.

The Socialist looking at modern capitalist societies sees them, no less than modern Communist societies, the prey of a profound neurosis. Their emphasis on a purely materialist standard of achievement, their insistence on competitive success as a proof of character: these in the Socialist view confine human personality within a framework rigid and mutilating—a framework in which the true values of civilization and the true warmths and generosities of human fellowship are placed in constant danger. He seeks to widen the democratic domain by giving values other than those of economic self-interest a new force in human society, because he refuses to accept the sceptical and pessimistic view of human nature from which the reliance upon self-interest as the primary motive power in society derives. In so doing he makes assumptions about human nature which carry with them attendant risks. But he believes that the search for a harmony more satisfying than that of the competition of the market place is part of the enduring adventure of mankind and that in that adventure Socialism has its own valid and durable part to play.

THE LIBERAL PARTY

I. HISTORY by the RT. HON. SIR HENRY SLESSER
II. PHILOSOPHY AND PRINCIPLES by DINGLE FOOT

I. HISTORY
by the RT. HON. SIR HENRY SLESSER

THE present position of the political organization which for over a hundred years has been known as the Liberal Party, despite many endeavours at explanation, presents an unresolved paradox. There is little doubt that the great majority of English people today accept the basic ideals of the Liberals, yet relatively few can be brought to vote for Liberal candidates or support the party between elections. What is the cause of this discrepancy between approval of Liberal objects and repudiation of its advocates? By many Liberals blame has been put upon our system of election which gives so little opportunity to a third party, but this surely begs the question. Granted that by proportional representation or some other method of alternative vote the Liberals were able to return Members to the House of Commons in proportion to their votes, even then, at the first election after the war they polled only 2,239,668 votes, while nearly 12,000,000 were Labour and eight and a half million Conservative; and in 1950, when more Liberal candidates were in the field, the result from a Liberal standpoint was certainly no better.

Despite the fact that the history of the Liberal Party has been written, both directly and in the many biographies and memoirs now accessible, it may be that the clue is to be found in the study of the development of the many different influences which in the past have gone to the formation of the party and possibly, in the end, have led to its partial disruption. Thus, to treat the matter chronologically, the Reformation, though in its result supporting authoritative states and sovereigns, at any rate in those countries which were moved by Lutheran influences in its more Puritan aspect, encouraged an individualism of judgment in matters religious which aroused apprehension among Elizabethan statesmen and was even then in danger of being regarded as seditious. We read of bills introduced as early as 1584 to substitute presbyterian government (a democratic form) for that of Bishops—then as now nominated by the Crown. Five Members, led by Peter Wentworth, perhaps to be regarded as the first Liberals, were imprisoned for this audacity. In the time of James I the Puritans became openly hostile to the Government, and in Coke the advocacy of a juridical foundation of liberal principles, challenging the royal prerogative, is to be found. Foreign affairs for the first time became a subject of Parliamentary debate, and we may surely call those Liberal who challenged the authoritarian Spanish influences, as Wyatt formerly had done in Mary's time.

So we come to the open breach with Charles I and the definite formation of parties for and against the King. With the suppression of Nonconformity attempted under the Clarendon Code, we see the work of the Tories, so first called in 1680 or thereabouts. The remnants of Puritanism and other sects came to be the Opposition, powerful under Shaftesbury for a season, and soon to be known as the Whigs. It will be noted how throughout this period the issue was presented, nominally at any rate, as one of uniformity or liberty in the religious sphere. Only in opposition to Catholicism did both sides agree.

Nevertheless this anti-Catholic unity resulting in the installation of William III, once the alleged peril of Popery was defeated, did not last. The attempts of William to govern by coalition did not succeed, and at length the Whigs, by calling in George I, established their long supremacy.

It is to be noted that once James had gone, the religious contentions largely disappeared; Locke, more particularly in his essay on Civil Government, had secularized the issues. Government was assumed to be based upon a "social contract" no longer on "divine right", and obedience to authority was conditional (as had long before been declared by St. Thomas Aquinas and the Jesuits—though few Whigs knew it) on legislation being for the good of the people as a whole. Interference with private property was only justifiable by consent of Parliament, and law must be impartial. Walpole, the great Whig leader (though perhaps he had never read Locke), and his associates, accepted these principles, sustained as they might be in practice by a large measure of material inducement to supporters, by preferment, honours, or direct monetary gift.

A new factor arose, the conciliation of the new affluent. At the time of the South Sea Scandal it is said that a seventh of the total wealth of the country was already invested in Joint-Stock undertakings, and the commercial class, as a whole, often in those days in religious dissent, supported the Whig administration while not venturing to claim an actual share in government. This they left to their betters, the Whig gentry; only in municipal affairs was the direct influence of the now powerful middle-classes felt. The only method of protest by the workers as yet was by riot.

From the time when Wentworth deserted the parliamentarians to support his King, it has been a characteristic of English progressive politics that the more cautious of what we now call the "Left" should leave their former enthusiastic allies; thus it was that after the French Revolution many Whigs abandoned opposition to form coalitions with the Tories. It is from the Whigs who remained steadfast to Fox that the Liberals derive. On the other hand we have to note the later tendency of Canning, in his support of Catholic emancipation and other matters, to depart from the authoritarian principles of his Tory predecessors; of Wilberforce to work with Radicals and Whigs in favour of the emancipation of slavery—a movement of enlightened Toryism, which ultimately brought such statesmen as Melbourne and Palmerston over to the Liberal side.

The agitation preceding the Reform Bill consolidated the Liberal position. Whigs, perhaps reluctantly, worked with

Radicals and Chartists to secure its passage. Never, till the rise of the Labour Party, were the Radicals again to secede, and the acceptance of Free Trade by the Tory Prime Minister, Peel, first by coalition of the "Peelites" during the Crimean period and later by complete assimilation, finally committed all Progressives to that Liberal Party led by Gladstone, himself once a "Peelite." This was the Party which dominated English politics during the greater part of the nineteenth century.

Meanwhile the economic situation was changing; in the earlier period, despite the Industrial Revolution, England was still largely agricultural, and the counties as always tended to Conservatism whether the electors were landlords or their dependants. It was the Tories under Disraeli who, in 1867, greatly extended the franchise. But as the demands of industry grew and the social problem of urban congestion became increasingly acute, the advanced Liberals began, hesitatingly, to doubt whether the *laissez-faire* principles of the Manchester school and the Utilitarians were not susceptible of modification in the face of the sordid misery of the industrial towns, most of which more or less loyally returned Liberals to Parliament.

The change in the opinions of their great thinker, John Stuart Mill, was symptomatic. He supported the right, belatedly, of the State to interfere to control manufacturing processes, and generally to interfere to protect the weak, and this in the ultimate interest of liberty. How different from the attitude of Bright in his opposition to the Factory Acts! The absorbing concern of the leading Liberals, such as Palmerston, in the liberation of foreign States now became domesticated. The removal of the excise on newspapers, introduced by Gladstone and rejected by the Lords, raised the issue as to how far the Liberals were prepared to go, for the aged Palmerston was still in control. But soon he died and after the general Election of 1865, by October, though the aged Lord Russell was Prime Minister, Gladstone was the effective and soon actual leader, and the independent Liberal Party had begun its career as one of the principal parties in the State, to last until 1915. During this period no more is heard of those coalitions and expedients and personal rivalries, such as that of Palmerston and Russell, which had been so customary since the fall of Peel's Ministry. Whether the principles of the contestants, Liberal and Conservative, were really opposed or not, they were presented and accepted by everyone as alternative systems of government, and the people as a whole were convinced that the much advertised antagonisms were fundamental, an acceptance of basic cleavage which had not fully existed since the days of the Jacobite rebellions.

Gladstone, pacific, a believer in free nations and in political democracy, was no friend to Socialism—or State activity—"To take into the hands of the State the business of the individual man ... has estranged me for many many years", he wrote in later years to Lord Acton. Evidently by then suggestions of a collectivist nature were beginning to manifest themselves among the younger Liberals.

Such State action, however, as did gradually win approval in both parties was in the nature of social amelioration in education, public health and cognate matters rather than in industry. The poor law still existed, as it had been framed in the thirties, to mitigate the severity of utter destitution, but the era was a commercial one. Neither political organization, save tentatively the Radicals in Birmingham, had it in mind to nationalize or in any way disturb that unfettered competition in industry which was still regarded as the only method whereby the wealth of the nation could be stimulated and reserved.

The formation of limited companies after 1860 had a far-reaching effect, though at the time unrecognized, in depersonalizing the old family businesses. Gradually the demand for capital equipment both here and abroad resulted in larger undertakings in which the shareholder tended to become a mere drawer of dividend. Agriculture for the most part was neglected and the Conservatives, whose dedicated task it had been to protect and foster it, failed in their endeavour. They turned their attention rather to the development of Empire and imperial trade, neglecting, almost as much as the Liberals, the welfare of the home countryside. The inclusion of the townsman Chamberlain in their ranks, after the Home Rule split, emphasized the urban interests of their party.

Many Whig families also, taking advantage of the Irish question to disagree with Mr. Gladstone, crossed the floor of the House, and, as the Liberals became more markedly democratic, the city and financial interests which had previously supported them tended to find a new political home in the now urbanized and commercial Conservative-Unionist Party. It was at this time, in the throes of the Irish controversy, that the Liberal Party began to show signs of disruption and weakness. Their predominantly middle-class support was one cause of all their failures to recognize the rising economic claims of the descendants of those Radicals and Chartists who had formerly supported them, albeit reluctantly, who already were now considering the formation of a new Independent Labour Party. But the final breach was slow in coming, and as late as the last triumph of the Liberals in 1906, their relations with Labour were comparatively friendly. The latter, now returned some thirty strong, were soon joined by the representatives of the miners. They had among them such later leaders as Ramsay MacDonald, afterwards Prime Minister, Philip Snowden and Arthur Henderson, and were an influence not to be despised.

Had Sir Henry Campbell Bannerman lived it is very possible that a concordat might have been achieved, but his successor, Asquith, was far less Radical; a Liberal Imperialist during the Boer War, he was quite incapable of appreciating the change of outlook which was familiarizing the mass of the workers in trade unions with Socialist aspirations.

Nevertheless, it cannot be denied that the 1906 Liberal Government was exceptionally strong in personnel, including as it did Lloyd George, Churchill, Haldane, Birrell, Burns, Samuel and Morley. It gave South Africa self-government, pleased the trade unions by emancipating them from the liabilities imposed by the Taff Vale decision (going too far in the opinion of many Liberals), and provoked a contest with the Lords over the land charges in the 1909 Budget. Old Age Pensions were first allowed out of State funds, workmen's compensation was extended, national health insurance and unemployment insurance introduced, and trade boards set up to fix minimum wages in sweated industries. Finally, after the prolonged dispute with the Lords and two elections in 1910, the Parliament Act restricted the veto of the Peers and altogether abolished their right to interfere in financial legislation. Again the Irish Question arose, but this time the Ulster Unionists went far further in opposition than had the opponents of Mr. Gladstone's measures. The leader of the Conservatives, Bonar Law, assured Sir Edward Carson that he would support him "whether his actions were constitutional or not." Drilling on both sides and the illicit importation of arms followed and, had it not been for the first world war, civil strife might well have broken out in Ireland. In fact the Home Rule Bill, passed under the Parliament Act, was to come into operation after the war, but by that time events in Ireland had gone beyond the scope of that measure. Welsh Disestablishment followed after long delay the disestablishment of the Irish Church by Gladstone, and with that Act the long tale of Liberal legislation came to an end; never since 1916 have the Liberals been in power.

There remains the melancholy duty of recounting their fall. In 1918 the number of Liberals following Asquith—for they alone deserved the title—fell to 34, their leader losing his seat. In 1923 after the break-up of the Conservative-Liberal coalition, they increased to 158. This was the occasion when they voted to bring the first Labour Government into office; at the ensuing election in 1925 they were again reduced in numbers, to 42.

What was more serious, the few who were returned were divided; while the views of Asquith and Simon on the handling of the general strike were those of the Government, Lloyd George was more desirous to effect a compromise. Nevertheless, after the death of Asquith in 1928, the Liberals were returned at the 1929 election 59 strong, and the number rose to 72 in 1931, when some entered a Coalition Government.

But the free-traders under Samuel soon resigned and in 1935 there were but 21 of them, in 1945 there were 12, in 1950 there were 9, and in 1951 only 6. Nor is this the end of this story of declination; of the negligible number now left in Parliament, the majority come from Wales and Scotland; England is almost unrepresented.

It remains shortly to discuss the reasons for this collapse, unique in political history. Many reasons may be advanced, the first and perhaps most persuasive being that the party has been killed by success. It has converted the whole electorate other than the Communists, it is said, to the belief in liberty, tolerance and opposition to authoritarian government. Secondly, it may be argued that the present democratized Conservative Party now affords a home for all those who fear the growth of Socialism, and that the many Liberals who emphasize that freedom requires a social as well as a political expression have already joined the Labour Party. Or again, it may be pointed out that both the Liberal and Conservative Parties are predominantly middle-class and that in their contest for supremacy with organized labour, they are forced by mutual need for protection from an aggressive proletariat to combine, that the so-called National Liberals have already recognized this necessity, as did the Liberal-Unionists before them, and that the remaining Liberals soon will. Lastly, there are those who maintain that the English party system necessarily involves a governmental party and a united opposition, that there is no room for a weak third party, such as the Liberal Party must now be. It may be that in all this the real explanation lies in the fact that all parties are in substance in agreement; that the differences between them are but those of emphasis which politicians by reason of their occupation are prone to exaggerate. Whatever be the cause, he would be a bold prophet who would foretell the return of a Liberal Government within the foreseeable future.

* * *

II. PHILOSOPHY AND PRINCIPLES

by Dingle Foot

Liberalism has always been, and still is, the creed of emancipation. Its aim is to strike off the fetters which bind the human body and the human spirit; to set free the slaves; to throw open the gaol gates; to abolish taxes on knowledge; to put an end to the disabilities of Jews, Roman Catholics and Dissenters; to pull down the barriers to international trade; to loosen the grip of landlords and monopolists; to get rid of all forms of race and class discrimination—these have been the historic aims of the Liberal movement.

The immediate objectives necessarily vary with each generation. But the Liberal attitude towards public affairs remains essentially the same. Its chief characteristic is a bias against authority. When Acton wrote that "All power tends to corrupt and absolute power corrupts absolutely," he was expressing the fundamental Liberal conviction. The king, the priest, the gauleiter or the commissar—they may not invariably be wrong, but there is always a strong presumption of error. Even where they have to be tolerated, their actions should be subject to the most jealous scrutiny and the most carefully devised restraints.

This attitude has always been manifest in the Liberal approach to foreign affairs. British Liberals have almost invariably sympathized with individuals or nations "struggling to be free". It is, of course, one of the crudest fallacies to suppose that a political movement never changes its ground, and that its leaders succeed one another in a kind of apostolic succession. "A party", said John Morley, "is perpetually being corrupted by personality", and the outlook of British political parties changes a great deal more than their supporters are generally prepared to admit. The Conservatism of Peel was a very different affair from the Toryism of Liverpool. The accents of Keir Hardie were hardly discernible in the budget speeches of Mr. Gaitskell. The outlook of Mr. Lloyd George was widely dissimilar from that of, say, Lord John Russell. Nevertheless the incontrovertible fact remains that

British Liberals have almost always been on the side of the oppressed. Charles James Fox rejoiced at the storming of the Bastille. From the moment when he wrote his letters to Lord Aberdeen on the Neapolitan prisons, Gladstone's whole career was a flaming protest against despotic cruelty whatever its form and wherever it might be found. Even in the last few years, when Liberal representation in Parliament has been reduced to a tiny handful, it has almost invariably been Liberal Members of Parliament who have been the first to protest against any example of race discrimination or any invasion of civil liberties in the colonial empire. No doubt such an attitude is frequently open to criticism. The oppressors are not always quite so lacking in justification nor the victims so entirely free from blame as British Liberals are given to imagine. Nevertheless, it is an extraordinary record. For a century and a half there has been a political movement in this country which has consistently proclaimed that foreign and imperial policy should be based not on expediency but on principle and (to borrow Macaulay's phrase) that "oppression in Bengal" is "the same thing as oppression in the streets of London".

Such a philosophy was easy to understand and justify as long as the tyrants who had to be resisted or overthrown could be readily identified. It becomes infinitely more difficult of application in a world of apparently impersonal forces. The individual oppressor, though not entirely extinct, is now a rare phenomenon. Abroad, the twin evils of Communism and extreme nationalism do not depend for their existence upon particular leaders or figureheads. At home, the enemy is no longer the ruthless, grasping or over-ambitious leader or class. The present danger, as British Liberals see it, is that we shall reach a state of affairs in which the individual will always be at the mercy of the organization. The food we may eat, the clothes we may wear, the news we may read, the films we may see, the broadcast programmes we may listen to, and the jobs we may take, will all be decided for us by some over-mighty authority, against whose decrees there will be no redress and no appeal. It will not always be a Government Department. It may be a quasi-independent public board, a private monopoly, or a giant trade union. But the effect will be the same. In every department of their lives ordinary men and women will be controlled by the anonymous bosses who run the managerial State. This is the hardest battle that Liberals have ever had to fight. The village Hampden resisting the little tyrant of his fields attracted almost universal sympathy. His cause is far less hopeful when the antagonist is the Ministry of Housing and Local Government or the County Agricultural Executive.

Here, nevertheless, is the first element which makes up the Liberal philosophy—the resistance to arbitrary or capricious power whatever form it may take. Hence the Liberal insistence, in both domestic and international affairs, upon the rule of law. Government is a necessary evil, and no modern community can avoid a considerable degree of regulation. But the essential difference is between government by law and government by caprice. Dictatorships take many forms, but they all have one feature in common—the dictator is above the law. No one in Hitler's Germany dreamed of applying to the courts for protection against the excesses of the Nazi party. It is inconceivable that a prisoner of the N.K.V.D. should apply to a Russian judge to secure his release. This is the fundamental difference. The essential feature of the Liberal state is that no man may be made to suffer either in his body or in his goods save for a distinct breach of established law and by the ordinary forms of legal process.

Now it is frequently argued by critics in both the other parties that this principle is universally accepted among the Western nations and it is, of course, perfectly true that it is rarely challenged in unmistakable terms. The Liberal answer is that of Lord Chesterfield:

> "Let us consider that arbitrary power has seldom or never been introduced into any country at once. It must be introduced by slow degrees and, as it were, step by step, lest the people should see its approach. The barriers and fences of the people's liberty must be plucked one by one,

and some plausible pretences must be found for removing or hoodwinking, one after another, those sentries who are posted by the constitution of a free country, for warning people of their danger."

Even in our own country the barriers have, during the past quarter of a century, been subject to a process of constant erosion. Parliamentary control over both legislation and administration is far less effective than it used to be. Ministers can impose the most far-reaching measures (e.g., the direction of labour) without any prior consultation with Parliament whatsoever. Great sectors of public administration, namely those under the control of public Boards as contrasted with Departments, are removed from any regular parliamentary or democratic supervision. Beside the ordinary courts of law there has grown up an enormous network of special tribunals whose members have not the same independence as Her Majesty's judges. It is difficult to point to any single development which, taken by itself, is open to overwhelming objection. But the general tendency is manifest. The protection of individual rights and liberties tends more and more to be subordinated to considerations of administrative convenience. To resist this tendency and to preserve and strengthen the safeguards of personal freedom has been one of the principal aims of the Liberal Party during the last twenty years.

The problem which has confronted Liberals throughout the present century has been the application of their well-understood beliefs in a rapidly changing world. How they endeavoured to solve it was expressed twenty-three years ago in the "Yellow Book":

> Faced by these conditions in modern industry, convinced that our present social order denies a real liberty to a great proportion of the population, anxious to effect the reforms that are necessary without at the same time injuring the springs of such efficiency (and it is not small) as that order retains, we have framed the constructive proposals, touching the many parts of the one great problem, which this book contains. Financial and in-

dustrial reforms, international trade and national development, the juster distribution of wealth, the worker's right to be a citizen and not merely a subject, in the world of production—the measures we advocate in relation to all these things spring from one clear purpose. We believe with a passionate faith that the end of all political and economic action is not the perfecting or the perpetuation of this or that piece of mechanism or organization, but that individual men and women may have life, and that they may have it more abundantly.

Perhaps the most significant words in this passage are "the worker's right to be a citizen and not merely a subject in the world of production." Ever since 1918 the principal matter of controversy between Conservatives and Socialists has been nationalization. The familiar clichés about the "wickedness of private profit" or the "dead hand of the State" have resounded from tens of thousands of platforms. Liberals believe that this sterile debate tends to obscure far more important issues. It makes little difference, for example, whether the railways are in the hands of four private companies subject to a considerable degree of public control or whether they are taken over by a single public corporation. What matters, both in public and private industry, is the status of the worker. The mere transfer of ownership accomplishes nothing. What matters is to build up a genuine sense of partnership between workers and management. This is the problem which, more perhaps than any other, has engaged the attention of Liberals during recent years. The result has been a series of proposals designed to increase workers' representation on boards of management of both nationalized and private concerns and to extend profit-sharing and every form of incentive to production. There is no copyright in political ideas and both the Conservative and Labour Parties have recently tended (with or without acknowledgment) to appropriate some parts of the Liberal "co-ownership" programme. Nevertheless Liberals believe that, in this as in many other spheres, it is they who have led the way and that they have discovered how to avoid the clash between capital and labour.

The second element in the Liberal philosophy has been the insistence on freedom of enterprise. Liberals in the nineteenth century were free-traders, not merely because they preferred a particular fiscal device but because tariffs, quotas and other impediments to commerce were, in their view, the economic expressions of privilege and restriction. To-day the same struggle is carried on in a different form. Protectionism no longer finds its expression merely in import duties. It is to be observed in almost every aspect of our national life. The number of protected occupations and industries constantly increases. The trade associations which engage in collective price maintenance, the boards of nationalized concerns which use their statutory powers to prevent competition by private competitors, the workers in heavy industry who, although fully employed, refuse to allow the introduction of foreign labour even though the need is manifest—all these are the modern protectionists. The Statute Book, during recent years, has been crammed with twentieth-century counterparts of the Corn Laws, measures which restrict free enterprise and injure the general public for the benefit of specially-favoured sections of the community.

This does not mean that Liberalism, as it has developed in our lifetime, is synonymous with *laissez-faire*. Indeed, ever since 1906 Liberal statesmen have taken a leading part in demanding certain forms of State intervention. In the modern world the question is no longer whether the State should intervene, but whether it should intervene in the public interest or on behalf of privileged economic groups. The outstanding Liberal contribution to political thought between the wars was the Lloyd George-Keynesian programme for an attack upon unemployment by great schemes of national development. If it had been adopted, it would have been a kind of British equivalent of the Tennessee Valley Experiment. Of course it involved deliberate State action on an enormous scale, but the result would have been to provide innumerable fresh openings for individual enterprise. Unfortunately this conception makes little appeal to the doctrinaires in both the other camps, with their unyielding insistence on the absolute virtues of nationalization or private ownership.

The third element in Liberalism is the belief in social justice. The social services are, broadly speaking, a Liberal achievement. It is true, of course, that the post-war improvements were mainly carried through by a Labour Government. For the most part, however, they commanded universal acceptance. Based on the Beveridge Plan, they were merely the logical fulfilment of the process initiated by Asquith and Lloyd George forty years earlier. Nevertheless, there is a vital distinction between the Liberal and Socialist attitude on these matters. It is expressed in the title of Lord Beveridge's second great report—"Full Employment in a Free Society." Socialists, and often Conservatives as well, frequently appear to believe that there is an inevitable conflict between freedom and welfare. This was made abundantly clear a few years ago in Parliamentary debates on the direction of labour. The favourite argument of those who defended industrial conscription was that direction by law was at least preferable to direction by economic circumstance. In other words, we must choose between hunger and servitude. Now it is true, of course, that schemes of social betterment may be carried through in such a way as to involve serious invasions of the individual's right of choice. The easiest way to avoid fluctuation in demand and in employment is completely to dragoon the consumer. In the short run the State planner can most easily succeed if everyone is compelled to fall in with his plans. But to the Liberal this is a counsel of despair. The problem of the modern world, as he sees it, is to combine three things—personal freedom, economic efficiency and social justice. Nor does he regard them as irreconcilables. In his view economic efficiency and social justice can only be fully secured in a free society.

THE MINOR PARTIES
Anon.

THE stability and forcefulness of British political institutions are said to depend on the existence of two great political parties competing for supremacy in Parliament and in the country. The electorate squeezes out any "intermediate, sectional or hybrid creed". The political history of the last 150 years confirms this thesis; many minority parties have flourished for a short space, but have eventually died away. During the last twenty years the two-party system has so increased in power against the minor parties that people often forget how frequently minor parties have arisen in the past, and how tenaciously some of them have clung to life. The purpose of this paper is to catalogue some of the minority parties of the last 150 years, to examine the reasons for their existence and for their disappearance, and to draw some general conclusions.

The earliest and most difficult to define of the minor parties in our parliamentary history is the Radical group. They lived on the fringe of the Liberals, and on most occasions voted with them. They had little cohesion in the House, were "singularly hard to unite on any practical course, and singularly given to riding individual hobbyhorses"; yet the items of their policy and their contribution to the development of the party system were so distinctive that they must be regarded as separate from their Whig and Liberal allies. The Whig aristocracy and the Tory House of Lords controlled the major parties to a greater extent than is generally appreciated, and the Radicals represented a policy and a section of the population whose aims were incompatible with that control. They inherited a Jacobin philosophy of the rights of man, and in particular the right of every man to an equally valuable vote (which implied equal constituencies and a secret ballot as well as universal suffrage). They had an egalitarian

THE MINOR PARTIES

dislike of all forms of privilege and patronage, whether in Parliament, the services, the church or in land tenure. They comprised dissenters with a puritan dislike of temporalities and ceremonial; they were inspired with Bentham's utilitarian principles. Had all these doctrines been pressed by a compact party based on a wide franchise, the resultant conflict would indeed have been revolutionary.

Their strength in the House of Commons is difficult to measure. Before the Reform Bill they numbered a few brilliant individuals—Burdett, Hobhouse, and Lambton (Lord Durham). After 1832 the ultra-Radical vote, for example on motions to reduce the Civil List, appears to have been about 30, rising on occasions to 50. On more popular issues—Grote's Ballot motion, or electoral reform—they obtained about 100-150 supporters. Their real strength lay not in the teller's count but in the persistence with which the motions were moved; in the intelligence, ability and singlemindedness of the Radical Members like Hume, Grote, Roebuck, Molesworth, Cobden, Bright, W. J. Fox and Joseph Chamberlain; and above all in the tremendous popular support which they could rouse from time to time on behalf of the Reform Bill, the Chartist Petition or the Anti-Corn Law movement.

Although they had no party discipline in the House, they can take the credit for originating modern "democratic" party organization in the constituencies. The National Political Union, started at the time of the Reform Bill, and Chamberlain's Caucus, originating in Birmingham in the 1870's, set the pattern for the modern ward—constituency—national party "pyramid". By demanding detailed pledges from candidates, they set the course towards political programmes.

Their policies, however, were so multifarious that they were often mutually antagonistic, and although they cleverly used outside pressure to force their way into the House of Commons their leaders, once elected, turned the machine of public opinion against abuses that were irrelevant to the main cause of radicalism. For example, Cobden and Bright captured the mass-meeting, mass-petition system for their campaign against the Corn Laws. Subsequently they turned their energies to a peace campaign. They, and Cobden in particular, neglected the need to widen the franchise and thus to increase the chance of forming a large and independent Radical party in the House. Just at the moment when household suffrage and the Ballot had been achieved, Joseph Chamberlain led the Radicals into the Unionist camp in a determined fight against Home Rule. Yet by 1886 they had achieved most of the reforming and Benthamite proposals of 1830. Britain was as "democratic" as France.

The longest-lived minor party was that of the Irish. They gave the party system what the Radicals lacked—discipline. The Irish problem proved the most intractable in British politics in the nineteenth century. From the rebellion of 1798 and the Union two years later, until the establishment of the Free State in 1923, neither country could find a common ground for lasting agreement. Nationalism was only one, and not the most important, cause of the quarrel. Religion was a barrier to sympathy. The Irish Catholic peasantry and their priests fought for Catholic Emancipation, for the abolition of the tithes collected by the Established Church of Ireland, and finally for the disestablishment of that Church. In this they were opposed by the majority of the Anglo-Irish aristocracy and of English voters. O'Connell achieved a rapid success in securing Catholic Emancipation; and his oratory, his mass meetings, his Catholic Association with its political fund, which set the pattern for the Anti-Corn Law League, were equally successful in using the threat of the unenfranchised to coerce the government.

In his success over Catholic Emancipation O'Connell conjured a spirit he could not control. The peasants and the peasant-priests wanted much more: tithe abolition, disestablishment (which did not come for forty years) and an agrarian revolution. The Reform Bill of 1832 raised the property qualification for Irish voters and thus counteracted to a certain extent the effects of Catholic Emancipation. The Whig and Tory landowners were still able to control many constituencies, and O'Connell's party in the House varied between forty and twelve in number. His caution and reluctance to face a violent solution led to his downfall. Repeal of the Union was unthinkable to the vast majority of the English, and without repeal, and the restoration of an Irish parliament, reform of other problems could not be obtained. Although the imperial parliament agreed to give way over the religious difficulty in the end, Ireland never achieved an agrarian revolution satisfactory to a peasant society until the Free State was set up.

The famine of the 1840's and the mass emigration which followed brought a new bitterness. Secret societies, murder of landlords, mutilation of cattle and coercive retaliation drove England and Ireland further apart. In 1870 the Home Government Association of Ireland was formed; in 1872 the Ballot Act was passed; and—cause and effect—in 1874, 59 Home Rulers were returned to Westminster. A new era began. Under the leadership of Isaac Butt and then of Parnell an implacable party fought bitterly against the English Parliament to which it had been returned. The pressure of public opinion, the force of extra-legal boycotts and the brutality of agrarian outrage had achieved a little: now it was the turn of obstruction. The result in the House of Commons was far-reaching; a gentleman's club was forced into becoming a businesslike legislative machine. However, even though Parnell and Redmond succeeded in persuading the Liberals to support Home Rule, they could not break the resistance of the House of Lords. The alliance cost the Liberals much in the long run—they could hardly expect gratitude from the Irish; they alienated Whigs and Radicals, and during a vital period they had their faces turned to Ireland and away from the social problems of English industrial democracy. The Irish alliance, eighty strong, allowed the Liberals to form a government in 1892 and in 1910, but their English supporters were in a minority in the House and in the country.

The sequence of Irish politics has carried us past the other important minor party of the mid-nineteenth century—the Peelites. In origins they are very different from either Radicals or Irish. They had no roots in the unenfranchised proletariat or in the land hungry peasants. They were members of the new gentry—the second generation of wealthy manufacturers—who had great intelligence and ability. Their intelligence was their downfall; they are almost unique in the history of party in the House of Commons in that they allowed themselves to be persuaded by debate into reversing a policy. The blandishments of Cobden and the famine in Ireland converted Peel, the respected leader of the Conservative (and Protectionist) Party, to the repeal of the Corn Laws. With a hundred followers, among them Graham, Gladstone, Goulburn and Sidney Herbert, and with the help of Irish, Radicals and Whigs, he carried repeal through. When the unlikely coalition broke up, he and his followers were elected as a distinct party. The result was an almost intolerable confusion in policies. Peelites, over eighty strong, refused to serve with Russell Whigs or Disraeli's protectionists. Radicals, about 100 strong, were highly unreliable in the division lobbies. The Irish would vote against any government which took steps to establish law and order in Ireland. Hence for ten years the business of arranging cabinets was as complex and tedious as it is in modern France, and governments fell as frequently. Since, however, the Peelites were predominantly men of administrative ability, they found arid opposition more irksome than others might have done. Since also their implacable enemies were the protectionists (in spite of Disraeli's attempts at reconciliation) they naturally tended to sink their differences with the Whigs and Liberals. The result was the Aberdeen coalition of 1852 in which the Peelites, although reduced to thirty Members in the House, took six out of thirteen seats in the Cabinet. The combined Whig and Radical strength at the same time was 270, yet they only held seven cabinet posts.

In 1857, after the General Election, the *Quarterly Review* reports the extinction of "the amphibious class" of Peelites, and comments:

> They were at once a sign of the prevailing disorganization and a cause of its continuance and extension. If they voted with the minister their adherence was deemed servile; if they voted against him their opposition was

thought faction. If they acted apart from all parties their
isolation was a proof of their self-conceit and of the extrava-
gant value they set upon themselves. ... The constituencies, locally organized under the forms of political dualism,
abhor the *tertium quid* ... not a single person has been
returned to parliament because he was a Peelite.

Those sentences describe in a nutshell the difficult and often
anomalous position in which a minor party finds itself. A
minor party will survive so long as the issue on which it
stands remains important in the eyes of the electorate: so
Peelites survived for a while as the protagonists of free trade.
But when the major parties start a serious battle over a
different issue, then the electorate is forced to take sides in
that battle and so to ignore the minor party's policy.

It is curious that the minor parties of the years prior to
1886 (the date of the first Home Rule Bill) all had a detri-
mental effect on the Conservative party: Radicals and Irish
almost always voted against them, and the Peelites robbed
them of all their leaders for fifteen years. Had it not been for
the minor parties the Conservative tenure of office in the
nineteenth century would have been almost continuous.
After 1886 the process worked against the Liberals. Some of
the Liberals seceded over Home Rule, and, after a period
as an independent party, joined the Conservatives.

Just as Free Trade had split the Conservative Party in
1846, and had distracted the Radicals from their primary
aim of universal suffrage, so Home Rule split the Liberal
Party in 1886, and led the Radicals away from liberalism into
the social reform camp of the Conservatives or the collectivist
camp of the Labour Party. The histories of the Labour and
Liberal parties are described in companion articles and it
would be impertinent to dwell on them here. They are, however, of considerable interest to a student of minority parties.
The rise of the Labour Party from minor to major status is
unique in our history, and so is the decline of the Liberals.
One also remarks that each, when in a minority, has proposed
adjustments to the franchise. Such proposals are characteristic
of a minor party which conceives itself to be in a helpless

position, yet feels it has a mission to fulfil. They are on a par with other attempts to capture the House of Commons from outside, though they are more in keeping with our time than the Chartist riots or Irish outrage.

The 1880's witnessed an interesting attempt to capture a political party from the inside. The so-called Fourth Party was short-lived, and was never seriously regarded as an independent entity in spite of the haughty treatment its members gave to the Conservative Whips. Composed of four brilliant individuals—Lord Randolph Churchill, Sir Henry Drummond Wolff, Sir John Gorst and A. J. Balfour—the group's purpose was to "ginger up" the official opposition which was being rather ineffectively led by Sir Stafford Northcote. Having joined forces and found common ground over the Bradlaugh incident, they began to form a policy of their own. They hoped to lead the Conservative Party back to Disraeli's Tory Democracy. After Disraeli's restraining influence was withdrawn on his death in 1882, their dispute with the official leaders of the Conservative Party grew more bitter and public. Lord Randolph's brilliant advocacy of the cause of social reform made him popular with the masses, and he evolved the plan of capturing the Conservative party organization. He hoped, by getting his own supporters elected to the National Union of Conservative Associations, to take the policy-making function out of the hands of the "Shadow Cabinet". He won, but as soon as he had done so he surrendered to the official leaders.

The twentieth century has so far produced five minority parties. The Welsh Nationalists, represented by Lloyd George, were soon swallowed up in the general "devolution" policy of the Liberals. The cause of Welsh devolution has been pressed by Welsh Liberal and Labour Members, but it has not inspired the same violent protagonism as nationalism did in Ireland. Indeed, once the Welsh Church was disestablished, neither religion nor economics supported nationalism. In the House Welshmen had achieved the addition of two Welsh members to the Select Committee on Kitchen and Refreshment Rooms.

The cause of Scottish nationalism has been little more successful. Motions in favour of devolution were carried by the Liberals in 1911-13. In the 1920's members of the Labour Party introduced "Government of Scotland" Bills but made little progress. There was no popular clamour in Scotland on their behalf. However, in the 1930's Nationalist candidates obtained a respectable number of votes at by-elections. In 1944 Dr. Robert MacIntyre was elected for Motherwell, and caused a sensation by refusing at first to accept sponsors when taking his seat in the House. He was defeated in 1945, and so far no Scottish Nationalist has taken his place.

The British Communist Party was founded in 1920. They have put forward a number of candidates at each General Election, but without much success. Saklatvala was elected for Battersea in 1929. Gallacher represented West Fife from 1935 to 1950. In the 1945 Parliament he was joined by Piratin. There is one point in their programme which links them with other minority parties: they propose to lower the age for voters to 18 years—once again the appeal for a change in the franchise.

The New Party was formed by Sir Oswald Mosley early in 1931, because he had been unable to get the Government to accept his solution of the economic crisis. It attracted five other M.P.s, but at the ensuing election all its 24 candidates were defeated. The party was already defunct when its founder went over to Fascism in 1933.

During the late war, in July, 1942, a Common Wealth Party was formed. This party had three Members in 1942, and put forward a programme of "greater equality of work, sacrifice and opportunity between soldiers and civilians, men and women, employers and workers". At later conferences they advocated a thorough-going socialist policy and a "Second Front". The party had twenty-three candidates in the field in 1945. Only one was successful, and he later joined the Labour Party. The Common Wealth movement appears to have drawn its main strength from its criticism of the Coalition's war policy and from the dislike of some of the electorate for the political truce.

From this short survey we can see that there are two kinds of minority party in English political history: firstly there is the party of the reforming or revolutionary type which tries to force the major parties to alter the franchise in its favour; this party is typified by the Radicals who were trying to capture Parliament from the outside. Then there is the party formed by a split over some important principle in one of the existing parties in the House of Commons. However strong in intellect and ability, this type of party is rapidly absorbed into one of the major parties, or is rejected by the electorate.

It is remarkable that none of the parties, except perhaps the Liberal-Unionists, was formed on a basis of some delicate logical difference in political philosophy, as are many Continental minor parties. A group of French or Greek or German politicians, finding themselves a shade to the left on social questions, or a shade to the right on economic issues, appear adept at coining a party name which, temporarily at least, defines those nuances of logical thought. One could easily perform the same service for groups inside the present British parties, but the groups, although they might agree that the logic was irreproachable, would reject the label and prefer to remain under the wide umbrellas provided by their present allegiances.

Apart entirely from the question of proportional representation, there is no doubt that the present financial necessities of party politics discourage minor parties. The complex party organization in the constituencies, the close discipline in the House, the appeal to an immense electorate, for all of which minor parties have been responsible in the past, have made party politics a whole-time business and cost money. The solution in Britain has been the political fund, which does not reward members directly, but enables them to set in motion a huge publicity machine at general elections, and to keep an agent to nurse their constituencies between elections. It is highly unlikely that any individual or group, however idealist or philanthropic, will continue to pay out the large sums needed, year after year, in order to support a party which stands no chance of carrying that individual's or group's political views into law. Only a minor party which is obviously in the ascendant can escape the blight of pauperdom.

THE INDEPENDENT IN POLITICS

by COMMANDER STEPHEN KING-HALL

The author of this article, who sat as an Independent M.P. from 1942-1945 and unsuccessfully contested the Ormskirk Division in 1945 and the Bridgwater Division in 1950 as an Independent candidate, thinks it desirable to remark that any views expressed in the following paper are personal and not to be regarded as in any way representing the policy or opinion of the Hansard Society, of whose Council he has been Chairman since 1944. He wishes to acknowledge his debt to a learned authority who desires to remain anonymous but who gave invaluable assistance by placing at his disposal the results of some historical research upon the subject.

THERE are some articles which, when the title is first mentioned, sound much easier to write than they turn out to be when the prospective author can no longer place in the Bring-Up file the impassioned appeals of the impatient editor.

This is one of those articles. The subject on the surface has a deceptively simple appearance. This is partly because the word *Independent* (in the political sense) has meant different things at different times. Originally it meant a person who was independent of the King or Queen and the great families, someone who was elected to the House of Commons under his own steam and who, once at Westminster, could not be relied upon to give consistent support to any particular policy or any particular personality.

During the first half of the eighteenth century the word came to have a new meaning. Now it meant somebody who was not in the pocket of the Government. During the famous debates in Parliament in 1741 on Walpole's conduct of affairs, Lord Carteret—who would probably have behaved no differently had the opportunity come his way—said that corruption was the only art of government which Walpole understood. "By corrupt means he gets his creatures and tools at most of the elections in the kingdom. Both Houses of Parliament are induced by a corrupt influence to approve of his measures." The few who stood out against this system were the Independents—which meant, in effect, the people who were rich enough to live without accepting sinecures or bribes.

Political parties had existed since the seventeenth century, but party was little more than a label for a particular set of ideas. When parties began to be organized in the second half of the nineteenth century, the word Independent took on a new meaning. An Independent was a candidate who sought election to Parliament (or, after 1888, to a local authority) without the backing of a party organization and without committing himself to giving unwavering support to any party policy. Of course, many who stood with party labels were independently-inclined, and their votes could not be relied upon. This did not matter much in the days when an adverse vote in the House of Commons did not necessarily or even usually lead to the downfall of the Government.

Independent, in the sense in which it has been used in the last eighty years, means a person who is independent of the party machines. Harold Nicolson distinguishes five different kinds of Independent.[1] There is what he calls "the fortuitously independent", the person elected during a period of Coalition government when there is a party truce, a person who merely expresses a feeling of discontent with things as they are. There are the "academic independents" who had increasingly after the first world war been returned for the University seats. There are the "temperamental independents", among whom Harold Nicolson includes Mr. Churchill and Mr. R. R. Stokes. Then there are the "forlorn independents", the survivors of a party which has died. Finally there are the "true independents", those who fight an election without a party machine and who, if elected, do not take a party whip in the House.

An Independent, then, first meant a person not dependent

[1] "The Independent Member of Parliament", in *Papers on Parliament*, Hansard Society, 1949.

on the King and Queen or the great families, then a person not dependent on the Executive Government, finally a person not dependent on the political parties. But whatever the Independent has refused to depend upon, he has always brought to the House of Commons that spirit of criticism which has long been its essential role.

This critical function of Parliament was coming to be understood as early as Tudor times. While it is fair to make the generalization that in broad political principles all members of Elizabethan Parliaments brought independence of mind to join with fervent loyalty to the Queen's Government, there were graduations of independence. Great men could influence the burgesses of boroughs, and could so recommend their friends and relations that no corporation dare refuse the proposed candidate. Young men so elected were dependent on the patron for further advancement. Great courtiers like Leicester increased their prestige by putting their nominees forward at elections: other grandees followed suit out of rivalry. The Queen's Secretary got his own friends and relations into the House. The Queen's Ministers were besieged with applications from their servants to procure seats. Parliament was fashionable, a seat was a mark of pre-eminence greater than knighthood; but the great man who helped the lesser man to get in could rely on the latter's support in the House. The number of courtiers who could be trusted to give a lead in supporting the Government was in 1584 little less than one hundred (that is, between one quarter and one fifth of the total membership). A very rough guess suggests that well over a hundred others were dependent not on government but on great families not directly connected with the court. The independent residue, after deducting the courtiers and the satellites of feudal aristocracy, were the country gentlemen whose settled fortunes and traditional standing enabled them to command a borough or the half share of a county.

The folly of Charles I and James II brought the Crown into conflict with these stubborn knights, and at intervals for sixty years they rebelled against attacks on their church, their property and their liberty. It is remarkable that they seldom led, and seldom governed: it is the great barons (great, even if recently ennobled), the lawyers, the secretaries, the priests and the diplomats who form the Government, and rule. Immediately the rebellion or crisis is over, the county gentlemen sink back into their bucolic routine and their suspicious attitude to the government they have just helped into power.

The conflicts of the Stuart period made independence difficult. When civil war is raging, it is unpopular if not impossible to be neutral. Circumstances forced people to take sides; and though it was possible to change sides, it was hardly possible not to be on one side or the other at any particular moment.

It was in Georgian times that the existence of placemen became a political issue. There were between two and three hundred of these men in the Commons during the reigns of the first two Georges. Government could not go on unless the Ministry could reward its political supporters in the House, and unless Members were able to lure freeholders to the poll by the promise of tangible rewards. There was no formed opposition. The King's Court and the dependents of the King's Friends formed the Government, both Ministry and Administration. Retired Ministers observed a passive loyalty. The opposition came from the rival courts—the heir to the Hanoverian throne maintaining a lively sense of favour to come—and from the "country interest".

An estimate by Professor Namier puts the number of Independents in 1760 at 60 to 80 (out of 588), most of them representing counties or large boroughs. In many cases they owned seats, where they had served a political apprenticeship, or had a traditional right to them, a right often only accorded when age had added dignity to hereditary right. An analysis in 1788 gives the number of Independents as 108.

With the French Revolution and Reform, two great issues of principle faced Parliament, and Members began to sort themselves out into what I should regard as the embryos of the present parties and the conception of "the Right" and "the Left". We thus come to the Independents and the quasi-

Independents of the late eighteenth and the nineteenth centuries.

Let us start with Sir George Savile, the last of a long line of Saviles, who sat for Yorkshire and was described as a "staunch Whig of independent character". Whig meant in these cases little more than loyal support for the dynasty: Savile was known as "Independent Savile" and his name and the fact that he had been independent was mentioned in an election song in 1807, twenty years after his death. He refused office, though offered it in Rockingham's administration. He criticized crown patronage, the "Indian influence", and the war with America.

Savile was far more intelligent than the majority of the independent country gentlemen. This group seldom attended the House, and when they did so caused raised eyebrows. Entering booted and spurred, swearing freely, boasting of their drinking capacities, they formed a somewhat uncouth section of a polished and aristocratic assembly. Their epitome was Squire Western; "I hate all lords, they are a parcel of courtiers and Hanoverians—my daughter shall have an honest country gentleman".

Then there was William Wilberforce who was elected for Hull in 1780. He was a friend of Pitt and opposed to the Government of Lord North, yet his first vote in the House was given *for* the Government against the re-election of Speaker Norton. He next sat for Yorkshire against the coalition, and led a revolt of the manufacturing interests against the great county families. He promoted several minor bills before taking up his great interest in suppressing the Slave Trade. He is classified as a Tory supporter of Pitt's Tory Government, yet he voted in 1794 and again in 1803, against the war with France, in spite of his own dislike of Jacobinism. He voted against Pitt on the impeachment of Melville, an occasion when his known impartiality is said to have influenced forty votes. He voted against the Government in 1810 in favour of an inquiry into the Walcheren expedition.

Cobden (1804-65) had a similar career. His three principles were Repeal of the Corn Laws, Free Trade, and no continental wars. Thus he was generally in agreement with the Whig-Liberal-Radical party. Yet he refused office when it was offered to him. He supported Peel over the Maynooth Grant (when Bright took the opposite side). He vigorously opposed the Crimean War against a Whig-Liberal Government. He carried a motion which resulted in Palmerston's resignation over China in 1857. In Palmerston's last Government he was again offered the Board of Trade. He refused, saying "In the last twelve years I have been the systematic and constant assailant of the principles on which your foreign policy has been carried on.... At the same time I have expressed a general want of confidence in your domestic politics."

Bright, Cobden's ally, also took an independent line. He voted against the "Tory" Ashley's ten-hour bills, but also against Whig education proposals in 1847; though he later sat in Liberal Cabinets.

Roebuck (1801-79) declared himself Independent when he was returned for Bath with the party tab of "Radical". Though he was a founder member of the Reform Club (the aim of which was to promote Whig-Radical friendship) he never liked the Whigs. He championed spirited action by England abroad, and his attack on the inefficiency of the Government during the Crimean War led them to resign. He violently supported slave-owners during the American Civil War, he made bitter attacks on the working-classes and on the House of Lords, yet his indifference to party was appreciated by the multitude who regarded him as a politician of stern integrity.

If I am reading my history aright, and I admit that I am navigating in seas which are somewhat uncharted, the nineteenth century "Independents" may be seen in retrospect to have been fighting a rear-guard action against the tendencies of the parties to crystallize into highly organized bodies. These men behaved in Parliament in a manner which had its origins in conduct of Members who, as far back as Tudor times, had asserted themselves against the wishes of the Monarch or the control of patrons.

It may surprise many people to learn that between the Reform Act (1832) and the outbreak of the Great War in

1914 there was never in the House of Commons a single Member who had stood for election as an Independent. In 1862 an Independent stood for Wycombe, Chipping, Bucks. He received one vote. I have been unable to discover whether it was cast by the candidate.

In the 1885 and 1892 elections there were six Independent candidates; all failed. During the latter part of the nineteenth century a handful of men secured election as Independent-Liberals or Independent-Conservatives, but they were party rebels and not true Independents.

If, however, the diligent reader examines *Hansard* for the century, he will come across examples of speeches in which Honourable Members rise to their feet and explicitly describe themselves as Independents. They sometimes spoke as if there were a recognized body of such men: here, for example, is an extract from a speech by a Mr. Whalley made on April 20th, 1877, during a debate on the adequacy of *Hansard*. He said: "I may be permitted to speak on behalf of an unfortunate, and it may perhaps be a small number of Members of this House— I mean the Independent Members. . . ."[1]

What did this use of the word Independent (and similar examples could be quoted) mean? How does this tie up with my statement that Independents—in the present-day sense of the term—did not appear on the parliamentary stage until the first world war?

The answer is, I think, to be found in the idea that Parliament's function is to act as a check upon the executive. I cannot improve on this description of the system by T. E. Utley in a Third Programme broadcast on "The Function of the Parliamentary Opposition". He said, after referring to certain quotations from Bagehot: "Obviously he [Bagehot] is thinking of the House as most of his contempories thought of it—as a corporate entity, a body with a will and soul of its own, existing in its corporate and individual state to choose, to criticize and, when necessary, to dismiss governments; standing in perpetual political opposition to the executive."

---

[1] The records show that Mr. Whalley did not stand for election as an Independent and that throughout his career he usually voted for his party.

T. E. Utley continued: "... This modern conception of Opposition[1] arises from the two party system and the two party system is another of those constitutional traditions which were, in fact, born yesterday. You may truly say that it did not begin to dominate British political life until 1931...."

It is against this background of a House of Commons which was *not* dominated by two great parties, which, like the top of icebergs, are the outward indications of massive party machines below the surface, that we must consider so-called Independents of the nineteenth century such as Mr. Whalley.

It is, I think, reasonable to deduce that in a general manner these Independents (up to the Great War of 1914) were simply men who because of their character or special interest in some great cause (e.g., the suppression of slavery) were distinguished from their colleagues by the fact that they behaved in Parliament in accordance with what had always been regarded as the business of Parliament, i.e., the expression of a collective "opposition". These nineteenth century Independents were men who put their party allegiances second to their independence of judgement and personal crusades. They were men who would have quoted with approval the words of Governor Pitt,[2] grandfather of Chatham, who wrote to his son in 1706: "If you are in Parliament show yourself on all occasions a good Englishman, and a faithful servant to your country. If you aspire to fame in the House, you must make yourself master of its precedents and orders. *Avoid faction, and never enter the House pre-possessed; but attend diligently to the debate, and vote according to your conscience and not for any sinister end whatever.* I had rather see any child of mine want than have him get his bread by voting in the House of Commons." The words I

---

[1] The pleasant conceit of paying the leader of the Opposition an official salary, a constitutional arrangement so mystifying to foreigners, only dates from 1937. In 1945 Russian post-graduate students at Sverdlovsk University asked me this question, "Is it essential in your opinion that an opposition should exist in Parliament in order that the Parliament should be democratic, and if no one wants to oppose, is it necessary to invent an opposition?"

[2] A gentleman whose activities were very far from conforming to the advice he gave his son. He was conspicuous for rascality even in the eighteenth century.

have italicized above seem to me to express the authentic creed of independence in an M.P.

But throughout the nineteenth century there was still plenty of room for manoeuvre inside the so-called parties, and it was not until our own times that the discipline of the Whips and the high pressure organization of the party machine came into being, together with the conception that the doctrine of Privilege might extend to party meetings.

It is in the twentieth century that the modern Independents first appear. In the course of my investigations I discovered that a young Member of Parliament called Winston Churchill was recorded for a brief period in the reference books as being N.P. The well-known but now extinct weekly *Vanity Fair* published a poem about this phenomenon which was evidently causing speculation in political circles. The paper surmised that it might be meant to stand for "Next Prime Minister". Others guessed it meant "No Party". In order to clear up this minor mystery I wrote to Mr. Churchill who has authorized me to say that he "thinks it meant Independent".

It was not, however, until 1915 that Mr. Pemberton Billing was elected as the first avowed Independent of what I shall call the modern variety of the Independent M.P.

In the post-Great War Parliament there were seven Independents and another thirteen who were described as Independents plus this or that. In 1922 there were three: Austin Hopkinson, Edwin Scrymgeour, a prohibitionist author who sat in several parliaments for Dundee, and G. M. L. Davies, who sat as an Independent (he was a Christian Pacifist) for the University of Wales. He is of some interest as he was the first avowed Independent to sit for a University seat.

The frequently-made claim that the University seats have been for centuries the refuge of Independents cannot be substantiated if the test of the contents of the bottle is to be the label. It is probably true to say that some of the University Members elected in the nineteenth century were men of exceptionally independent minds; but others were Ministers whose minds, however independent, had to conform to the then almost sacred doctrine of collective Cabinet responsibility.

Sir Oswald Mosley was returned at a by-election as an Independent to the 1922 parliament. In 1923 there were again three Independents. In 1924 there were four—Hopkinson, Scrymgeour, Ernest Graham-Little, and Shapunji Saklatvala (later Communist). There were also four Constitutionalists. In 1929 there were four Independents—Graham-Little, Sir Robert Newman (previously a Conservative), Eleanor Rathbone, and Scrymgeour. In 1931 there were three—Eleanor Rathbone, Hopkinson, and Graham-Little. Already the University representatives predominate among the Independents. In 1935 there were two—A. P. Herbert and Eleanor Rathbone plus two Irish Members.

At the Dissolution in 1945 there were twenty Independents, quasi-Independents, or persons not members of recognized parties: Sir Richard Acland (Liberal-Common Wealth-Independent-Labour), Vernon Bartlett, W. J Brown, Sir Stafford Cripps (ejected from Labour Party), A. S. Cunningham-Reid (former Tory), P. Cunningham (Irish Nationalist), Tom Driberg (later Labour Party), Graham-Little, E. L. Granville (former Liberal), T. Edmund Harvey, A. P. Herbert, Austin Hopkinson, Leslie Hore-Belisha (previously a Liberal), Kenneth Lindsay, D. L. Lipson, Sir Murdoch Macdonald, Anthony Mulvey (Irish Nationalist), Eleanor Rathbone, Sir Arthur Salter (later Conservative), and myself.

At the General Election of 1945, twelve Independents (excluding the Irish) were returned (eleven if we exclude Cripps). Of these Bartlett, Brown, Wilson Harris and Herbert were journalists and authors; Graham-Little, Kenneth Lindsay, Boyd-Orr, and Eleanor Rathbone were all, if they will excuse the description, ex-dons and intellectuals sitting for University seats; W. D. Kendal, D. L. Lipson and Sir M. Macdonald might be called territorial—they had either manufacturing interests or land or an exceptional record of public service in their constituencies.

In the 1950 election there were twenty candidates who described themselves as Independents with or without qualifying appendixes to the term. The electorate cast

Independents and Communists into a common grave. At the dissolution in 1951 there was one Independent Member in Parliament (Mr. Raymond Blackburn) who had left the Labour Party in 1950 and assumed the description of Independent. There were ten Independent candidates in 1951, of whom none was elected.

An attempt will now be made to sum up the question as I see it, with the reservation that no exactitude is possible since the application of the word Independent to an M.P. has meant different things at different times in our history.

In Elizabethan days it would have been applied to an M.P. who, like Peter Wentworth, resisted the wishes of the Crown even at the cost of imprisonment in the Tower. Wentworth was, to my way of thinking, expressing the true spirit of Parliament when he declared: "Two things do great hurt in this place, of which I do mean to speak. The one is a rumour which runneth about the House, and this it is: 'Take heed what you do, the Queen liketh not such a matter. . . '."

Then there were men who were independent of the great patrons. Then, in the nineteenth century, there were the men like Wilberforce who were party men with reservations.

Finally there were the modern Independents who were non-party men without reservations. These modern Independents—perhaps the late Miss Eleanor Rathbone and Sir Alan Herbert can properly be used as examples—were making the last stand on behalf of the theory that Parliament as a whole—and not a party therein—is the opposition to the executive.

To put the matter crudely, it is an Independent attitude which starts with the assumption that the first duty of an M.P. is to guard the liberties of the subject, that practically all legislation restricts liberty, that all proposals of the executive should be regarded with suspicion, and that it is the duty of the King's Government to prove its case for more powers before it is given those powers.

But although the party system has—for the time being—obtained such a grip on Parliament that it seems almost impossible for a candidate to obtain the necessary number of votes if he bases his appeal on his avowed intention of speaking and voting on each issue according to his own opinion and without regard to whether or not it is part of a political programme, it is also right to point out that in times of crisis the House of Commons can still burst out of party chains. The most notable recent example of this event was the Tory revolt in 1940 when a considerable number of Members (Tory, Liberal and Independent) who had usually supported Mr. Chamberlain's administration either abstained or went into the Lobby with the Socialists and so reduced the Government majority that it resigned and was replaced by an administration led by Mr. Churchill who had made the winding up speech in support of the Administration!

For those few historic hours, during which decisions of world-wide importance were reached, the House of Commons was the great Council of State at whose bar the King's Government stood on trial for its life. Whatever one may think about the present state of affairs in which membership of one of the great parties seems to be almost essential to membership of the House of Commons—and to enlarge on this subject would lead me into controversial channels which I do not propose to explore—I have no doubt that in an emergency similar to that which faced Parliament in 1940 there will always be sufficient of the spirit of independence from party discipline to ensure that national interests will predominate over purely party considerations.

Without transgressing the rules of fair comment it may be useful to conclude this sketch with a few questions which seem worthy of consideration by all those who have the welfare of Parliament at heart.

First, to what extent is the extraordinary growth of the political party organizations a reflection of the state of the electorate? There is grumbling about the rigidities of party discipline even from the party men, but does not the evil—if it be an evil—arise from the fact that the mass electorate has come to regard the M.P.s and their parties as persons and bodies conducting an auction for its favours? Given the demand for this kind of politics—inelegantly referred to as belly-politics—the parties, with their programmes and promises, organize themselves to meet it.

Secondly, does the present state of affairs tend to make the personality and character of candidates of less importance than is desirable? In this connection both the great parties have been at pains to reform the method of selecting candidates. In particular the Conservative Party has made it increasingly difficult for their candidates to put up much, if any, money. This apparently democratic and progressive measure has of course the paradoxical effect that the M.P., being obligatorily financed by the party, is that much more in the power of the machine. Furthermore, the conception of the deposit of £150 in order to make each candidate think at least twice before he goes forward on the serious enterprise of seeking to represent his fellow citizens in Parliament is now meaningless in so far as the party is concerned. It is the party not the man who risks the money.

Lastly, and perhaps most important of all, is the new problem of the relationship between Parliament and the publicly-owned industries. There is general agreement that this problem is important and has not been solved. There are many reasons why it is not susceptible of solution along party lines; and several reasons why it would seem that Parliament should deal with its responsibilities in this matter as a watchdog on behalf of the nation as a whole. If and when the principle of the public ownership of an industry or service has been accepted by the parties, the question of parliamentary control and criticism of broad (as opposed to detailed) matters of administration does not seem to raise issues of political principle but rather calls for that independent investigation characteristic of such bodies as the Public Accounts Committee. It can be argued that if the party organizations are enormously strong and especially if the Government majority is small, the party point of view makes it extremely difficult for Parliament as a whole to act as the supreme independent investigator.

PARTY ORGANIZATION
By R. T. McKenzie

THERE has been no systematic examination of the structure of the political parties of this country since Ostrogorski published the first volume of his classic *Democracy and the Organization of Political Parties* in 1902. This is easily the most striking omission in the study of politics in Britain; it is particularly surprising when one reflects that whatever yardstick one uses, the British party system is one of the most successful that has emerged in any democratic state. Only the briefest sketch of party structure is possible in an article of this length but it is hoped that this outline may suggest some of the avenues which deserve further exploration.

This article deals only with the three major British parties, the Conservative, Labour, and Liberal Parties. Each of them consists of three distinct sections:

(*a*) The party in Parliament; (*b*) The popular organization of the party outside Parliament which represents the rank and file membership of the party and its affiliated organizations; and (*c*) The Central Office of the party, a full-time professional organization.

The first of these sections, the party in Parliament, antedates the other two by over a century; the party system in Parliament can be traced to the factional struggles and parliamentary controversies of the seventeenth and eighteenth centuries, while the formal party organizations outside Parliament did not appear until after the Reform Bill of 1867. This article is concerned almost exclusively with the extra-parliamentary structure of the parties; their function is fourfold. The first, bluntly, is to win elections. The second, closely related to the first, is to educate or propagandize the community on behalf of the party's principles and programme. The third function of the party organization is to act as a two-way channel of communication between the Leader of the Party and his colleagues in Parliament on the one hand and the rank-and-file members of the party organization on the other. The fourth function is to enable the politically-active section of the party's supporters to play some part (however small) in the selection of the party's leaders and in the formulation of its policies. These functions (particularly the third and fourth) are fulfilled in significantly different ways in the three major parties.

THE CONSERVATIVE PARTY

(a) *The Role of the Leader.*

The most striking fact about the Conservative Party is the pre-eminent role assigned to the Leader under the constitution of the party. As the Maxwell Fyfe Committee noted in its recent review of the Conservative Party structure[1] the Leader is "the main fountain and interpreter of policy". The decisions of the party conference and of the various organs of the party are "conveyed" to him so that he may be kept constantly aware of the mood and opinions of his followers. But the Leader is in no way bound by these resolutions—however emphatic they may be—which are laid before him, and he alone is ultimately responsible for the formulation of the programme on which the party goes to the country. In addition, all of the key offices at the Central Office (the Chairman, Vice-Chairman, and Treasurers of the Party Organization as well as the Chairman of the Policy Committee) are direct personal appointments of the Leader. Through these appointments the Leader controls the entire Central Office machinery with its research and policy-making committees, its educational and propaganda functions, and the spending of party money.

The Leader is elected in the first instance by a body constituted (since 1937) as follows: the Conservative and Unionist members of the two Houses of Parliament, all prospective Conservative Parliamentary Candidates, and the Executive of the

[1] *Interim and Final Reports of the Committee on Party Organisation, 1948 and 1949*, London, The National Union, 1949, p. 2.

National Union. This election is usually not much more than a formality. If the party is in power when its Leader dies or retires, the new Leader is virtually determined by the Sovereign's action in calling (on the best advice available) the Conservative front-bencher who is most likely to be able to command the support of his party. If the party is in opposition, one candidate again becomes an almost inevitable choice because he has emerged (as Mr. Eden has today for example) as the acknowledged heir-apparent.

The Leader's work in Parliament is not subject to any formal review by those who have elected him. Indeed he does not normally attend the Annual Conference of the National Union. He appears only after the Conference has adjourned and customarily delivers a major address which is not of course subject to debate by the Conference.

This is, as Nigel Birch has called it, "leadership by consent"; however, a subtle but very important change has occurred in recent years in the Conservative doctrine of leadership by consent. Perhaps few Conservative leaders would ever have gone as far as the Duke of Wellington: "The party", he once said "what is the meaning of a party if they don't follow their leaders? Damn 'em, let 'em go". One suspects, however, that there has always been (until recently at least) a good deal of sympathy among the Conservative Leaders with Mr. Balfour's scornful reflection that he would as soon take advice from his valet as from the Conservative Conference. But the present Leader of the Party, Mr. Churchill, even though he is one of the most powerful personalities ever to hold the position, has encouraged his lieutenants to give the party membership a sense of participation in the formulation of party policy.

(b) *The National Union of Conservative and Unionist Associations*.

The National Union is the most broadly representative of the party's organs. It is a federation to which are affiliated constituency associations and central associations (in boroughs with two or more constituency associations) throughout England, Wales and Northern Ireland. (There is a separate Scottish Unionist Association.) The National Union's main function is to advance the cause of the party and to serve as a deliberative and advisory body which keeps the Leader informed of the mood and opinion of the party.

The National Union meets in *annual conference* at various points in England and Wales. Those eligible to attend this Conference include the members of the Central Council of the National Union (see p. 118) and three additional representatives of each constituency association, together with certificated party agents. The chairman of the 1948 conference defined the purpose of these conferences in colloquial but apt terms: "In a way", he said "this is the power house for next year's propaganda for the good old Tory Party." In a two and a half day meeting the Conference receives and discusses (as a rule very briefly) the report of the Executive Committee of the National Union and it debates about a score of resolutions scattered across the whole range of public affairs. With three to four thousand delegates attending the annual Conference (the present rules of the National Union provide for a possible maximum attendance of 5,600) serious and thoughtful deliberation is impossible. Sir David Maxwell Fyfe warned the 1950 Conference that it had "grown into a great and continuous mass meeting . . . [through which] enthusiasm runs . . . like a great prairie fire". As a rule all but three or four of the resolutions presented to the Conference are passed unanimously; the meetings appear to serve mainly as a demonstration of solidarity and enthusiasm for the party's own leaders. Yet the Conference decisively rejected an effort made at the 1950 meeting to reduce its size to more manageable proportions. As one delegate, a Mrs. Joan Benton, put it, "This is my first Conference. It is the most exciting thing that has ever happened to me; and Mrs. Benton wants to come again."

It was at this same Conference that a revolt from the floor forced the platform to accept the specific figure of 300,000 as a target for the Conservative housing programme. Subsequently the Chairman of the Young Conservatives boasted that on this occasion the Conference had "educated the platform". These events raise the interesting possibility that this sleeping giant, the Conservative Conference, may eventually awaken and insist upon playing a more decisive part in the affairs of the party. If it did so, it might prove rather difficult for the party leaders to assert their control because of the system of voting used at the Conference. Each constituency association regardless of size has equal representation at the Conference and each representative has equal voting rights. There is no equivalent to the Trade Union block vote on which the platform could rely to defeat a popular rebellion among the constituency representatives. Those who attend the Conference on behalf of their Associations are not, incidentally, "delegates" in the ordinary meaning of the term; they are not mandated as to how to vote by their associations. "They are free" as the Conservative Party literature puts it "to speak and vote according to their consciences". It can be argued in reply, of course, that this system is workable only so long as the Conference has no real power to determine policy, but in the meantime the system of voting encourages the theoretical possibility that the Conference might suddenly decide to try to play a much more dynamic role in the affairs of the party.

The other main organs of the National Union include the *Central Council*, a body almost as unwieldy as the annual conference, which meets twice a year in London. It considers the report of the *Executive Committee* of the National Union, reviews the motions which have been submitted by the lower echelons of the party, and conveys its decisions to the Leader of the party. The *Executive Committee* which normally meets monthly, consists mainly of the representatives of the provincial Areas (who in turn of course represent the constituencies in the areas). It deals with resolutions submitted by Provincial Areas, Constituency parties and in addition it has the right to admit Constituency Associations or expel them from the National Union. The Executive Committee has a number of Advisory Committees, Central Committees and Boards, the most important of which is the *Advisory Committee on Policy*. The Chairman of the Committee (at present Mr. R. A. Butler) along with the Vice-Chairman, is appointed by the Leader, and the Committee is responsible to him.

Provincial, Area and Constituency Organizations.

England and Wales have been divided into twelve areas and in each of these a voluntary federation of constituencies has been set up to plan the most effective use of the party's financial and other resources in the area. In addition, there is also in each area an Area Office which is under the direct control of the Central Office. The basic unit of the Conservative Party is of course the Constituency Association whose purpose, as described in the party literature, is "to form a centre of political strategy and activity and to stimulate and coordinate the work of the various branches and sections." The members of the Association elect their own officers, adopt their own candidate, select their own certified agent, administer their own funds and conduct their own education and propaganda work.[1]

(c) *The Central Office.*

The Conservative Central Office (along with its twelve Area Offices) is, in effect, the civil service of the Conservative Party. It provides a cadre of full-time, professional party workers who operate the machinery of the party organization under the ultimate direction of the Leader of the Party. The Central Office staff do not so much duplicate the functions of the voluntary section of the party organization (the National Union); they see that its jobs get done. The Central and Area Offices are in a sense the steel skeleton on which the rather flabby flesh of the National Union hangs. And the brain which directs the movements of this skeleton is the Leader of the party acting through his personal appointee, the Chairman of the Party Organization. If the Chairman does his job well, there need be no friction between the Central Office and the National Union since every opportunity is provided for liaison between the two organizations. Indeed, a smoothly functioning Central Office should give the members of the National Union the feeling that they themselves are fulfilling their own functions in a satisfactory fashion. As the Maxwell Fyfe Committee noted, "The role of the Central Office is to guide, inspire

[1] The total membership of Conservative Associations in November, 1951, was 2,763,968.

and coordinate the work of the Party throughout the country".

The critic has no difficulty in showing, as Sir Charles Marsden argued, that the Conservative Party "is democratic until it reaches the top", or in proving as two American observers (Professors Ranney and Carter) have claimed, that "essentially the system is one of autocracy tempered by advice and information." There can, I think, be no doubt of the validity of these criticisms and indeed most Conservatives in reply content themselves with Mr. Nigel Birch's argument that the Constitution of the Conservative Party symbolizes the Tory ideal of leadership by consent.

But the critics may easily overlook the profoundly difficult question: what *are* the limits of democracy within the mass political party? And above all, what are these limits when the mass party is merely the external agency of the party within a parliamentary system such as that in operation here in Britain? Even after one has proved that the relationship of the Conservative Leader to his party outside Parliament is in theory not very much more than that of a benign and benevolent dictator, this does not prove that a fully "democratic" structure in which the rank and file of the party controlled the actions of the party Leader is either feasible or desirable. Indeed, one may well ask whether such a relationship is by any definition "democratic." Why should the relatively few active party members control the actions of the party Leader whose position in Parliament is after all determined by the vastly larger number of citizens who voted for the party? And when the party Leader becomes Prime Minister, he cannot serve two masters. He must above all be responsible to the House of Commons and through it to the nation. As party Leader the Prime Minister wants and must have the approval and active support of his party organization outside Parliament, but he cannot possibly submit himself to the control of that organization.

In a sense, therefore, it can be argued that the Conservative constitution merely protects the Leader against the day when he becomes Prime Minister. And since the party appears to operate on the tacit assumption that it alone is the natural ruler of Britain, it is perhaps not surprising that it should have included this provision in its constitution. On the other hand, no part of this defence justifies the extreme over-centralization of power in the hands of the Leader. There seems to be no good reason why the Central Office should not be responsible to the National Union nor why the Leader should not report directly and in person to the Party Conference on the work of the party in Parliament. These changes could be made without in any way endangering the independence of the Leader from extra-parliamentary control when he becomes Prime Minister. Until these changes are made the party cannot complain if the sincerity of its devotion to popular democracy continues to be questioned by its critics.

THE LABOUR PARTY

It should be emphasized that the rank and file of the Labour movement has been slow to recognize the autonomy of the Parliamentary Labour Party (hereinafter the P.L.P.); there has been a persistent tendency to treat the P.L.P. as the servant of the Labour movement and to argue that it should accept the instructions of the Annual Conference and the National Executive Committee of the Party (N.E.C.). In the 1945 election Mr. Churchill claimed that this possibility represented a serious threat to the British parliamentary system. He suggested that a Labour Government would be responsible not to the House of Commons but to what he seemed to imply was a rather sinister body, the N.E.C., which that year was presided over by Professor H. J. Laski. But in fact, of course, neither the ill-informed but enthusiastic Labour supporters who have sought from time to time to control the P.L.P., nor Mr. Churchill, were right about this. Once a group of Labour M.P.s had been elected to Parliament, these M.P.s ceased to be, in the last analysis, servants of the Labour Party organization outside Parliament. However much weight the Parliamentary Labour Party might choose to give to the views of the party outside Parliament, it could not allow itself to be bound irrevocably by the decisions of any extra-parliamentary body. And what is true of the Parliamentary Labour Party is even more true of a Labour Government. It is solely responsible to Parliament; it can accept from the Labour Conference only advice and suggestions for action.

It is not surprising that misunderstanding should persist on this subject when Mr. Attlee himself has written about it in a rather misleading fashion. For example in *The Labour Party in Perspective*, 1937 (re-issued 1949: see p. 78 of latter edition) he wrote: "In contradistinction to Conservative conferences which simply pass resolutions which may or may not be acted upon, the Labour Party Conference lays down the policy of the party and *issues instructions which must be carried out* by the Executive, the affiliated organizations, and *its representatives in Parliament* and on local authorities". (Italics mine). The Labour Party itself has done its best (since 1945 especially) to discourage this interpretation, at least in so far as it applies to "representatives in Parliament". A surprising phrase occurs in an official party publication *The British Labour Party* ("prepared for the guidance of foreign visitors desiring to know more about the structure of our Movement"). After explaining the provision for liaison between the National Executive and the Labour Government, the publication adds "In this way, at least, Parliament and Government are *not unaware of* the decisions and deliberations of the Party's governing body". (Italics mine). The phrase "not unaware of" would no doubt have startled some of the founders of the Party, but it does reflect a realistic recognition of where the real centres of power in the party lie.

However, after the most emphatic recognition of the autonomy of the Parliamentary Labour Party and its Leader, where their actions in Parliament are concerned, it must be stated equally emphatically that there can be no doubt that the extra-parliamentary organs of the Labour Party play a much more important role in determining the electoral programme of the party and, indeed, in influencing the activities of Labour M.P.s and of a Labour Government, than does the National Union in the case of the Conservative Party.

(a) *The Role of the Leader*

When the P.L.P. is in opposition, it elects annually a Leader who normally serves also as Chairman of the P.L.P. Originally, it was apparently intended that the office of Leader of the P.L.P. and Chairman of the N.E.C. should be of equal rank. But this prospect was undermined by the fact that the Leader of the P.L.P. was a potential, and eventually an actual, Prime Minister. The Leader of the P.L.P., therefore, came to be accepted as the national Leader of the Party even though the party outside Parliament plays no part in his election. The Leader of the P.L.P. is an *ex officio* member of the N.E.C., and continues of course to remain a member if he becomes Prime Minister.

While the party remains in opposition the Leader of the P.L.P. has nothing like the authority granted by the Conservative Party to its Leader. He is expected to keep within the broad definition of party policy as determined in the first instance by the Annual Conference and the N.E.C. and as interpreted and applied in the House of Commons by the P.L.P. He cannot declare policy by himself and he does not control the Central Office machinery. He may in fact become not much more than an official mouthpiece for the party and may even find himself at times the mouthpiece for a policy with which he disagrees completely. George Lansbury's experience provides an interesting illustration. When he finally resigned the Leadership of the P.L.P. in 1935 over the issue of sanctions, he explained to the Party Conference the dilemma in which he had found himself:

> Often—and only the Executive and my colleagues know how often—I have disagreed with their policy, and because I was a member of the Executive and lately because of my other position [Leader], I have remained silent during the whole of the Conference. During the six years—first in the Labour Government, and secondly, as Leader of the Party—I have been in a kind of Dr. Jekyll and Mr. Hyde position. I have tried to speak for the Party . . . and on each occasion when I have spoken for the Party . . . I tried honestly and straightforwardly to

state the Party's position. My own position has never shifted.

Unlike his Conservative opposite number, the Labour Leader (while in opposition) does not choose his own deputies and front bench associates; they are elected annually by the P.L.P.

When Labour is in a position to form a government, the Sovereign as a matter of course calls the Leader as Prime Minister. A Labour Prime Minister then follows the normal British constitutional practice in the selection of his ministry. The P.L.P. and the party outside Parliament have no voice whatever in the formation of the Government (in contrast to the procedure followed, for example, by the Australian Labour Party). Thereafter, the Cabinet to a large extent supersedes the Executive of the P.L.P., although an elaborate effort has been made in each of the four Labour Governments to use the machinery of the P.L.P. to provide a system of liaison between the Cabinet and the back benches.

(b) *The Popular Organization of the Party Outside Parliament: the Annual Conference, the National Executive Committee, and the regional and local organization of the Party.*

The position is that there are today three main types of organization affiliated to the party: *Trades Unions* (affiliated nationally in respect of all of their members who have not signed a form "contracting out" of the political levy); secondly, certain *Socialist Societies* (the Fabian Society, the Jewish Socialist Labour Party, the Socialist Medical Association, the National Association of Labour Teachers); and thirdly, the *Constituency Associations* (including Federations of Labour Parties, constituency and borough Labour Parties). There is in addition one Co-operative Society directly affiliated.

The Annual Conference

The Annual Conference is sometimes described as "The Parliament of the Labour Party", but the analogy is a dangerous one since it may suggest to some the conception of a sovereign organization with final authority over all organs of the party and this, as has been emphasized, is far from being the case. Still, the Conference is the great annual assembly of the party and it is certainly very much more powerful than the equivalent annual conference of the Conservative National Union. The principal duties of the Labour Annual Conference are to receive and debate reports from the N.E.C. and the P.L.P., to discuss the various reports and policy statements submitted by the N.E.C., to debate resolutions submitted by the various affiliated organizations and constituency parties, and to elect annually the N.E.C. which administers the affairs of the party outside Parliament during the ensuing year.

This Labour Annual Conference is considerably smaller than that of the National Union (the average size in recent years has been about 1,200), but it is still too large for really effective discussion. Only a tiny fraction of the Conference can participate in the debates, especially since so much of the very limited time available ($4\frac{1}{2}$ days) is taken up with major expositions of policy by members of the N.E.C. or, when Labour is in office, of the Government. Despite these limitations the Conference debates are as a rule much more vigorous and colourful than the debates which take place at the conferences of the National Union. This is partly, no doubt, because among the delegates to the Labour Conference there is a much wider variety of strongly-held opinions. It is partly also because of the tradition of radical dissent and of opposition to established authority which still permeates the thinking of many of the more militant members of the party.

Despite the verbal fireworks which take place in many debates, the Conference usually acts as its Executive advises. At the 1937 Annual Conference, Herbert Morrison defined his conception of the N.E.C.'s duty as follows: "This Executive is the servant of the Conference. But it has a duty to lead the Conference, to advise the Conference in the way it ought to go, and I hope that every Executive that has responsibility will never hesitate to give the Conference firm advice as to what it ought to do". Usually the Conference accepts this advice. For example, in the years 1932–37, a period of very considerable turmoil within the party, the N.E.C. was overruled by the Conference only ten times and then not as a rule on major matters of policy. Since 1945 the N.E.C. has been defeated on very few issues and certainly on nothing which could be called central to the policies recommended by the N.E.C. or the Government. The basis of representation at the Annual Conference of each affiliated organization and constituency association is as follows: one delegate for each five thousand members or part thereof (with an additional woman delegate if women members number more than twenty-five hundred). Each affiliated organization may also cast one vote for every one thousand members and these votes must be cast "en bloc." Thus a constituency party with two thousand members would have one delegate and two votes. At the other extreme the Transport and General Workers Union with 830,000 members affiliated to the Party (1949) would have the right to one hundred and sixty-six delegates who between them would cast a bloc of eight hundred and thirty votes.[1]

It is inevitably the case that the two or three largest unions always dispose of more votes than all the constituency parties taken together. Since, in addition, the Trades Unions contribute by far the largest proportion of the funds, it seems an obvious conclusion that the Trade Unions in fact control the Labour Party. This is sometimes treated as a rather sinister charge against the Labour Party; but in itself it would not be particularly serious (since, after all, there is nothing sinister about trade unionists controlling a party in which they constitute over five-sixths of the membership) were it not for a further consideration which cannot be so lightly dismissed. It is claimed by some critics that a small group of professional Trade Union leaders in fact dispose of the huge block votes of

[1] Some idea of the comparative voting strength of the constituency and trade union wings of the party is given by the following membership figures for 1949. Total membership, 5,716,947. Of these, 4,946,207 were members of Trades Unions affiliated to the Labour Party, 729,624 (439,591 men and 290,033 women) belonged to 660 constituency parties (or groups of parties), 41,116 belonged to the affiliated Socialist and co-operative societies. See 1950 *Labour Conference Report*, p. 35, and *The British Labour Party, op. cit.*, p. 2.

their Unions. In other words it is argued that a tiny oligarchy of Trade Union "bosses" holds final control of the party machinery.

It is difficult to get reliable information on this point, but there appear to be widely differing degrees of consultation about party policy within the various Unions prior to the party conference. In some unions the agenda is discussed at several levels prior to the mandating of the Union's delegates. In other Unions only the national executive is likely to discuss the Agenda and in some instances they appear to accept the advice of the senior officials of the Union on almost every item. After reviewing this problem in his *The Labour Party in Perspective* (1937) Mr. Attlee arrived at a characteristically moderate conclusion: "I think on the whole", he wrote "it will be found that Trade Union leaders do not exercise their power tyrannically".

Recent experience demonstrates beyond doubt that the real centre of power in the Conference lies in the hands of the leading parliamentary figures in the N.E.C. (who were also, in the period 1945-51, usually Cabinet Ministers). They wielded this power with the support, or at least the acquiescence, of the leading members of the Trade Union delegations. It was in fact the bond of confidence and mutual respect between the leading "political" figures on the N.E.C. and the leading Trade Unionists which ensured consistent conference support for the Labour Government.

The National Executive Committee.

From what has been written above about the N.E.C., its functions should be fairly clear. A further word should be added, however, about its composition and committee structure. The N.E.C. consists of twenty-seven members, one of whom, the Leader of the P.L.P., is an *ex officio* member. The other twenty-six are elected annually by the Party Conference on the following basis. Twelve are elected by the Trade Union delegates. Since the General Council of the Trades Union Congress precludes its members from standing for the N.E.C., this means that the Trade Union representatives on the N.E.C. tend to be second (or third) rank Union leaders. Seven are elected by Constituency Party and Federation delegates. This group normally includes three or four prominent parliamentary figures along with several of the more colourful and militant of the left-wing leaders (the latter have included in the past men like Professor Harold Laski, D. N. Pritt, and journalists such as Michael Foot and Tom Driberg). Five women are elected by the Conference as a whole, as is the Treasurer. One additional member is elected by the Socialist, Co-operative and Professional Association delegates. The N.E.C. (which meets at least once a month) chooses its own chairman, generally on a seniority basis.

The N.E.C. is responsible for carrying out the decisions of the Annual Conference, for interpreting policy, and for administering the affairs of the party, including especially the work of the party headquarters at Transport House. The N.E.C. carries on most of its work through a series of standing sub-committees, which correspond with the major divisions of the Party's work. The Labour Party maintains close liaison with the Trades Union Congress and the Co-operative Union through the *National Council of Labour* which normally meets monthly to review matters of common interest.

Regional Organization and the Constituency Parties.

There are nine Regional Councils in England and one each for Wales, Scotland and Northern Ireland which coordinate and further the work of the Labour Party within these regions. The basic party units are of course the constituency parties which have been established in almost all of the parliamentary constituencies. A Central Labour Party is usually set up in boroughs with more than one parliamentary constituency and in most counties there is a Federation of Constituency Labour Parties to co-ordinate the work of the Party in contesting County Council elections.

The Co-operative Party.

There are in all, over 1,000 retail, wholesale and producer co-operative societies, with a total membership of approximately 11,000,000, affiliated to the *Co-operative Union*. Of these in 1949, some 671 co-operative societies with a membership of 8½ million were affiliated with the *Co-operative Party*. It maintains several joint committees with the Labour Party to consider matters of common concern and it has been agreed that Co-operative Party candidates will not at any time be set up in opposition to Labour Party candidates. Normally, a number of parliamentary candidates are jointly sponsored by the parties (in the 1951 election there were for example some 38 candidates jointly sponsored).

* * *

In this highly complex structure, initiative and leadership clearly comes from the parliamentary leaders of the Labour Party. They are the dominant members of the N.E.C. and usually the outstanding figures at the Annual Conferences. They are normally able to rely on the support of the principal Trade Union leaders and this in turn enables them to carry the Annual Conferences on virtually every major issue. They have to contend, however, with a strong tradition of socialist militancy among the constituency parties; although this is to some extent counter-balanced by an even stronger tradition of loyalty to the party leadership. Yet the situation is not without its awkward possibilities. At the 1951 conference, for example, the "rebel" wing of the party led by Mr. Aneurin Bevan, captured four of the seven places on the N.E.C. reserved for constituency party representatives. If, as is quite conceivable, such a rebel movement captured all of these seven places, the Leader of the P.L.P. (who is also, of course, the Prime Minister when the party is in power) might find himself alone on the N.E.C. without any of his senior parliamentary colleagues to support him. He could still, no doubt, rely on the support of the Trade Union and women's section of the Executive, but the Leader's position would be a most uncomfortable one in such circumstances. A description of this possibility again throws into bold relief the contrast in the role of the Leader in the Conservative and Labour parties. Both are the dominant figures in their respective parties. But the ascendancy of the one is protected and buttressed by the constitution of his party and the tradition of "leadership by consent". The other is exposed to an inevitably more complex set of pressures and potential challenges to his authority. Yet oddly enough, after sixteen years as Leader of the Labour Party Mr. Attlee's position seems at least as secure as that of Mr. Churchill who has led his party for ten years.

(c) *The professional organization of the Labour Party outside Parliament, the central office or party headquarters (popularly called "Transport House").*

The party headquarters works under the direction of the N.E.C., implementing its decisions, undertaking research and educational work at its direction and generally attending to the affairs of the Party. The secretariat, which works under the supervision of the General Secretary, comprises a number of departments including Research, Press, Publicity, Organization, Finance, International, and the Women's Department.

"Transport House" comes under frequent criticism from both friend and foe. Mr. Nigel Birch has borrowed from a great predecessor to call it a "Venetian Alegarchy", to quote but one Conservative gibe; but much more lurid descriptions are common in the literature of the socialist dissenters. The gist of these latter criticisms seems to be that the Party headquarters is weighted down with "officialism" and unimaginative bureaucracy and that it invariably throws its weight behind the moderate, and indeed the conservative, elements within the party leadership. Mr. Attlee in reviewing these criticisms (in *The Labour Party in Perspective*, p. 85) remarked that "much of it is not deserved", but he added, "it must be admitted that all political head offices are apt to develop certain tendencies... There is necessarily developed in such organizations a certain amount of routine, officialism and caution . . . [all officials] tend to be conservative in regard to their methods and to regard innovations with suspicion". Then Mr. Attlee added sagely: "This is not surprising when one remembers the amount of ill-digested suggestions which they receive from members". In reply to the charge that Transport House is a soulless machine which has long since jettisoned its socialist idealism, one may quote the comment of Mary Agnes Hamilton in *The*

THE LIBERAL PARTY

Labour Party Today, (p. 51.) "It is a machine only in the sense that it is an instrument shrewdly adapted to its purpose".

(a) *The Leader and the Liberal Party Committee*

The Leader is elected by the Liberal Members of Parliament and thereafter he is recognized (as is the Leader of the Parliamentary Labour Party) as national leader of his party. The coordination of the Liberal Party's work inside and outside Parliament is undertaken by a rather complex body known as *The Liberal Party Committee* which is presided over by the Leader. Its members include the Chief Whip, the Leader of the Party in the House of Lords, the President of the Party Organization, the Chairman of the National Executive, the Chairman (or other representative) of the Liberal Candidates' Association. The Leader also appoints additional members of the Committee as follows: twelve from a panel of forty Liberals, twenty of whom are nominated by the Parliamentary Party and twenty of whom are elected by the Council of the Party Organization. In addition, the Leader may (in agreement with the President of the Party) co-opt up to ten further members. This Liberal Party Committee clearly provides a much more elaborate structure for the co-ordination of party activities inside and outside Parliament than exists in either the Conservative or Labour Parties. The existence of this Committee does not, however, modify the ultimate autonomy of the Party in Parliament.

(b) *The Liberal Party Organization*

This term is used by Liberals to describe the whole structure of the popular organization of the party outside Parliament. The President and other officers of the Liberal Party Organization are elected annually by the Assembly.

The Assembly is the Annual Conference of the Party Organization. Those entitled to attend include the representatives of all Constituency Associations together with certain *ex officio* members such as Members of Parliament and candidates. In addition to electing the officers of the Liberal Party Organization, the Assembly receives from its Council a report on the work of the Party and debates policy resolutions proposed by the Constituency Associations or other organs of the Party. The Assembly is thus responsible for determining the broad outlines of Party policy.

The Council, which meets quarterly, includes thirty representatives elected by the Assembly, along with representatives of the Party in the Commons and the Lords and members elected by the Area Federations, the Women Liberals, the Young Liberals and others. According to the Party Constitution, the first duty of the Council is "to stimulate militant Liberalism in every part of the country" and express the views of Liberals on current political questions as they arise. The Council is also responsible for maintaining the party headquarters, for raising funds, and for publicity and propaganda work. In addition, it appoints a smaller body, the *Executive Committee*, which meets at least once a month, to look after the day-to-day affairs of the Party.

The Constituency Associations are banded together into a number of Area Federations to coordinate and extend the work of the Party within their respective areas. The Constituency Associations themselves are responsible for their own organization, working arrangements and finance. They also undertake the usual educational and propaganda work and, of course, they sponsor Liberal candidates in local and national elections. An unusual feature of the Liberal Party constitution is the wide range of additional responsibilities laid on the Constituency Associations. According to the Party Constitution, they must "keep watch upon the legislative and administrative work of the Government especially as it affects the needs and interests of the district and to direct the attention of local authorities, the public and the press to the importance of these subjects, and to the methods by which Liberals believe they should be handled." They must "keep all citizens *without respect of party*, creed or race, to secure their rights, and to protect them against oppression." (Italics mine). They must, finally, "demonstrate that Liberals desire to help their neighbours by providing, wherever possible, such social services as are not otherwise available." This is a surprising outburst of radical idealism to discover in a party constitution and, on paper at least, it appears to set the Liberal Party rather apart from the narrower political preoccupations of the other two parties.

(c) *The Professional Organization of the Party: The Party Headquarters*

The Party Headquarters is responsible to the Executive and Council and through them to the Assembly. It provides secretarial and executive assistance to all the national organs of the Party and their committees and, in addition, the headquarters is responsible for publicity, propaganda and research.

* * * * * *

To summarize this discussion of party structures, it can be argued, I think, that the great growth of the extra-parliamentary organization of the British parties since 1867 has in no way destroyed the autonomy of the parties in Parliament. On the contrary, the party organizations outside Parliament have provided most valuable channels of communication between the party leaders and their most active supporters. They have also enabled the politically-active section of the community to play a definite though not a decisive part in determining the policies of the party they support. Perhaps the most apt conclusion can be borrowed from Lord Bryce's foreword to the first English edition of Ostrogorski's *Democracy and the Organization of Political Parties*. Bryce had praised Ostrogorski's work very highly, but he questioned whether Ostrogorski had not taken a much too gloomy view of the threat to democracy represented by the growing power of the party caucus. Bryce concluded: "In England, happily for England, the [party] organizations have not ceased to be controlled by men occupying a position which makes them amenable to public opinion, nor have they as yet departed far from the traditions in which the strength of English free Government lies."

A NOTE ON PARTY FINANCE
By R. T. McKenzie

THE subject of party finance awaits a full-scale study and anything short of it is bound to be tantalizing and inconclusive. The subject bristles with problems: what can be said of the Conservative Party which refuses to publish its accounts? How can one decide what is legitimately to be included under the heading of expenditure for party purposes? In the case of the Labour Party, does one include the expenditures for propaganda and educational work of the organizations which co-operate with Labour for political purposes such as the Trade Unions, the Co-operative Union, and the socialist societies such as the Fabian Society? There is a similar problem in the case of the Conservatives in determining how one classifies the organizations (such as "*The Aims of Industry*") which propagandize on behalf of the system of society which the Conservatives advocate. This note can do no more than discuss the sort of information that is at present available and point to the areas of uncertainty which require further investigation.

CONSERVATIVE PARTY

The Maxwell Fyfe Committee on Party Organization has recently undertaken an extensive review of the Conservative Party's financial methods. This Committee warned (p. 15 of its Report) of the dangers of the present policy of secrecy in financial matters: "In the past, no information about the expenditure or income or requirements at the centre has been available to responsible Constituency Officers, Members of Parliament, Candidates or ordinary members of the Party. The advantages of secrecy," the Committee argued "are outweighed by the disadvantages of failing to tell Conservative supporters frankly what bill they must foot if they want the country properly governed ... The Treasurer of the Party should publish an annual financial statement ... people will subscribe more generously when they can see how their contributions are spent." In moving the adoption of the interim report of the Maxwell Fyfe Committee at the 1948 Conference, Mr. Henry Brooke added the further warning that "lack of information ... engenders suspicion."

In launching his appeal for a £1,000,000 fighting fund in 1947, Lord Woolton admitted: "It is a new thing for the Conservative Party to make a public appeal for money.... In the past the party has been shy of asking for money and it has collected for its Central Fund from a few hundred people." It would not seem unreasonable to assume that these were the people who responded to the famous appeal by Mr. Baldwin in 1926: "We need funds and I look to the City of London to give a lead in providing that support which as business men they should be prepared to give, in view of our efforts to make their business safe." (*Daily Telegraph*, 2nd February, 1926.)

Lord Woolton warned at the 1947 Conference, however, that the Conservatives were not "the rich man's party" and he claimed indeed "we are over-spending ourselves five times." The Maxwell Fyfe Committee estimated "the gap" in national party finances (i.e., the difference between assured annual income and what the party "ought to be able to spend") at £200,000. The Committee argued that this sum should be raised by the constituency associations through a "voluntary quota scheme" related to the Conservative voting strength in each constituency at the immediately preceding General Election. The Maxwell Fyfe Committee subsequently reported that "a great many Associations are accepting freely and generously their new responsibility." However, since the Party still does not publish its accounts, it is impossible to know how far the Constituency contributions have helped in the closing of the £200,000 annual "gap" in the Party's funds.

The Conservative Party has also recently re-examined another financial problem: the question of contributions to party funds by candidates and M.P.s. Lord Woolton admitted at the 1947 Annual Conference: "In the past it has cost a good deal of money to be a Conservative candidate" and he added the warning "we cannot afford only to draw for candidates from the people with money." To meet this problem the Maxwell Fyfe Committee recommended, first, that the entire election expenses of Conservative candidates should be the responsibility of the Constituency Associations; second, that candidates should not be permitted to contribute to the funds of their Association more than £25 per year and M.P.s should not be permitted to contribute more than £50 per year. In any case, the question of an annual subscription to the funds of the Party must not henceforth be mentioned by any Constituency selection committee to any candidate before he has been selected. These provisions were to apply to all candidates selected after 31st December, 1948. After a spirited debate this Report was adopted by the Annual Conference in October, 1948.

The officials of the Conservative Party continue, however, to argue against the publication of party accounts. Thus the General Director of the Conservative Central Office wrote in *Parliamentary Affairs* for Autumn, 1948: "The idea of publishing the accounts of political parties is superficially attractive. It arises from the instinctive curiosity about other peoples' affairs which we all share." He claimed, however, that the public welfare would not be advanced in any way by such publication because "the publication of comparative figures . . . would be completely misleading. There can be no standard form of comparison owing to the fundamental differences in the composition and functions of the different party organizations and their relations with quasi-political bodies."

In the same vein, the Conservative Handbook for 1950 argues that in fact the Labour Party is only a section of the Socialist Movement as a whole and therefore the money which it confesses to spending is only a small part of the funds expended on propaganda for socialism. "In 1948," the Handbook claims, "the combined income of the political funds of the Trades Unions amounted roughly to £399,000, of which

£113,000 went to the Socialist Party in affiliation fees. The whole of the balance of £286,000 was also available for the propagation of Socialism." In the same year, the Handbook points out, the subscriptions of the Retail Societies to the Co-operative Union amounted to over £100,000 and of this sum a "substantial part," it is claimed, is applied to the furtherance of the Socialist cause. In addition, the Handbook argues that the £370,000 a year spent by the Retail Societies themselves on educational work, "cannot be anything but a powerful auxiliary of the Socialist propaganda machine". The Conservative Handbook therefore concludes that "the Socialist Movement has at its disposal an income little less than £1,000,000 a year quite apart from what is raised and spent by the Constituency Labour Parties."

Because the publication of party accounts would be liable to be "highly misleading", the Conservative Party opposed the motion moved by Mr. Geoffrey Bing, a Labour M.P., on 15th December, 1949, "that in the opinion of this House, political parties and all other organizations having political action as one of their aims should publish annually full and adequate statements of their accounts."

LABOUR PARTY

The National Executive Committee report to the Annual Conference includes a statement showing the Labour Party's current financial position. The 1950 Report showed a credit balance at the end of 1949 amounting to nearly half-a-million pounds. The statement indicates the Party's principal sources of revenue which for that year were as follows: The Trade Unions provided £124,000 in affiliation fees, £27,000 towards the Party's Development fund and £148,000 towards the General Election Fund. Constituency Labour Parties contributed £18,000 in affiliation fees, £7,500 to the By-Election Insurance Fund and £7,000 to the Development Fund.

The full subscription payable by each member of a constituency party is a minimum of six shillings per year of which 6d. is sent to Party Headquarters and 2d. per member is payable by local parties to the Regional Councils. Members who pay the political levy through a union affiliated to the Party do so at rates which vary from union to union from one penny per week to one shilling per year.

Constituency parties are responsible for their own financial arrangements, including election expenses, although various forms of assistance in money and in kind (printed material, etc.) are provided in certain circumstances from central party funds. Where a candidate is specifically endorsed by a particular Trade Union or Co-operative Society, it is customary for the sponsoring organization to make a money grant to the funds of the constituency party and to contribute a special sum towards election expenses. Oddly enough the Labour Party appears to have placed no limit on the amount of money a candidate or M.P. may personally contribute to his constituency party's funds. As Mrs. Mary Agnes Hamilton admitted (in *The Labour Party Today*), at the Constituency Selection Conferences, "There will, as a rule, be some [questions] about finance—how much, if anything, could the would-be candidate contribute, either to election expenses or the normal running of the Party Machine?" She added, however, "it is not the rule that the answers [to these questions] settle the fate of [would-be] candidates".

The Labour Party *Handbook* ("Facts and Figures for Socialists" 1951) argues vehemently that "the nation should know what groups and organizations are specially anxious to have a Conservative Government". The Handbook meets the Conservative charge that Labour has powerful financial allies whose support is not reflected in the Party's budget by alleging that "big business is actively helping the Tories.... The Aims of Industry and the Economic League are two organizations engaged in anti-socialist propaganda. They have the strong support of the powerful Federation of British Industries". The Economic League, it is claimed, has ninety-two permanent full- and part-time speakers and during 1948 it distributed $9\frac{1}{2}$ million leaflets and secured over 25,000 inches of press publicity. The Aims of Industry is described as "a propaganda body in the interests of big business" and the Handbook quotes the organization's 1948 report in which reference is made to the fact that in that year the press gave the Aims of Industry over 78,000 column inches of space ("worth no less than £780,000").

LIBERAL PARTY

Each Constituency Area pays an annual affiliation fee, the amount of which is fixed by the Association each year (the present fee is five guineas per year). Half of this sum is paid to the party central office and half to the Area Federation in which the Association is situated. In addition, donations and annual subscriptions from individual subscribers are contributed to the central office. On 31st May, 1946, the Liberal Foundation Fund was launched to commemorate the founding of the Liberal Federation on 31st May, 1877, and in connection with this Fund both Associations and individuals have made special contributions to the work of the Party. The Liberal Party Organization operates on an annual budget of approximately £50,000 (1949). The constituency parties raise funds through individual subscriptions (one shilling and upwards), profits on publications, and social activities.

Mr. Philip Fothergill, formerly President of the Liberal Party Organization, has claimed (*Parliamentary Affairs*, Autumn 1948) that "The Liberal Party is poor, only because it has no wealthy pressure group to finance it" and he adds the warning: "Today, in the fierce competition for political power, it would seem that a party must secure the support of a wealthy patron or languish in honest but ineffective poverty. . . . No party has yet solved the problem of deriving a really big income from so large a number of small (without strings) contributions that it can be both effective and untrammelled".

THE FORMULATION OF PARTY POLICY
by H. G. Nicholas

NO political party can do entirely without a policy; every political party, at one time or another, will find itself wishing it could. The function of a policy is not only to tell the voter what he may expect; it is also to remind the party itself of what it is and what it is for, to prevent it degenerating into a mere agglomeration of power-seeking adventurers. It is thus the party's response to the need for self-expression and a kind of guardian of the party's self-respect. But since the future cannot be predicted, circumstances are bound to arise for every party in which facts clash with theories and hopes, or in which the path to power seems to deviate from the path of policy; then develops the familiar cleavage between intention and execution, programme and performance, and the inevitable rationalizations, the adjustment of the party "line" or the denunciation of "saboteurs" or, in less crude communities, the plea that circumstances alter cases, the appointment of a Royal Commission or, most popular of all, the putting of the blame on the Opposition. Thus the role of policy in party life partakes simultaneously of the real and the sham. Parties cannot exist without it, they can never fully live up to it.

In another sense, too, the element of the sham creeps in. In varying degrees parties in a democratic state claim themselves to be democratic organs, seeking to express the will of their members. But policy cannot spring spontaneously from an inchoate mass; initiative must usually come from above and direction in a crisis must always come from a few. Pressure is thus constant on parties in power (or in sight of power) to put the active part of policy-making in the hands of a few and to reserve for the rank and file the passive roles of acceptance, more or less qualified by criticism. Moreover, just as the democratic aspirations of sovereign states are qualified by the fact of living in a warring world, so the democratic formulation of party policy is limited by the need to win elections. A policy which is merely and entirely what the party membership wants may not win many of the vital floating votes when the election comes; for success at the polls the commander-in-chief, the electoral strategists and tacticians, must be allowed a dominant voice about what goes into, or is left out of, the programme.

British political parties exemplify these characteristics in different ways and degrees. Traditionally it is the parties of the Left which have taken policy-making most seriously; the Right, priding itself on its empiricism, retains a distrust for policy even when it perceives its necessity. Thus there is for the student of British politics more to be seen and said about the mechanism of policy-making in the Liberal and Labour parties than in the Conservative. At the same time it should be remembered that appearance may not always accord with reality and until the full history of party conclaves is known (if ever) one cannot always be sure where the real decisions were taken and where the real springs of action lay.

Every party makes formal provision for the formulation of policy. The Labour Party constitution, in its 5th Clause, empowers the party conference to "decide from time to time what specific proposals of legislative, financial or administrative reform shall be included in the party programme" (the general objectives of which have, of course, been defined in the preceding clause on "Party Objects"). For such inclusion any proposal requires a two-thirds vote of the conference. This however is the long-term programme of the party. The responsibility for deciding "which items from the party programme shall be included" in the election manifesto rests with the National Executive Committee and the Executive Committee of the Parliamentary Labour Party. "The joint meeting of the two executive committees shall also define the attitude of the party to the principal issues raised by the election which are not covered by the manifesto". Since the National Executive Committee is elected by the Conference and Labour M.P.s by the electorate, the chain of democratic control might appear to be as strong as any constitution-maker could devise.

The Liberals endow the Liberal Party Committee with "responsibility for policy". It is also responsible for securing "liaison between the parliamentary party and the party organization" and expresses the Liberal attitude on questions of immediate urgency as well as acting on matters of long-term policy. Its membership, one-third consisting of party officials and two-thirds of elected and co-opted persons, appears to represent a compromise between continuous popular control and the need for leadership at the centre.

The Conservative Party has never felt it so important to construct a continuous chain of policy control from its National Union of Constituency Associations, through its Central Council, to its Parliamentary Party and its Leader. To a far greater degree than its rivals, it reposes authority in its Leader and in its M.P.s, accepts the formulation of policy at the top, and relies much less upon formal machinery of control even where that machinery exists. There is no requirement that the party should have a "programme", still less that it should receive the detailed endorsement of the party conference. The resolutions passed at the conference are "submitted to the Leader of the Party" who (e.g., in 1950) "discussed them with the Chairman of the National Union, the Chairman of the Party Organization and the Chairman of the Executive Committee". Mr. Churchill indicated that they had his "full approval". In similar fashion the resolutions of the Central Council were "communicated to the Leader of the Party" who "expressed himself in agreement with them". There is, however, also a Committee on Policy, consisting of seven representatives of the executive committee of the National Union and five of the Conservative M.P.s Committee, plus two representatives of the Conservative Peers. But, in keeping with the tradition of not trammelling the Leader and his fellow M.P.s, the Committee is called "Advisory".

Such, broadly, is the machinery at the parties' disposal. How do they use it? The defeat in 1945 produced among the Conservatives, as defeats generally do within parties, a demand for a new statement of policy. (Incidentally, one may note, as a verbal reflection of the continuous play between the ideal and the actual, that parties never demand "a new policy" —it is always "a new *statement* of policy"; the creed is fixed, it is only the theology that requires modification.) Since what was involved was largely a readjustment of the party's own ways of thinking about social and economic issues, the party's "progressives" in effect began a process of persuasion and conversion within the party. Mr. R. A. Butler, as Chairman of the Advisory Committee on Policy, was the spearhead of the movement. The weapons were the issuance of documents such as the *Industrial Charter* which, by discussion in the press and debate at the party conference, gradually got themselves accepted not so much as detailed statements of what the party would do when it obtained power, but rather as indications of the changed temper and mood of the Conservative Party and of a future Conservative government. But, as the 1950 election approached, those members of the party who were most convinced that Labour's 1945 success was due to their election programme, became loud in their demands for a comparable Conservative document. Here, one may note, was not the familiar pattern of division between party leaders who want a free hand and the rank and file seeking a formula for their control. The disagreement in the party ran vertically; at each level were to be found advocates of either side. In March, 1949, at the annual meeting of the Central Council, several resolutions were tabled demanding a "clearer formulation of policy" with an indication of the legislation this would imply from a Conservative government. Mr. Butler promised a "restatement" soon and the result was *The Right Road for Britain* published on July 23rd, something half-way between a general statement of aims and a detailed programme. This was presented to the party conference, which met in October under the shadow of the approaching election, and was debated in general terms. The only amendment (which was virtually a proposal to reject) came from Sir Waldron Smithers. This having been defeated without a count, the statement was "accepted" by the conference. But to the demands for more detail Mr. Churchill in his final speech rejoined, "Today the Conservative Party has neither the power nor the responsibility to decide the policy and shape the fortunes of the State. . . . At this moment we can only utter words, but the national safety requires deeds. . . . A programme of words can be pulled to pieces one item at a time without any corresponding results to show in the general welfare of the state. That is why I have advised you consistently during these last four years not to commit yourselves to detailed, rigid programmes, but to let the nation learn from the hard teaching of facts". The appearance in the following January of *This is the Road* demonstrated the party's adherence to Mr. Churchill's precepts; it was, in essence, merely a concentrated version of the early document.

The failure of the Party to oust Labour in February, 1950, provoked a repetition of the earlier debate within the Conservative ranks, leading the "progressives" to conclude, as Mr. R. A. Butler put it, that to win the extra seats needed "we have got to make a closer appeal to the industrial voter". However, this did not lead the Conservatives, like Labour, to produce a new "statement" for their annual conference in October. Mr. Butler explained why: "We deliberately did not issue a statement of policy before this conference. Our statement of policy will be issued, to use the words of the Prime Minister, 'at the right time and in the right way'; and it will be on the lines of *The Right Road*; and it will achieve the right result! I would like to tell you that one reason we did not issue a statement of policy or a charter or anything else for you to approve . . . is that we thought we would wait for reactions at this Conference. Thank God you have given us some good reactions on which to work. [One of them was the demand for the insertion of the figure of 300,000 a year in a resolution on the party's housing programme—a demand "gladly" accepted by Lord Woolton, as party Chairman.] Our job now is to carry forward those ideas, which you have given us at this Conference, into the field of Party Policy. I can undertake to do that with as much success as we did in furnishing you with *This is the Road* on the last occasion".

One of the incidental tributes paid in Mr. Butler's speech was to the authors of *One Nation*, a volume of policy essays by a young "ginger group" of back-benchers, and this is as good a place as any to point out the value to party policy-framers of unofficial trial flights of this kind. All established parties are suspicious of new and untried ideas; as repositories of a faith and a tradition they have to be. Yet without new ideas parties die. If a way can be found for trying out novelties, both on the party and on the electorate, without committing the party to them in advance of their general acceptability, then much anxiety and recrimination is spared. One of the established ways of doing this in British politics is the political pamphlet or the volume of essays. The well-timed speech may also be used to advantage, as Mr. David Eccles demonstrated in his advocacy of a higher productivity. A newspaper crusade is more dangerous. If launched by an independent organ, like the Beaverbrook "Empire Free Trade" campaign of the thirties, its failure may turn the journal into positive hostility; if launched by an "official or semi-official" party organ, its failure will blunt the paper's usefulness for other jobs of propaganda. Most dangerous of all is the adoption of a new policy by a party conference in advance of its real acceptance by the leaders or the rank and file. This has happened to the Liberals twice in recent years. In 1947 the Liberal Assembly resolved to support conscription against the advice of the parliamentary party; a year later, in an endeavour to harmonize both points of view, it passed a very loosely-worded resolution which was mainly directed at the way in which the government had operated conscription. Again in 1948 the Assembly endorsed the principle of compulsory co-ownership in industry against the advice of several of its leaders; in 1949 the Assembly reiterated its approval, but when the vote was taken there were some notable abstentions. In 1950 when the election manifesto *No Easy Way* appeared, it simply said, "The Liberal Party is prepared to introduce co-partnership and profit-sharing into major units of industry". The 1951 election manifesto, *The Nation's Task*, remarked merely that "Increased efficiency and production must also be obtained by bonus systems and profit-sharing schemes on top of the standard trade union wages".

If these two instances of hastily-considered policy-making appear surprising, regard must be had to the parliamentary position of the Liberal Party. Its small representation in the House, the certitude that in normal times its votes will not affect measures or governments, encourages—and even to some extent justifies—a relatively light-hearted flirtation with experimental policies. In relation to the other two parties the Liberals are, in some sense, the explorers, the pioneers, one might almost say the test pilots. The price they pay for their role is, of course, that if their inventions are a failure they are involved in the ensuing crash; if a success they cannot avoid the patents being stolen by their rivals.

The Labour Party, as a party of doctrine, has an even greater appetite for policy-framing than the Liberals, but as a party in office or seeking office it has to limit its diet to ideas which are administratively practicable and electorally acceptable. The party has generally preferred to entrust the inventive role in policy-making to others than its political leaders—to a Sidney Webb or a Harold Laski. Here it has been greatly helped by its "federal" structure; to have a group like the Fabians running as it were a policy laboratory, whose products could be adopted when useful and ignored when inconvenient, has been an inestimable boon to the party. But thanks largely to the fertile genius of Sidney Webb, whose 1918 *Labour and the New Social Order* represented a capital stock of ideas which is only now beginning to run low, the Labour Party has never suffered from a poverty of policies; its problem has always been to relate its policies to the political exigencies of the hour. This has generally expressed itself in a clash of opinions, in turn usually appearing, as the party constitution might lead one to expect, at the point where membership and leadership connect, the National Executive and the Annual Conference.

The formula for resolving such differences has generally taken the form of saying that while the Conference may decide a principle, it must be left to the Executive or the Parliamentary

Party to decide on its application or timing. Thus in 1947 when the Westmorland Divisional Labour Party moved a resolution for nationalizing the nation's water supplies "at once", Mr. Bevan for the Executive replied that: "If this resolution were carried the Executive would be instructed to approach the Government 'at once' to nationalize the water supplies of Great Britain. It is the function of Conference to move a decision of principle, but it must be left to the Parliamentary Party to decide Parliamentary priorities, because some things are more important than others."

The resolution was withdrawn, but an equally unacceptable resolution, urging the abolition of the tied cottage, was carried over the Executive's opposition. What then? No action was taken. The following year, 1948, saw the resolution moved again and opposed in similar terms. Mr. Bevan said, "When the appropriate moment arrives we will legislate to abolish it. But while it is the task of the Conference to decide policy, it is the onerous task of the Government and the Parliamentary Party to decide how and when to implement it. For the Conference to decide the Parliamentary time-table would be impossible."

None the less the resolution was carried again. Brought up again at the Blackpool Conference in 1949, it was again deferred by the Executive for "reconsideration" in the next Parliament. In the 1950 election manifesto, *Let Us Win Through Together*, reference to the tied cottage was confined to similarly general terms; "When the Rent Restrictions Acts are dealt with in the new Parliament, the position of tied cottages will be reconsidered and the Unions consulted about the best means of giving to farm-workers the security in their homes enjoyed by other workers". In the ensuing parliament no legislative action was taken, though of course the Government's slim majority may well provide explanation enough of that.

However it is not over specific legislative proposals but over administrative or diplomatic issues, involving the often intangible elements of the more or the less, of emphasis and priorities, that policy differences generally emerge in a party. Here the device of the representative party conference has served Labour well (despite the occasionally misleading effects of the card vote). Conference debates can be real soundings of party opinion, invaluable to the Executive and the Government as a guide to feeling in the party. The Lansbury-Bevin debate in 1935, and the debates involving the "Keep Left" group in 1947 and afterwards, not only settled issues of foreign policy quite decisively but also did so in a way which fairly revealed the proportion of support which each side enjoyed in the party. This is particularly valuable where, as with the "Keep Left" group, a minority's policy enjoys the support of highly vocal spokesmen and two influential weekly papers—factors which otherwise would make the movement appear far more consequential than it actually is. No doubt resolution of differences by open debate advertises a party's rifts to the world, but the advantages of such a process generally far outweigh the losses—provided the party possesses, as in the main Labour does, a strong overriding feeling for unity.

Sometimes of course the necessity of unity dictates an opposite course, and the open discussion of policy is deliberately subordinated to the necessity of not dividing before the enemy. The handling of the case of Mr. Bevan and his friends in the 1951 election provides an instance of the alternative method. Three days after the ministerial resignations, the National Executive (of which Mr. Bevan and three members of his group were members) held a meeting and decided against summoning a special party conference to thrash out their differences over the rearmament programme, although the previous conference, in October 1950, had not, of course, had the issue before it. The Executive did not even consider the question of holding a smaller conference, like the Dorking "house-party" of the previous year, to meet in private. Instead it issued a statement endorsing the budget and advocating party unity; the statement was carried by majority vote, Mr. Bevan and his supporters voting against the budget paragraphs and in favour of the unity clauses. This provoked a disagreement between Mr. Bevan and Mr. Morgan Phillips, the Secretary, on the role of the Executive in policy-making. Mr. Bevan insisted that in issuing this statement the Executive had "exceeded its proper function"; "it should not be called on automatically to endorse Government policies, even major policies, which have not been pronounced upon by the party conference". Mr. Phillips seemed on firmer constitutional ground when he replied that the Executive is "free to comment on the work and policies of any government" and "as the elected authority responsible for representing the Labour party between conferences the National Executive Committee has not only the right but also the duty to publish its views, especially on matters which might be the subject of controversy and confusion in the movement". In fact, of course, owing to the imminence of the election, the Bevan case against the rearmament policy was not brought to the arbitrament of the Scarborough Conference.

Mr. Mikardo has certainly gone too far in asserting (as in *The Tribune* of May 28th, 1948) that "with the Labour Party in governmental power, the Annual Conference as a policy-making institution is as dead as a dodo". Yet it is certainly true that the nearer Labour has got to office the more conscious it has become of the difficulties and dangers of policy-making by conference. Before the Conferences of 1943 and 1944 were laid a succession of policy reports, the bricks out of which the 1945 election manifesto, *Let Us Face the Future*, was later to be fashioned. Most of them went through Conference without much discussion and without any amendment. Professor G. D. H. Cole says in his *History of the Labour Party*: "It was practically impossible, under the procedure adopted, to discuss specific points; for the Reports were moved not directly but in the form of summarizing resolutions, so that they could be effectively challenged only on very broad grounds". Yet by the appeal to results it could be partly claimed that the product of this process, *Let Us Face the Future*, was a great success—it was a manifesto of a triumphant election and a precise legislative agenda of the ensuing administration.

It is interesting to note the process that has operated since. It reflects Mr. Morrison's warning to the 1948 Conference that the policy statement for the next election would be more difficult to prepare than the last. It must be "attractive to ourselves, but also attractive to the general level, the general body of public opinion". As before, a sub-committee of the National Executive was made into a policy-drafting committee, served by the highly efficient Research Department team in Transport House. In preparation for the 1950 election this sub-committee (on which was represented a very fair cross-section of party opinion, under Mr. Herbert Morrison's chairmanship) began its operations as early as 1948-9, having joint meetings with the T.U.C., individual unions and the Co-operative movement. In February, 1949, it drew up a draft which was considered by the whole Executive. Then followed the interesting experiment of the Shanklin Conference, a weekend private meeting of the Executive, the Prime Minister, the Cabinet and almost all other Ministers as well. This implemented Mr. Morrison's observation to the 1948 Annual Conference that it would be unwise to come to final conclusions on policy without consulting the members of the government because of their special knowledge and, if re-elected, their future responsibilities. After Shanklin came a final meeting in March with the T.U.C. Economic Committee and, on the following day, the issuance of the statement under the title of *Labour Believes in Britain* to constituency parties for their consideration. In June it was debated at the Annual Conference at Blackpool. The Executive decided that no vote should be taken and no amendments accepted for debate, but Mr. Morrison assured the delegates that their views would be fully considered when the next electoral equivalent of 1945's *Let Us Face the Future* was prepared. In the two-day debate only minor criticisms were heard, of which the most serious was the Co-operatives' objection to the proposal to nationalize industrial assurance. Certainly when the Executive (working again through its sub-committee) came to draft the final election manifesto this complaint received full consideration, for when *Let Us Win Through Together* appeared on 18th January, 1950, "nationalization" had been converted to the less offensive "mutualization".

The system of conference and consultation employed in 1949 was apparently thought generally satisfactory, for it was in substance repeated in 1950-51. Two differences, however, may be noted. Firstly, greater care was taken to canvass all interests in the Labour movement at an early stage, and so to avoid the back-tracking that occurred in 1950 over the proposals which affected the Co-operatives. The house party at Dorking in May, 1950, which was the counterpart to the 1949 meeting at Shanklin, was larger and more representative. Fifty-six persons attended and there were three T.U.C. and three Co-operative representatives, in addition to any spokesmen they might happen to have in the Government or the Executive. Secondly, the published product of their deliberations, *Labour and the New Society*, was couched in even more general terms than *Labour Believes in Britain*; no doubt the Executive, bearing in mind the failure of the nationalization proposals in the previous document to arouse any electoral interest, wished to keep their hands as free as possible. Mr. Morrison expressed the position to the Conference in these terms: "It is designed to expound the fundamental principles and purpose of the Labour Movement. It is therefore not necessary, in such a general statement, to particularize on certain industries. . . . Now we may be asked specifically whether cement, sugar, and industrial assurance are dropped. The answer to that is 'No'. They are within the field of eligibility for consideration, as are some other industries or services. But we do not think it wise, at any rate at this stage, to commit the Party to a time-table for socialization".

The document was given a two-day debate in general terms and a motion was carried that it should be "received". The election manifesto when it appeared on 30th September of the following year was, as before, the product of the National Executive, working through a sub-committee of four, but, owing to the timing of the election, it was also available in time for "submission" to the Annual Conference. Naturally, however, with the enemy at the gates, no real debate was attempted; instead it was received with acclamation. Those members of the party, like Mr. Bevan, who had only a few days before been conducting a vigorous movement of dissent on at least one section of the party's policy, endorsed it along with the rest.

PARTIES AND THE PEOPLE'S MANDATE
by Cecil S. Emden

REPRESENTATIVE government in this country has long been subject to an increasing measure of direct popular influence in the form of public opinion. That kind of influence is, of course, unsystematic. Within a few years of the passing of the Great Reform Bill of 1832, a new feature in our constitution was introduced; and it was admitted that the people should have a systematic influence on the course of national policy. For more than half a century now, there has been a steady practice whereby the electorate is consulted at general elections in regard to fundamental legislative changes. This development is obviously one of large significance for democracy. How far, it may be asked, has this interesting experiment in direct government extended; and has it worked successfully? In order to attempt an answer to these questions it is desirable first to glance at origins, and then to make a brief survey of the progress of the people's mandate.

Soon after the Restoration there was some talk in political party pamphlets about the ability of the electorate to determine the main lines of policy on occasions when the public interest was closely involved. About 1679-81 the choice of members of Parliament was described, in such tracts as *Advice to Freeholders*, as being a likely reflection of the views of the nation at large. Anti-papist tracts suggested that the right choice of Parliament-men would result in the adoption of policies salutary to the nation. William Penn in his *England's Great Interest in the Choice of this new Parliament* (1679) claimed a right in the people to share in legislation, and alleged that their fundamental rights of liberty should not be infringed upon by legislation without their consent. Sometimes political periodicals or pamphlets described general elections as displaying the "sense" or "disposition" of the nation without actually implying that there was an obligation on Parliament to give effect to any particular policy.

In 1701 there was an official pronouncement which seemed to imply a notable democratic advance, and which was exceptionally explicit. The Royal Proclamation of the dissolution of Parliament invited the electors to choose their representatives with the expectation of securing a particular policy. The Royal "We" "thought it reasonable at this extraordinary juncture to give Our subjects the opportunity of choosing such persons to represent them in Parliament as they may judge most likely to bring to effect their just and pious purposes". Defoe hailed the Proclamation as "a glorious recognition" and "an unexampled testimony of the just rights of the People". It was, he asserted, proof that "the people are in some measure judges of the actions and management of their representatives".

These principles were again ventilated (for they cannot be said to have been put into operation) in the reigns of George I and George II, when attempts were made to treat legislative proposals as issues in general elections. Periodical-writers tried to make the Septennial Act an issue in 1722, and the Excise Scheme an issue in 1734. In 1739 and 1740, the Opposition claimed that the people had the power to insist on the passing of a Bill to reduce the number of placemen in Parliament by showing a preponderance of votes in favour of it.

We have to hark back to the late seventeenth century not only for the first traces of issues being submitted to the people, but also for the first traces of the corollary, the pledging of the Ministry to act in accordance with the people's decision shown by their majority vote. The pledge given nowadays by Ministries is referable to a widespread practice of constituents exacting pledges from individual Members. As early as 1681, many newly-elected Members were pledged to uniform lines of policy by means of common-form instructions. These instructions were prepared and disseminated by a rudimentary party organization set up by the Earl of Shaftesbury. This practice, with some variations, was repeated in the eighteenth century, though many protests were made against the principle of rendering Members of Parliament mere delegates, acting under the instructions of their constituents. But the practice of pledging Members persisted, subject to the retention of reasonable freedom in the interpretation of obligations. Meanwhile the spread of the principle, that every Member represented the whole nation and not merely his constituency, helped towards transforming a number of individual pledges into a general one.

There were many circumstances in the eighteenth century which were obstructive to democratic development. Lip service was often paid to the people's influence over policy for party reasons. Votes were wanted in elections; and they could be secured by pretending that they were capable of doing more than the mere choice of Members of Parliament. Sometimes the apprehension of a Ministry that popular frenzy at public scandals might have ugly repercussions led to nominal appeals for popular support. In 1774, when the seriousness of the situation regarding the American colonies was growing extreme, Lord North wrote to the King informing him that he advised a general election "lest popular dissatisfaction, arising from untoward events, should break the chain of those public measures necessary to reduce the colonies to obedience". It rarely happened that a statesman seriously intended that attention should be paid to the attitude of the people. In 1768 and after, the agitation respecting Wilkes and the Middlesex election led to numerous petitions from counties, cities and boroughs begging for the dissolution of Parliament; and in 1770 Lord Chatham proposed that His Majesty should "take the recent and genuine sense of his people, by dissolving the present Parliament". This proposal, we may be sure, was an honest one.

Furthermore, such issues as were raised at general elections in the eighteenth century tended to be negative in form, turning on resistance to allegedly unpopular policies. There was but little idea of constructive legislation, such as we have nowadays. Nor were there any adequately developed party organizations to thrash out and elucidate positive issues, for issues for popular decision can only be properly formulated by the interaction of competent political parties. Even the membership of parties was loose and vague. Party discipline was hardly effective; and more unfavourable still to democratic development was the fact that the electors often did not know the party affiliations of the candidates at parliamentary elections.

As so far described, the principle of the people's mandate has been discernible only in embryo. The great turning-point which enabled it to come into genuine operation was the passing of the great Reform Bill in 1832.[1] It then began to be an integral element in our constitutional system. The intense popular excitement prior to the passing of the Bill, and the profound significance of the proposed measure rendered a submission to the people essential. They were admitted to be capable of deciding at the general election of 1831 whether the Bill was to be passed or not.

Subject to some hesitations and delay, the election of a majority of representatives pledged to a particular measure was in future to be interpreted as an obligation on the Ministry to introduce it. The happenings of 1831 and 1832 were of such vast constitutional implication that the full effect of the people's promotion to a direct part in government was not generally recognized for some few years. The great step in democratic development was thought at first to be a final settlement of the franchise question, and thus incapable of being a precedent.

Some delay in progress was naturally due to the confined outlook of conservatively-minded statesmen. The conservatism of such so-called Liberals as Melbourne, and the even more deeply ingrained conservatism of Peel were handicaps. They both clung to the eighteenth century notion that Parliament should not, if possible, be dissolved for an appeal to the people unless there was a strong likelihood of victory. A defeat, they thought, would be injurious to the authority of the Crown. Peel showed his limitations in other ways. In 1846 he refused

---

[1] Historians are now in general agreement that the election of 1784 did not, as was at one time supposed, mark a notable stage in the extension of the political power of the people.

to consult the electorate in regard to his vitally important proposal to repeal the Corn Laws on the ground that "such an appeal would ensure a bitter conflict between different classes of society".

Other influences hindered the principle of mandate in the nineteenth century. The lack of party organization and discipline still remained. Peel's political apostasy in regard to free trade encouraged confusion of party allegiances. And, soon after, Palmerston became for a decade or more the predominant political figure, and one of immense popularity, with the consequence that issues had for a time more relation to personalities than to measures.

But the extensions of the franchise in 1867 and 1884 produced a radical change in the constitutional balance. These extensions coincided with an upsurge of social reform; and party leaders were prompted to advance programmes of amelioration of the conditions of the workers. They found it expedient to court the electorate by promises of material benefits. In 1868 Disraeli considered the advisability of including some proposal of social amelioration in his election programme. In 1874 Gladstone tried to improve his chances at the polls by promising the repeal of the income-tax and other attractive measures. Thus it came about that party manifestos, making submissions of proposed items of policy to the electorate, became normal features in general elections. When the Liberals came into power with a large majority in 1906, there was a notable increase in legislation conferring social benefits; and there were not lacking critics who accused the Ministry of bribing the electorate. The process continued after the vast extension of the franchise in 1918, and has since become intensified. It cannot be denied that the principle of the mandate is in some danger of being prostituted owing to the temptation of party leaders to put forward programmes designed to attract the masses without due regard to national interests.

In the late nineteenth century the Tories became as much committed to the principle of mandate as the Liberals, but rather as a means of curbing legislation than of pledging themselves to it. They tried to thwart Liberal legislation by rejecting it in the House of Lords, where they had a permanent majority. They alleged that it was the duty of the House of Lords to keep the Liberal Ministries within the limits of their mandates. In 1872 Lord Salisbury asked the House of Lords to reject a bill for the introduction of the ballot on the ground that the question had never been an election issue; and in 1884 he tried to delay the passage of a measure for a large increase in the numbers of the electorate because, as he insisted, the Liberals had no right to make vast constitutional changes without formally consulting the opinions of the people. Conservatives argued on these lines down to the time when the powers of the House of Lords were curtailed by the Parliament Act, 1911. Lord Curzon asserted in 1909 that it was "inherent in the rights of any Second Chamber" to "compel a reference to the polls" where the Ministry of the day introduced an important measure such as the Parliament Bill for which the mandate of the people had not been obtained.

Even down to the early twentieth century the old-fashioned Liberals retained some relics of Whig principles. In appropriate circumstances they denied any need for specific mandates. Some of them genuinely believed that, when a Ministry gained a majority at an election, it had implied authority to undertake any legislation it pleased, provided that it was in the spirit of the party principles. Even as late as 1907 Campbell-Bannerman, the Liberal Prime Minister, denied that the people's mandate was necessary for the introduction of such measures as his Ministry's Education Bill. He said: "The Constitution knows nothing of this doctrine of the special mandate, nothing whatever". But it was, in fact, becoming impossible for statesmen to maintain such reactionary doctrines. Extensions of the franchise had involved all political leaders in the practical wisdom of appealing to the people; and dependence on the people's decision for the main outlines of policy had, by the early twentieth century, become firmly established.

In normal circumstances election issues tend to be raised by the Ministry; but there is no objection to the issues being raised by the Opposition. The matter may be settled by vigorous personality and by ability to impose a subject on the attention of the public. A forceful statesman like Gladstone was able, as Leader of the Opposition, to make the Irish Church question the dominant issue in 1868, in spite of the efforts of Disraeli, the Prime Minister, to concentrate attention on the achievements of his Ministry. Disraeli was able to reverse the position in 1874, for he, as Leader of the Opposition, proved that he had adequate dynamic force to insist that the prevailing issue should be Gladstone's past record, and not the tempting baits with which Gladstone tried to woo the electorate.

On some few occasions Prime Ministers or their colleagues have publicly taunted the Opposition for their lack of a positive programme to place before the electorate. The question has, therefore, been mooted—is there an obligation on leaders of an Opposition party to produce a positive programme of policy, or can they confine themselves to criticizing the Ministry's future policy and past record? The answer seems to be that the Opposition is only under an obligation to state its views with any particularity on subjects which have previously been in controversy in Parliament and which remain undetermined.

From the time of Disraeli down to that of Mr. Winston Churchill, leaders of the Opposition have occasionally refused to make a declaration of policy at the outset of a general election on the ground that they have not access to the secrets of government, largely kept in Government Departments. Oppositions are not, however, in such a difficult situation in this respect as they used to be in Disraeli's time, for nowadays they themselves maintain research staffs qualified to collect and assess data.

Sometimes other influences have affected the raising of issues. Democratic elements in public bodies and in party organizations are outstanding examples. Various societies and leagues have been powerful in enforcing issues, from the time of the Anti-Slavery Society in 1832, and the Anti-Corn Law League a little later, down to the League of Nations Union, and, perhaps most powerful of all, the Trades Union Congress.

Since the later part of the nineteenth century the pressure

of democratic elements in party organizations has caused some of the party leaders to modify their election manifestos. In 1877, Joseph Chamberlain founded the National Liberal Federation; and he then emphasized the right of the people to have a part in the framing of issues. Party discipline was tightened so that pledges should be strictly complied with. From 1880 onwards many Liberal local associations chose candidates on condition that they adopted the party programme. The periodical meetings of the Federation soon became concerned with the "planks" in the party "platform". In 1891, the Liberal Party Conference prescribed the "Newcastle Programme" with a heterogeneous list of proposed measures which involved the party leaders in considerable embarrassment.

The Conservative Party, too, saw the advantage of tightening party discipline and of the democratization of party management; but they succeeded in keeping the latter within limits.

The youngest party, the Labour Party, has gone furthest in admitting popular influence in the framing of issues. The Constitution of the Party provides that the choice of items for the Party Manifesto, published prior to an election, must be made by the Executive Committees of the Party from the proposals advanced by the democratically-elected Party Conference. The Executive Committees also define the attitude of the party to the principle issues raised outside the party. Exceptional provisions are made in the Constitution that the mandate undertaken by the Party shall be made effective. The strictest of all Party disciplines is imposed on M.P.s of the Labour Party, who as candidates have to pledge themselves to "accept and conform to the Constitution, Programme, Principles, and Policy of the Party".

Experience seems to have shown that unrestricted initiative by local party associations and by party conferences is not beneficial to national interests. Such initiative may produce programmes with unwieldy and conflicting items, adopted without the adequate data and background which are only available to the leaders of the party.

The operation of public opinion, intractable as it is, has frequently modified the balance of issues shortly before and during general elections. It is a temptation to party leaders to fly such kites as "Hang the Kaiser" with the hope of gaining a last-minute accession of votes. But courting the people can seldom lead to the sober conduct of politics.

Almost any important issue of policy *can* be submitted to the electorate for their decision; but there are some kinds of issue which experience indicates *should* be so submitted. The circumstances leading up to, and the passing of the Great Reform Bill of 1832, suggested that, thereafter, matters affecting the liberty of the subject and the structure of politics required the popular mandate. Even Sir Henry Maine, a great constitutionalist who was suspicious of unduly rapid democratic progress, recognized as early as 1885, that owing to recent changes, "the electoral body must supply the House of Commons with a mandate to alter the Constitution". This principle was plainly admitted in 1909 and 1910 in regard to the Parliament Bill, which curtailed the powers of the House of Lords. It had previously been conceded in Victorian times in regard to extensions of the franchise; but, oddly enough, no specific mandate was considered necessary for the vast extensions of the franchise in 1918 and 1928. Perhaps the approval of the electorate was so obvious as to require no testing. It is also difficult to understand why no mandate was obtained for the settlement of the Irish question in 1921, when Southern Ireland was given Dominion status. The probable excuse would be that the matter was an urgent one.

On one or two occasions urgency has also been assigned as a reason for neglecting the need for the people's authority in regard to measures of defence; and the inability to refer to the people before a declaration of war has been obvious in the two World Wars.

The main reason, perhaps, for the close interest of the people in any alteration in the Constitution is the possibility that their liberties may be endangered. A rather similar reason renders it obligatory on a Ministry to obtain a mandate before introducing legislation which will affect matters closely relating to the life of the people, such as the price of food. This obligation was explicitly admitted in the discussions on proposals for tariff reform in 1903-1905, and on similar subsequent occasions when Baldwin was Prime Minister.

There are some kinds of issue that have been generally regarded as outside the scope of the people's decision, on the ground of being too technical or abstruse. Whereas, for instance, the people have the capacity to decide on the general principle of a Bill, they are not able to investigate the advantages and disadvantages of the details of legislation. The great Reform Bill of 1832 was supposed to be submitted with all its eighty-two long clauses for the consideration of the electorate—an obvious impossibility. In 1892, it was argued by Gladstone's opponents that the terms of his Home Rule Bill were incapable of being referred to the electorate, but that they might perhaps be able to give an answer, "Yes" or "No", in relation to a brief summary of the Bill.

After the second of the two general elections of 1910, in which the Parliament Bill was the issue, the Liberals maintained that they were given specific authority to pass the Bill, which had, in terms, been referred to the electorate. The Conservatives, on the other hand, denied that the people had been able to consider the Bill in detail, and merely admitted that the people had shown themselves to be in favour of some amendment of the relations between the two Houses of Parliament. Incidents of this kind prove either the incapacity of the people to deal with details, or the need for clear, authoritative and impartial summaries of detailed legislation so as to enable a Ministry to claim that they have some specific authority to pass a Bill which has been challenged by the Opposition.

Many vitally important administrative changes have been undertaken without any mandate, presumably for reasons of urgency and, even more, of technicality. Such were the departure from the gold standard in 1931, and the devaluation measure in 1949. Furthermore, the technical questions involved in many great social reforms prevent their being submitted for popular decision.

In the period in which the principle of the mandate was

in its early, experimental stage, it was often remarked that foreign policy was outside the people's scope; and this view is still largely maintained, partly no doubt because foreign policy must of necessity be arranged in a confidential atmosphere. However, the First World War and the subsequent operations of the League of Nations Union created so vivid an interest in foreign politics that the maintenance of the Covenant of the League of Nations and the doctrine of collective security became a predominant issue in the election of 1935. The Baldwin Ministry said in its Manifesto: "The League of Nations will remain, as heretofore, the keystone of British policy". This adventure in the submission of matters of foreign politics to the electorate proved to be a failure, because the expressed desires of the people were flouted by the Baldwin and Neville Chamberlain Ministries. The Hoare-Laval terms for Ethiopia of 1935 involved a flagrant violation of the League's Covenant, and were rightly characterized by Mr. Attlee in the House of Commons as "a betrayal of the electors who were induced to support the Government". Though Sir Samuel Hoare's immediate resignation seemed to imply some respect for the people's mandate, Neville Chamberlain again violated the Covenant in June, 1936, by denouncing the régime of sanctions. In 1938 Neville Chamberlain went from bad to worse by agreeing to negotiate with Italy on the basis of the *de jure* recognition of the Italian conquest of Ethiopia.

It seems unlikely that questions of foreign policy will be submitted to the people as a matter of routine for some time to come. When Neville Chamberlain's Munich Agreement was concluded in 1938, Mr. Winston Churchill said it would be "constitutionally indecent" for Chamberlain to appeal to the people for support of his policy. Mr. Churchill was, indeed, rightly apprehensive that a wave of pacifism might lead the country into a dangerous attitude towards the Nazis. But, on broader grounds, there remains a widespread general opinion that the people's views about international questions in an atmosphere of tension are apt to be unreliable.

Such questions as the extent of popular influence in the

choice of issues, and the extent of detail and technicality with which the people are capable of dealing, are perhaps less critical to the useful survival of the practice of the mandate than the persistent problems of interpretation. In most general elections circumstances have conspired to render the interpretation of the mandate confused and debatable. Sometimes this may be unavoidable; but often it seems that, with sensible regulation and some impartial control, ambiguity could be largely eliminated. Statesmen continue to adopt a fatalistic attitude in this matter. Balfour, when trying to evade the conclusion that the second general election of 1910 produced a mandate for the passing of the Parliament Bill, alleged that all the general elections which he remembered had had mixed issues, and must have had mixed issues. That may be true as regards the past, though he possibly overlooked the election of 1868, which happened when he was a young man. This election provided a rare example of a straightforward and simple issue about the Irish Church; and it was, moreover, an issue in respect of which the people of England could obtain no direct benefit, so that self-interest and partiality were excluded in an exceptional degree.

Even if it were admitted that general elections cannot be confined to one issue, it might be possible for one predominant issue to be given special validity. Ministries advancing policies in loose and vague terms or keeping them in the background should not be allowed to claim specific mandates in respect of them. As a result of the election of 1950, therefore, the Labour Ministry could not, and perhaps would not, claim that they had popular authority for the nationalization of the sugar and cement industries.

Various statesmen (Balfour and Curzon, for instance, in 1910 and 1911) argued that questions could be put to the electorate much more concisely and decisively in a referendum than in a general election. This view does not seem to be supported by experience in countries in which the referendum is regularly used. Inevitably, personal factors and party prejudices obtrude themselves and blur the issue.

When there is a party leader of exceptionally forceful

personality, or with particular claims to the attachment of the people, issues of policy may give way to those of leadership. Palmerston, as already remarked, was such a leader. In two elections, those of 1929 and 1935, Baldwin's reputation as a safe and trusted national figure, with pipe and homely, fireside manner, was exploited by the Conservative Party organization and became a dominant issue. Again, in 1945, the Conservatives tried to adopt the same tactics so as to make the election turn on the nation-wide popularity and immense prestige of Mr. Churchill. Perhaps these occasional deviations from issues of policy are unavoidable; but they may be regrettable as tending to introduce sentiment at the expense of sober intellectual judgment.

Another divergence from issues of future policy is that in which party leaders deem it prudent to try and make the past record of the Ministry the prevailing issue. Sometimes an Opposition has preferred to blacken the past record of a Ministry which has been losing the confidence of the people, rather than to raise a positive issue or to combat one raised by the Ministry. In 1880 the Liberals decided to rely chiefly on the alleged delinquencies of the Beaconsfield Ministry and to refrain from advancing positive proposals of their own. On the other hand, Ministries have sometimes preferred to rest their hopes of a majority of votes on their past achievements rather than to formulate positive issues which might not attract a sufficient proportion of the electorate. In 1950, the Labour Party "soft-pedalled" nationalization and placed much reliance on their past record, both in their election Manifesto and in their party broadcasts. Indeed, little attempt was made by the leaders of the Labour Party to formulate any positive issues, with the result (as in similar instances) that the people's mandate could hardly be claimed to be operative in its full sense in the ensuing Parliament.

All these variations from the normal type of issue which have been mentioned tend to make the interpretation of the result of a general election difficult. Even if several co-ordinated items of a party programme represent the main issues of an election, doubt has been cast on the continuing validity of the mandate when some of the items have been left to a period shortly before the next general election is due. It is a mistake to assume that a mandate authorizes a succession of items of policy being passed into law year after year regardless of changing circumstances and changing public opinion. A mandate can lose its force owing to its becoming stale. The heated discussions in Parliament and in the country about the Steel Nationalization Bill, towards the conclusion of the Parliament of 1945-50, will be remembered as an instance of this argument being raised by the Conservatives against the Labour Party.

Expediency has been a frequent factor. Development of the people's part in government was delayed for many years by reason of Peel's repeated tergiversations regarding the propriety of appeals to popular decision at general elections. In 1834, he was unexpectedly appointed Prime Minister; and it was convenient to him to issue to the electorate a manifesto stating his future policy. This Tamworth Manifesto was regarded as a bold democratic enterprise; but Peel soon came to the conclusion that he had been unduly progressive, and he regretted the precedent he had created. In 1846 he laid himself open to much pertinent criticism by introducing free trade legislation without obtaining the sanction of the electorate. But in the next year, in the election of 1847, he once more performed a *volte face* when he found it expedient to issue to the electorate another manifesto of his political principles.

Gladstone, also, on a historic occasion, gave the appearance of rejecting and adopting the principle of the mandate in accordance with the convenience of the moment. When, shortly after the election of 1885, he suddenly introduced his momentous Home Rule proposals without previous reference to the people, he was severely criticized by Lord Hartington and others. But Gladstone described Hartington's doctrine as an extraordinary one, not laid down by any constitutional authority; and he denied the need for a mandate. But, when political circumstances had changed two months later, and his Home Rule Bill had been defeated in the House of Commons, he advised a general election, and did not display the least hesitation in referring the issue to the people in the most explicit way.

This tendency to opportunism has continued, in less flagrant form, into recent years. When in power, party leaders have sometimes argued, with scant grounds, that they have popular authority for proposed legislation. When in opposition they have expressed themselves as shocked at the absence of a specific mandate for a measure of legislation which was in fact well within the general principles advanced by the Ministry at the preceding general election.

The people's direct influence on national policy cannot operate satisfactorily without high principles and vigorous, constructive leadership in statesmen. Failure to submit to the electorate issues involving national safety, because such a submission might prove disadvantageous to party prospects, is reprehensible. We know now enough of the facts about Baldwin and his feeble attitude on the crucial subject of defence in 1933-36 to charge him with lack of a sense of public duty. He had adopted the view that a policy of rearmament required the authority of the electorate. When speaking in the House of Commons in November, 1936, he excused himself from telling the people the facts in 1933 on the ground that there was then a strong pacifist feeling running through the country. If he had appealed to the electorate on rearmament in 1933, he said, he would have lost the election. He remarked in his speech in 1936 that he put these views before the House "with an appalling frankness". His frankness was more appalling than he realized. If, in 1933, he had aroused the people's patriotism with the facts about Nazi Germany as he knew them, he might well have won the election and provided the country with proper protection. If he had lost the election, the country would have been as well off with some other statesman at its head as with a Baldwin in his 1933 attitude of mind. His behaviour was an almost tragic example of the way in which inadequate leadership can render the mandate principle a source of national peril.

There is another example of party opportunism which seems not to have raised as much remonstrance as it should, perhaps because it is accepted as inevitable. By constitutional convention Prime Ministers are permitted to choose the time for general elections; and this choice has often been admittedly made to some extent for party purposes. If, as may be hoped, the mandate comes to operate according to more public-spirited principles, Prime Ministers will naturally determine the time of elections in the interest of the nation alone.

A final word must be devoted to the problem of how to make the people's mandate more efficient than hitherto. In the first place, too much should not be asked of the people. They should not have abstruse or confused questions put to them. Secondly, such straightforward questions as are asked should be framed fairly without bias or distortion. It is perhaps unreasonable under present conditions to expect party manifestos to be free from all undesirable forms of special pleading. But these elements might well be reduced by the application of some impartial guidance in the formulation of issues, which should be fairly and lucidly explained, when not self-evident.

Although confused issues have frequently led to bitter and unprofitable recriminations, it must be borne in mind that over-simplification has its dangers. Nationalization, in the election of 1945, was submitted to the electorate's determination in a misleadingly simple form. The question could not be fairly put if it did not explain the degree as well as the extent of the proposed nationalization.

The problem of the proper working of the people's mandate requires a good deal of thought, much more than it has yet received. If it were sensibly managed, our frail democratic structure could be invigorated. Democracy can never succeed without an electorate that is genuinely interested in politics. If the people feel that they have a part in the process of government, their interest will be stimulated. So far in its history, the people's mandate has been of dubious value. But it is not yet necessary to abandon it, either as unduly ambitious or as hopelessly discredited.[1]

---

[1] Readers who wish to find references for items in this article should consult Cecil S. Emden, *The People and the Constitution* (1933), where the treatment of the subject is fuller than is possible here.

THE PERSONNEL OF THE PARTIES
by J. F. S. Ross

LIKE every human organization, a political party is ultimately composed of individual people. So in considering its philosophy, history, and constitution, we must not lose sight of the actual men and women on whose experiences and ideals, hopes and fears, the whole thing is based. Let us, then, have a look at the personal backgrounds, educational, occupational, and social, that lie behind and give colour to the activities of the parties.

In each case, of course, we must distinguish between the parliamentary (House of Commons) party on the one hand, and the aggregation of electors that supports it, on the other. These two entities may be and in fact usually are very differently composed. Moreover, while we are on fairly firm ground in dealing with the parliamentary parties, since their membership is clearly defined and its characteristics have been pretty fully studied, when we turn to the electorate we find the bounds of party membership nebulous, and relatively little precise information available as to its characteristics.[1] Even here, however, we have some useful indications, from a variety of sources, and can gain a general idea of the position. We are, of course, concerned with the vast body of electors who support with their votes each of the political parties, and not with the tiny minority of enthusiasts who register their names in the party books, pay subscriptions, and toil for the cause between elections. We shall realize, too, that no party, in or out of parliament, has anything like a single uniform type of personnel: in each there is diversity of membership.

Let us begin with the Conservatives, taking first the parliamentary party. Educationally this is remarkably homogeneous, for six out of every seven Conservative M.P.s

[1] It is to be regretted that the official statistics relating to elections in this country are so meagre in comparison with those issued elsewhere.

have had a public-school[1] education, and one in every four was at Eton, while only one in forty is the product of the elementary school. Moreover, more than half the members were at Oxford or Cambridge, and more than half the rest were at some other university, or at a service college, or at one of the inns of court.[2]

Occupationally perhaps the most significant fact is that one-third of the party consists of regular officers of the fighting services and of practising barristers (in almost equal numbers). Another third is composed of farmers, journalists, manufacturers, civil servants (including diplomats), solicitors, stockbrokers, and merchants. Further, while a typical three dozen Conservative M.P.s would include eleven employers and managers and twice that number of professional men, it would contain only one solitary rank-and-file worker. We may note, also, that one in every four of the party is a lawyer, practising or non-practising, and that three in every eight are company directors.

Another factor in the party make-up is the close connexion that nearly a third of its members have with families of hereditary title. This strong "aristocratic" element is all the more noteworthy because it is practically confined to the Conservatives: fewer than one in twenty of such members in the 1950 House of Commons belonged to any other party.

[1] A "public school" in the English sense is an independent school, not run for profit, which admits its pupils at about 13 years of age and trains them chiefly for admission to the universities and the public services. Many of these schools are residential. For convenience, membership of the "Headmasters Conference" is here taken as the criterion of public-school status. For other selective schools providing a type of education roughly similar to that of the public schools, though more varied in character, and admitting their pupils at about 11½ years of age, the term "secondary schools" is employed. Most of these are grammar schools, owned and run by local education authorities, and most of them are non-residential. (Under the Education Act, 1944, a secondary school is merely a school for pupils of 12 years of age and over; but that Act is too recent to affect the education of the adults with whom we are concerned.) "Elementary school" denotes a non-selective school providing a simpler and less academic type of education. (For a fuller discussion of this classification, see my book *Parliamentary Representation*.)

[2] The inns of court are responsible for the training and examination of intending barristers.

Lastly we observe that of every four Conservative M.P.s in the 1950 House one had seen service as a member of a County Council, Town Council, District Council, or other local authority.

Social classes still exist in this country, though they are neither sharply-defined nor exclusive; and we can sum up the position by saying that the parliamentary Conservative party is pre-eminently recruited from the upper and upper-middle classes. That is demonstrated in many ways, but most significantly perhaps by its near-monopoly of the M.P.s who are regular officers of the fighting services and of the M.P.s belonging to titled families. Plentiful on the Conservative benches, such members are exceptional elsewhere in the House.

When we turn from the House of Commons to the electorate we find a very different state of affairs. Let us start from one basic fact; that in the 1950 general election the Conservative party and its auxiliaries polled over 12½ million votes. That tells us some interesting and important things about the Conservative voters.

First as to education: of the 28¾ million electors of all parties who went to the poll, it may be estimated that only about 3 million had had full-time education beyond the standard of the elementary school. So if every one of these voted Conservative there must still have been some 9½ million Conservative voters with only an elementary-school education. But there is reason to believe that at least a million and a quarter electors with a grammar-school or public-school education voted for other parties; so for 9½ million we must substitute 10¾ million. That means that roughly six out of every seven Conservative voters were elementary-educated, against the mere one in forty Conservative M.P.s—a sharp contrast.

Next as to income: we know that fewer than four million of the voters had an income of £500 or over. So if every one of these better-off electors gave his vote to the Conservatives, that party must still have drawn over 8½ million of its votes from people below the £500-a-year level. But though it has been well established, by means of "sampling" investigations, that the higher the income people have, the more they tend to vote Conservative, it has also been shown that an appreciable proportion of "well-off" people vote for other parties. It seems probable that not more than three million of the electors above the given income level support the Conservative party: hence that party must have drawn over 9½ million votes from the poorer classes; that is to say, more than three-quarters of its total strength. So here again we have a marked contrast between the Conservative voters and the Conservative M.P.s.

We cannot analyze in detail the occupations of the electors, as we can those of M.P.s. But it is clear, from the facts given above, that large numbers of Conservative voters must belong to what used to be called the "working classes", and must be engaged in manual, clerical, or other subordinate occupations; and this is confirmed by the results of various "sampling" investigations. In particular, it has been found that clerks and shop assistants are predominantly Conservative.

Two other well-established facts should also be noticed. The first is that the older the electors are the more they tend to vote Conservative. The other is that Conservatism gets much more support from women than it does from men.[1] Roughly three women vote Conservative for every two men who do so. The greater number of women in the electorate—now about ten women to nine men—only partly accounts for this.

Now let us turn to Labour; and again we take first the parliamentary party. Educationally, and indeed in many ways, this is nowadays less homogeneous than the Conservative parliamentary party; though thirty or forty years ago that was not so. In the 1950 House of Commons rather more than half the Labour members had had only an elementary school education, while of the remainder rather less than half had attended public schools and rather more than half other types of selective secondary school. About four out of every eleven Labour M.P.s had had some kind

[1] This phenomenon seems to be world-wide; it has been verified statistically in many countries and at many elections.

of university education, but only one in six had been to Oxford or Cambridge. No account of the educational background of Labour members would be complete, however, without a reference to the efforts that many have made to remedy early educational deficiencies by attendance, mostly part-time, at technical and commercial colleges, W.E.A.[1] classes, and other comparable institutions.

As with education, so with occupation: the 1950 parliamentary Labour party background was very different from that of the Conservatives. Lawyers, of course, abounded in both; but the regular officers, farmers, stockbrokers, etc., of the Conservatives were replaced on the Labour benches by teachers, miners, railwaymen, and so on. About a quarter of the party consisted (in almost equal numbers) of teachers and miners, while another two-fifths was made up of barristers, journalists, clerks, metal workers, solicitors, and railwaymen. The proportion of manual workers was much lower than it used to be, but, even so, the contrast with the Conservatives was still striking. The Labour M.P.s of professional status outnumbered the rank-and-file workers by fifteen to fourteen; but the comparable number of employers and managers was only three—a very different state of affairs from that on the benches opposite. Lastly we may note that one in seven of the party was a lawyer, practising or non-practising, and that, while one in eleven was a company director, one in three was a past or present trade-union official.

Another contrast was to be found in the almost complete absence from the Labour ranks of the "aristocratic" element that is so conspicuous in the Conservative make-up. On the other hand, the Labour members were more generally experienced in local government work, four out of every seven having served on local councils, against the Conservatives' one in four.

It will be seen that, whereas by far the greater part of the Conservative parliamentary party is fairly homogeneous in its composition and outlook, there is no such uniformity in the Labour party. Here we can clearly distinguish two main

[1] Workers' Educational Association.

streams. The first is that of the rank-and-file workers, mostly of elementary education and manual occupation, who have risen to prominence through their trade-union activities. The second is that of the "intelligentsia", typically (though not invariably) men and women of lower middle-class or working-class origin, who have climbed up by means of school and university scholarships, have graduated (often in economics or allied subjects), and have become school-teachers, adult education tutors, journalists, civil servants, and lawyers. Though these streams differ widely in experience and outlook, neither has much in common with the typical Conservative M.P.

In the Labour party, then, the social disparity between M.P.s and electors is less striking than in the Conservative party. Disparity there is, but in the main it is between those who have risen above their initial environment and circumstances and those who have remained there; whereas in the Conservative party it is between people who are, and have been from birth, of different social classes.

As we have seen, the Conservative electorate includes a substantial part of the lower middle classes and working classes; but the larger part of those classes supports the Labour party. What the proportions are it is almost impossible to say—especially as there are no water-tight definitions of the classes. We can, however, usefully notice certain facts ascertained by "sampling" investigations. It seems clear that Labour's strongest hold is over the men employed in the "heavy" industries—coal, steel, and so on—and over the unskilled workers. Moreover, unlike the Conservative party, Labour has a stronger hold on men than on women. It is reported that in the 1945 election 53 per cent. of the male electors voted Labour, but only 45 per cent. of the female; and there seems some probability that in the 1950 election the disparity was even greater.

It is curious that while the average Labour M.P. is over four years older than the average Conservative, amongst the electors the position is reversed, and the average Labour voter is nearly three years younger than the average Conservative. Hence the age-gap between electors and M.P.s is some seven years greater in the Labour party than in the Conservative party. On the other hand, as we have seen, the social gulf between Conservative M.P.s and Conservative electors is much wider than that between Labour M.P.s and Labour electors.

When we turn to the Liberal party we are, of course, up against the difficulty that its 1950 membership in the House of Commons was so small as to afford little reliable basis for generalizations. But we have also available full particulars both of the very much larger number of candidates who stood at the previous two elections, and of the many Liberal members of the inter-war parliaments. So from all these sources together we can form a reasonably clear picture of the normal educational, occupational, and social make-up of the parliamentary Liberal party. We soon see that in each of these respects the party comes somewhere between the other two parties, though not necessarily midway.[1]

So just as we may call the Conservative party in parliament the "public-school party", and the Labour party the "elementary-school party", the Liberals may be termed the "secondary-school party"; though perhaps not with quite so much force. In university education, again, the Liberal position is roughly half-way between those of the other two parties. Similarly the occupational background of the party has a character intermediate to those of its rivals. It lacks alike the army officers, diplomats, and stockbrokers of the Conservatives, and the miners, weavers, and railway clerks of Labour. Lawyers, business-men, civil servants, and journalists: they are the sort of people from whom Liberal M.P.s are chiefly drawn. Socially, again, the party is between the others. It lacks, nowadays, the aristocratic element that is still so strong on the Conservative benches, but it equally lacks the manual workers who are so powerful in the Labour party.

---

[1] If A and B are points taken to represent the respective positions of the Conservative and Labour parties, then the point C representing the position of the Liberal party does not necessarily lie on the line AB: it may well be the apex of a triangle having AB as its base.

Indeed one might almost say that the most marked characteristic of the parliamentary Liberal party's background is that it has no very marked characteristics.

When we turn from the parliamentary party to the electors we find a similar state of affairs. Where the Conservative electorate is predominantly female and includes a high proportion of the old and elderly and of the better-off, while the Labour electorate is predominantly male and draws more on the younger age-groups and the worse-off, the Liberal electorate appears to draw equally on both sexes and all ages, and not to depend for its members on any particular income-group. Indeed Henry W. Durant goes so far as to say that the party is unique amongst British parties in that its support does not seem to be conditioned by sex, class, or age. But a fuller investigation would be necessary before we could accept unconditionally this striking dictum. It may be noted that another investigation reports the Liberal voters as "the most election conscious and the most informed".

All these things really tie up together. Because of their respective positions on the Right and Left in politics, both the Conservative and Labour parties necessarily attract to their ranks a proportion of the more aggressively class-conscious and the more extreme in opinion. Because of its more central position, there is nothing to attract to the Liberal party either the violently partisan or the bitterly class-conscious. Obviously, then, the Liberal electorate might be described either as colourless and nondescript (by its enemies) or as sane and level-headed (by its friends). Certainly its characteristics are not as boldly marked as are those of the other two party electorates.

Here, then, is a sketch of the kind of personnel to be found in each of the three parties, in and out of parliament. Even such a brief survey serves to show that there are salient personal differences not only between parties but also, within a party, between its members in the House of Commons and its supporters in the country. (Indirectly these differences reflect the fact that parties in this country are doctrinally distinct in a way that parties in the United States and Canada are not.)

Of the Conservatives we may say that, in both spheres,

they attract to themselves the greater part of the more aristocratic, better-established, and better-off elements. But whereas in the House of Commons these elements almost monopolize the party membership, in the electorate they are greatly outnumbered by people of the lower-middle and working classes. We note, too, that whereas Conservative M.P.s are relatively young and almost all men, Conservatism in the country attracts to its support fifty per cent more women than men, and exerts an increasing pull on the electors as they grow older.

Labour, on the other hand, attracts to itself a great proportion of the more plebeian, more discontented, and worse-off elements. Its greatest strength lies in the manual and unskilled workers. Differences of background between M.P.s and electors are less fundamental than with the Conservatives, but differences of age are greater. Reversing the Conservative tendencies, Labour draws more support from men than from women, and from the younger electors than from the older; though, in curious contrast, the Labour M.P.s are considerably older than the Conservative.

Of the Liberal personnel, both in and out of parliament, the most characteristic quality is the absence of extremes. Here are neither aristocrats nor sansculottes. Here we can trace little effect from age or sex or income. Both in and out of the House, this is the least class-conscious, the least partisan of the three parties.

The study of the electorate and its behaviour, however, is still in its infancy. The various investigations so far reported, though highly interesting and instructive, leave an immense field almost untilled, and it is to be hoped that the subject will receive more comprehensive and detailed attention than it has yet had.

THE PARTY SYSTEM IN LOCAL GOVERNMENT

by J. H. WARREN

IN British government at the national level, the party system has in all essentials been with us for two hundred years or more. Although its existence goes for the most part unacknowledged in the forms and precepts of our constitution, we know it to be the engine which supplies the motive force to national government. The nation recognizes and accepts it as such; and its effects are all-pervasive. In its total play, behind and through the mechanisms of constitutional government, it can be pictured, indeed, as Hardy pictured "the anatomy of the immanent will" in the forescene to "The Dynasts".

In British *local* government, the situation is not quite the same.

In the first place, to the extent that the party system exists, it is of much more recent development. Roughly speaking—how roughly students of British Local Government will know—our modern system of democratic local government was inaugurated by the Municipal Corporations Act of 1835, establishing a new model for town government on a basis of election, since widened to adult suffrage; but although, in the succeeding portion of the nineteenth century, there were many localities in which municipal elections had come to be run on party lines, producing Conservative and Liberal party groups in the local council, it was not in all of these localities that the party groups so acted or inter-acted as to manage the council's business on party lines. The Conservatives were, it is true, running Liverpool in this way well before the close of the century. Birmingham, in the seventies, was being similarly run by the Liberals—the activities of Chamberlain, Schnadhorst, and their caucus of Birmingham Radicals being responsible, indeed, for an important chapter in British social history. In the London County Council, two groups had established themselves almost immediately after the creation of the Council in 1888: the Moderates (afterwards Municipal Reformers) who were mostly Conservatives; and the Progressives, who were mostly Liberals; each group making an organized approach to Council business. On the other hand, while the Manchester City Council comprised Conservative and Liberal groups throughout the latter part of the century, "neither party" at that period, says Lady Simon, in *A Century of City Government*, "used its majority to run the Council on party lines". And over large parts of the country many councils remained "non-political", even in composition, until well after the close of the century; though some were captured by the Liberals in the Liberal heyday of 1906 to 1914.

Party sway in local government is still not complete today. There are few areas in which the Labour Party has not entered the lists, but a fair number in which it has secured only a fractional representation. And there appear to be some areas where the Conservatives have not yet put forward party nominees. The Councils in such places are comprised, as to a majority at any rate, of "independents". It is difficult to assess their number. They are to be found mostly among the small boroughs and the urban or rural districts, and, among these types of local authority, more in the South than the North; the North as a region, and the larger towns and cities as a class, being mostly "political". Such "independent" Councils may amount perhaps to a half of the 572 urban districts and three-quarters of the 475 rural districts, but probably only account for a tenth of the counties and the larger towns. Labour Party propaganda frequently dubs independent councillors as Conservatives in disguise, or avers, at any rate, that when put to the test of their reaction to the policies of minority Labour groups, they show themselves to be anti-Labour. There is some truth in this. The areas in which "independents" survive are not, on the whole, those which have proved very favourable ground for the Labour Party. Having no strong challenge to meet, independents in such places, who may in fact be Conservatives (or Liberals), have not felt the need to resort to party support at the polls, or party organization on the Council; and their attitude seems, until recently at any rate, to be one in which the local Conservative or Liberal organization has been prepared to acquiesce. Be all this as it may, the fact remains that a fair number of Councils still exist in which there are large, and often majority, groups of "independents" who stood for election on no party ticket. Curiously enough, however—or is it but a sign of the inevitability of party in the long run?—there are places in which even independents with no personal allegiance to any national party have come to act very much as a council party; the thrust of the political party groups forcing them to take concerted action on the Council, and in some cases to subscribe to a joint election manifesto by way of counterblast to the election programmes of the political groups.

Even today, party sway over representation does not always produce the same results. There are still some places in which the situation is not unlike that described by Lady Simon as characterizing Manchester in the nineteenth century. There are many more, mostly, it would seem, among Conservative Councils, in which, although the dominant party group orientates council policy along party lines, it does not carry the philosophy of party control to its logical conclusion. We can say, indeed, that the party system in local government has a good number of variants; but in view of present tendencies it is perhaps better to confine the term "party system" itself to the cases where the Council is run on strictly political lines with all the characteristic practice which this implies. We shall say more fully later on what practice *is* implied, but for the moment we may take the term "party system" as implying (1) that elections are conducted by the local machinery of the national parties on behalf of party nominees; (2) that the party group which is in the majority on the Council assumes political responsibility before the electorate for the conduct of Council business and uses its majority to ensure the adoption of the party policy in Council affairs; (3) that the majority party establishes a watch over administration to ensure that administration shall conform with party policy as approved by the Council and (4) that the party group or groups in the minority function as an Opposition. These are the broad essentials; but it could be added that where the system is, or becomes, deeply rooted, both (or all) the party groups are commonly found to observe certain conventions—e.g. as to balance of representation on committees, alternating choice of Mayor, and proportionate aldermanic strength —irrespective of which group is in power, or which in opposition, at any particular time.

Though not yet universally established, the party system in this full sense has spread rapidly in the last twenty-five years or so; and indubitably the spread is due to the rise of the Labour Party as a new major party of the Left. The introduction of the party system in local government has from the first been part of that Party's creed. It has conceived of Parliamentary and Local Authority activity as but two phases of the one political effort. In the endeavour to permeate national thought and sentiment with new doctrines, any new party of the Left can, indeed, be expected to seek all channels of influence, and to try to establish a hold upon local institutions no less than central—a course which, inspired with a missionary spirit, and pursued with a disciplined approach, as it usually is, is bound in itself to stimulate the Right to react along similar lines. All this is not to say that the Labour Party's philosophy rests on mere party spirit. It has seen no reason to believe that the party system need be less desirable in local than in national government. Its leaders have upheld the party system in local government as preferable in the wide public interest, and on grounds of efficient local government and administration. And the Party appears to accept fully the logic of its own philosophy by according customary "opposition rights" to an opposing minority council group, by accepting the system when it is applied by a dominating opponent group, and by recognizing such conventions as were developed by the older parties to regulate the working of the system *as* a system.

Nevertheless—and here is the further difference between national and local spheres—party government in the local sphere is not quite so unquestioningly accepted by the nation as it is in the national. There is still a sector of public opinion which regards the party system as out of place in local affairs. The survival of independent councils and candidatures is in itself evidence of this; for whatever may be the truth as to the real allegiance of some independent councillors, others are known to have resisted on principle the endeavour to build up a council group representative of a national party to which their own personal allegiance does not stand in doubt. The sentiment against party politics in local government is known, however, to be considerably more widespread than is indicated by any visible tokens of it such as independent councils or councillors. Those who best know local communities know that, even in places where the party system has been deeply rooted for years, there are many citizens who cast their votes on party lines but express open doubt of the virtues of the party system. Indeed, there are voters whose national vote is known to go invariably to the one party but whose local vote is known to go, either regularly or on occasion, not merely to some "independent" candidate but to some candidate of opposite political creed. Quite a large number of local government votes are cast, indeed, on purely "personal" grounds; and this, incidentally, is the factor which makes local election results so uncertain a guide to the fortunes of the parties in elections for Parliament.

The factual situation just sketched clearly marks out the further topics which should be discussed in an article such as this: How does the party system work in local government? And what are its merits and demerits for securing local government of a kind which is at once responsive to local need and efficient from the administrative standpoint?

II

The manner in which, in Great Britain, a Local Authority can be "run" politically cannot be understood, and may, indeed, by foreign readers be seriously misunderstood without a clear perception of the salient features of its constitutional mechanism, and an appreciation of how this mechanism differs from that of national government in Britain and from that of Local Authorities in most other countries of the world.

In Britain, the elected council is constitutionally responsible for both the policy and the administration involved in the discharge of the Local Authority's responsibilities. There is no separate executive organ, such as the Government in the British Parliamentary system, or such as is constituted, in one way or another, in many foreign systems of local government. There is no office corresponding to that of burgomaster, with independent executive powers, such as exists in many continental countries. The functions of an English Mayor (or in Scotland a Provost) are quite different from those of a Mayor in the United States under the "Mayor—Council" constitution not yet wholly supplanted in that country by the City Manager system. Apart from traditional social duties, they go little beyond the duties of a presiding chairman of the elected council. And although, in English Local Authorities which have the "Borough" type of constitution, there is a body of aldermen, chosen by the elected councillors and enjoying a longer term of office, they too, like the Mayor, lack any executive functions such as those exercised jointly with the Burgomaster by the "Vethoulders" of the Dutch Towns, or by the "magistraats" of towns in Denmark or other countries of Northern Europe.

To remove any misunderstanding, it should also be said that although in British Local Authorities there are certain offices which are filled, under the party system, by nominees of the dominant party, and others (such as the office of Mayor and Aldermen) which are filled by the parties in alternation or in proportion to party strength, under conventions which the parties mutually observe, these are elective offices and in no wise extend to the paid officers. The paid officers of a British Local Authority are employees who stand in the relationship of master and servant to their employing councils. They discharge their functions with responsibility to the council. They constitute a body of trained and impartial "professionals", akin to the civil service in the national sphere; and, subject to good behaviour and efficiency, they enjoy in practice security of tenure. There is in British Local Government nothing like the "spoils" system.

Although, as we have said, the elected Council as a whole is responsible for all phases of activity involved in the discharge of the functions entrusted to it as a "Local Authority", the tasks falling to British Local Authorities are so large and varied that the Council finds it essential to discharge its work through the medium of a series of standing committees. These committees advise the Council on matters of policy, but their other important function is to supervise the execution of approved policy and to exercise a general oversight over the services or functions allotted by the Council to be their concern. A large part of administration is left to the paid officers as part of their managerial functions; but the officers keep the committees informed of their activities by way of periodical report, and bring up in their reports issues which arise in the application of policy, or which may lie along the indeterminate borderlines of policy, administration, and pure management, and take the committees' instructions. There are large powers enabling the Council to delegate executive powers to the committees. The general flow of business is upwards—from the departments to the committees, in matters not settled at departmental level; from the committees to the Council, in matters not within the delegated powers of the committees. The committees are the real "workshops". The Council agenda largely resolves itself into a review of the Standing Committees' proceedings and into the consideration of their recommendations, as embodied in their minutes or reports.

These, then, are the salient features of the constitutional and administrative mechanism through which the party system must work.

Political control by a dominant party group is exercised through and by the party caucus, which is simply the periodical assembly of the dominant party group and is naturally held in private. The opposition groups work through a similar caucus. How far is the control of Council affairs the responsibility of the Council group itself, exercising an informed judgment on data assembled through constitutional channels, such as the reports of the expert staff, as considered in committees and tested there by discussion and debate; or how far is responsibility thrown back on the local party organization, entirely ignorant as it must often be of the facts and issues involved in some specific project or administrative task? The question is obviously one of importance for sound standards of governance and administration. There is some reason to believe that, in the uprise of the Labour Party some twenty-five years or so ago, Council Labour groups introducing political control into Councils which they had captured, had often to submit to the dictates of the local party organization, with much embarrassment to themselves, grave danger to sound administration, and an unwelcome prospect that the discharge of the Local Authority's responsibilities would be seriously warped by party spirit. Eventually, the Labour Party dealt with this issue (and others) in Model Standing Orders for Labour Groups which it formulated to define their status and govern their practice. These provide that representatives from the party may sit with the caucus, but without vote; that the local election programme shall be formulated by the Party organization, but that the Council group is to be responsible for the conduct of Council work. The Conservative party claims that its Council groups have never been tied to the dictates of the local party organization and that even today their groups are left a much freer hand.

Somewhat similar considerations of principle, likewise with an impact upon sound administration, arise out of the practice of the caucus as to the juncture at which it determines its attitude to business passing through the constitutional machinery. Here again, in the early days, many local Labour Parties were insistent that the Council group should review beforehand, with them, the business arising *in the committees*. In other words, the group was to pre-determine its attitude before committees met. The effect was that decisions were taken before the facts and the issues had been sorted out in the work of the Council's committees. Such a practice was certainly a wide aberration from the practice built up by the older parties. Here again, the dangers were keenly appreciated by the Party's local Council groups themselves, and the Model Standing Orders referred to now provide that the caucus meeting shall be held at a convenient time between the issue of the Council agenda and the Council meeting. What we have said about the mechanics of Local Authority administration and the flow of business shows this juncture to be the right one; it is at this stage that a caucus can fittingly review the proceedings of the committees and the proposals arising for the Council's determination, as embodied in the committee minutes and reports circulated with the Council agenda. Much of the disquiet at one time felt about the impact of the party system upon sound Local Government and administration arose from the practices just mentioned, but these may now be counted as abuses of the party system rather than as incidents of its present normal operation.

Notwithstanding the arrangements now generally operative as to the time of the caucus meetings, it is evident that the control of a dominant group might be seriously impaired if it is left entirely ignorant beforehand of matters arising in the upflow of business from departments to committees and committees to Council. If a party's members on a committee have done something, or passed something, which the caucus eventually questions, it is open to the caucus to secure the "reference back" when the Council meets. But such a course does not cover the possibility that the committee may have been acting under delegated powers and that action has already been taken. Moreover there are many matters which arise between meetings of committees on which officers may feel the need for guidance—difficulties arising in some particular task, issues arising in the application of policy as lawfully determined by the Council's majority, and the thousand and one problems that arise in day-to-day administration. It has been a fairly long, and certainly a growing, tradition in English Local Government, that such matters can be brought to the notice of the Chairman of the Standing Committee concerned, and that he can convey to the officers what he thinks would be the sense of the committee, relying upon subsequent ratification when the action taken is reported to the committee by the officer. The Chairman of a Committee, although he has no legal powers, and as an individual cannot legally be given any, and although he is not yet in the position of "political head" to a Local Authority Department, as a Minister of the Crown is in relation to a Department of State, is accorded something of the functions of a "porte-parole" and is expected to make himself knowledgeable in the work of the department and keep in touch with all its activities. In this way, the office of the Chairman of a Standing Committee is very much an "organic" one in local authority administration; and one with functions naturally falling in with the objects of party control. If the chairman of the Committee is a party nominee he can discharge the traditional functions of the office and at the same time act as something of a rapporteur to the party group, the group being thus enabled to maintain a continuous conspectus of Council activity. For all these reasons it is common practice for the dominant party, not only to secure a party majority on each committee, but to secure the chairs of all the Standing Committees, or certainly the more important ones. There is also a growing tendency for minority groups to decline to accept chairmanships even on the sufferance of the dominant group. There is on principle nothing to object to in such an attitude. If one of the virtues of the party system is that it makes responsibility visible to the electorate, the picture may become considerably confused if a minority party chairman is dealing with matters arising between committee meetings without a majority at his back; and on the other hand, there can be all round embarrassment if a minority party chairman has to present to the Council committee proposals which reflect the views of the dominant group on the committee but which his own group on the Council decides, in caucus, to oppose. The Labour Party's Standing Orders, however, make no rigid prescription on this aspect of the matter. They provide that when the party group is in a minority members shall not accept chairs without the consent of the group.

A caucus usually works with a chairman, secretary, and

"whips" drawn from its own number. It also appoints a leader of the group in the Council; and, when leading the majority group, this member of the Council has come in many places to be openly styled "Leader of the Council". He is accorded a general guidance over the strategy of debate adopted by the dominant party in the council chamber; and, without displacing the functions of the chairman of committees in submitting the proceedings of committees, will often act as the party's chief spokesman on major issues. In addition, he plays the key role in maintaining the group watch over the flow of current business; and just as the officers may resort to a chairman of committee so those chairmen often resort in turn to their leader, keeping him generally informed, and taking his guidance on the more important matters.

To round off this sketch of the system as it works, we may note the conventions which relate to the choice of Mayor and Aldermen. The filling of these offices sometimes creates difficulties and controversy between the parties, because in the "borough" type of constitution the elections are annual and the strength of the parties often changes from year to year. In such circumstances, it is sometimes really difficult to decide whose rightful turn it is to nominate for the mayoralty, or to fill vacancies at the periodical aldermanic elections, or on the occurrence of a casual vacancy. But while difficulties of this kind can and do arise, they do not detract from the truth of the general proposition that the party system has succeeded in developing conventions which regulate the filling of these offices on fair lines, determined by the proportionate strengths of the party groups in the Council. Nor does the acknowledgment of this principle fall short of giving "turns" to independent members if such exist.

III

One line of criticism directed against the party system relates to its effect upon the calibre of Council personnel. Undoubtedly, it must have a restrictive effect upon the field of candidature in some directions. Once firmly established, it places the independent candidate at considerable disadvantage in the electoral contest as compared with party candidates that have the backing of an organized machine, and, very largely indeed, discourages independents from coming forward. Moreover, there are certain layers and classes of a local community which will always hesitate to label themselves politically, even though they may feel attracted to the service of a local public and have a party allegiance. Considerations of this kind affect, for example, certain classes of tradesmen, a variety of professional men, and some classes of salaried employees whose employers feel that entanglements in local politics may detract from the service to be given to themselves or their customers. Against this line of criticism it may be argued that, even if all Councils were non-political, not every type of difficulty which confronts these sections of the community would be removed. What is more, it can be argued that the party system, while it may have restrictive effects in some direction, has a widening effect upon the field of candidature in other directions. The expense of fighting a local election is not inconsiderable, and the defrayal of expenses out of party funds attracts many candidates who would otherwise not come forward.

Further criticism of this kind fastens upon the sacrifice of independent judgment which the party system entails. Some such sacrifice there must indeed be, beyond the point when the Council group has taken a decision; for the party system involves a fair measure of discipline, particularly in Labour groups; although even here the Labour Party's Standing Orders make provision for abstentions on conscientious grounds, and contain a provision that members of the party group must exercise a free judgment in considering matters which fall to be dealt with by the Council in a quasi-judicial capacity. Though dissident individuals are often proved right, it may be doubted whether sacrifices of this kind have a serious impact upon the efficient discharge of Council business; and the criticism must in any event be tempered by the consideration that, although political control may extend to all the Council's business, a large part of this turns out to be uncontroversial, the Council proceedings resolving themselves into debate upon issues isolated after both caucuses have sifted the proceedings of committees, and probably found nine-tenths of them a matter of general agreement.

Couched in general terms, the most important criticism of the party system, however, is that it introduces artificial issues into local government, and clouds with party spirit many issues which could be easily and satisfactorily settled if objective judgment had free play. Put shortly, the implication is that party politics in local affairs are a needless intrusion. Such a view is altogether too sweeping. There is no doubt a large branch of local government business which does not raise issues of the kind which divide the national political parties. The provision of sewers, drains and a good water supply does not in general (though on occasion it could) involve party politics. There are other branches of municipal responsibility which indubitably do involve issues of the kind which divide the parties nationally. The extent and nature of housing provision, housing rents, school standards, the scale of public assistance when that function fell to local Councils, and in general the extent, scope, and standards of welfare and health services, are all matters which can raise issues of this kind, and have indeed frequently done so. Projects such as new social services, and the scale of provision which these shall make, have indeed been subjects of keen political division in the past. And, while the functions of Local Authorities do not change every day, no one can be sure that new functions may not develop which will strike, from time to time, a new balance between political and non-political business.

In crystallizing opinion, and in singling out the issues for public debate and public judgment, the party system fulfils a function well recognized in our political philosophy. And if the party system fulfils a function of this kind in regard to local matters of a "political" complexion, and to that extent is acceptable in principle, it is not necessarily a bad thing if, in addition, its ambit extends in practice to business of a non-political character. For if responsibility before the electorate be assumed over the whole field of the work of local authorities, the party effort, and the party concern, are broadened. The party group must endeavour to impress the electorate by the whole range of its trusteeship. This is good in itself because its effect on the party is good; but it also has the virtue of making responsibility all the more visible to the electorate, and of facilitating public judgment of the party's all round calibre by bringing this to the test of well-marked signs of success or failure, as the case may be, in the total impact of Local Government upon the local community. This is precisely the process that democratic machinery should make possible.

In any event, the intrusion of "artificial" issues is not the peculiar vice of political councils. Personal antagonisms often introduce them into independent councils, and such antagonisms often find fuller play in independent councils because they go unchecked by the disciplines applied by the party caucuses.

We saw in the last section that the party system had led in most places to the appointment of a "Leader of the Council" whose functions under the system obviously place him in a position of considerable influence. In so doing, the party system, it has been alleged, gives rise to a real danger of Caesarism. Undoubtedly, some instances of this sort of thing have been revealed from time to time, usually in places where the general tone of public life has deteriorated, or where the political sentiment of the area is so overwhelmingly in favour of one party that the Council is almost entirely of one colour, or the Opposition ineffective. There have, in recent years, been a few lurid instances of regimes in which the dominant party leadership has fallen little short of "ward boss" standards, not free from the taint of malpractice. Conditions of this kind do not appear to be widespread or to persist for very long; and the parties appear to be guarding against the danger by encouraging local party groups to fix a maximum term of office for the group leader. It should not be supposed, however, that independent Councils are necessarily immune from this kind of danger. Intrigue, the growth of personal cliques, and the exercise of personal pressures have been known to carry individuals of forceful personality but dubious character into positions of something like personal dictatorship in some independent Councils; and the safeguards there can often be the less effective, in the absence of organized and watchful party opposition, or party discipline.

Having considered some of the dangers of the party system and some of the criticisms directed against it, we may turn now to catalogue its positive virtues, for positive virtues it undoubtedly has.

Recapitulating some points already made, we may say that in the sphere of policy it has on the whole a beneficial effect because, like the party system in national politics, it arouses electoral interest, segregates issues of a genuinely political kind for popular judgment and, at the same time, tends to produce an integrated policy for the locality as a whole; and that in doing all this it renders responsibility for the general level of Council achievement visible to the public, facilitates judgment at the polls, and through the ups and downs of party fortunes at successive elections, brings shifts in public feeling forcibly to the Council's notice. While the system may confer roles of prominence and influence upon leading personalities, either as "Leaders of the Council" or Chairmen of Committees, it does so by democratic group vote and on lines which are at any rate capable of securing the necessary restraint over purely personal dominance; whereas in independent Councils dominating personalities can attain to a personal rule which owns no kind of responsibility to others. In enabling matters such as the choice of Mayor and Aldermen to be settled on understood lines the system saves much of the time which independent Councils frequently spend on such matters, and often eliminates much of the purely personal feeling (much of it disturbing to administration) which business of this kind so often generates in such Councils.

The system has also beneficial effects in the administrative sphere. It ensures that policy, integrated in the way mentioned, is vigorously pursued. The organized team-work of the groups orientates the Council's time and attention to the attainment of definite objectives and programmes; whereas, in Councils which are an assembly of unorganized individuals, effort tends to drift and, indeed, to veer, and any integrated policy or ordered programme which may with difficulty be built up may still lack the necessary impetus, and the officers of the Council are often left in doubt as to where the Council wishes to steer. The system also organizes debate in the council chamber and increases vigilance over administrative action.

IV

On the whole, there is much reason to think that, if party spirit is not carried to excess, the party system makes for good and efficient Local Government; and there are in fact many local government officers who say—and their judgment should be as knowledgeable as it is objective—that they have found the "political" Councils they have served more efficient as a rule than the "independent".

It can be said that party spirit, on the whole, is not carried to excess, as matters stand today. There is friendly collaboration in the committees. While Council debates emphasize party differences, the great bulk of municipal business passes through Council by agreement (with all the greater warranty of sound handling after the organized scrutiny of opposing caucuses). One or the other, and sometimes both, caucuses will often leave suitable issues to a "free vote". The caucuses, or their leaders, often exchange views; and one or the other will often initiate an arrangement for united approval to some course of action. The caucuses being usually thrown on to the same evening for their pre-Council meeting, there are places where they meet in adjoining rooms at the Town Hall, without any disturbance to the Queen's Peace. It is not improbable that each knows a good deal about the other's proceedings before the evening is over; and it is certainly no strange thing to find a fair sprinkling from all camps in congenial intercourse at the same hostelry on the way home. All this seems fairly in keeping with the British tradition, and with the peculiar character of British local life—where, if anywhere, personal relationships can transcend (and sometimes overshadow) the differences of party.

REFLECTIONS ON THE PARTY SYSTEM
by Sir Ernest Barker

IN thinking about the development and the significance of the party system in Britain, one may begin by drawing a distinction—a distinction which is far from precluding connection, and even co-operation—between Society and the State. Society is the area of voluntary groups and voluntary effort: the State is the area of legal rules and of action under those rules. One of the features of British history, during the last four hundred years, has been the large part which Society has played in the development of Britain. Voluntary combination, issuing in voluntary effort, has determined much of the life of our country. On the other hand it has also been a feature of British history that voluntary Society and the legal State have seldom been in conflict. On the contrary, as Sidney Webb wrote some forty years ago, "Voluntary association and Government action ... go on side by side, the one apparently always inspiring ... successive developments of the other." The party system reflects, and indeed it has helped to cause, these features of British life.

Party began in the area of Society, and in that area it may already be traced as early as the Middle Ages. It was in its origin, and it still remains in its core, a *social* formation. A party begins as a set of connected and coherent political ideas, formed and enunciated in the process of social discussion. It becomes, in the course of its development, a body of persons permanently united in entertaining such a set of ideas: a body of persons, forming a social group in the area of Society, who discuss and clarify their common ideas among themselves, formulate them in a policy or programme, and defend that programme in discussion against other similar groups in the same social area. Finally, and in the culmination of its development (which does not come, as we shall see presently, until the idea and practice of cabinet government has been attained), party becomes an organization, with its own recognized leaders, for the purpose of carrying a programme into effect, first by securing a majority of the votes of the political electorate, and then by proceeding to turn its leaders into the political government. It thus serves as a mediator between the process of social discussion and the practice of political action. We may accordingly define a party as a social formation which has two distinct but complementary functions—first that of serving as a *social reservoir* for the collection of a set of connected political ideas from the area of Society; and secondly that of serving as a *political conduit* by which the ideas so collected flow from their social reservoir into the system of the State and turn the wheels of political machinery in that system. So conceived, party performs the service of enabling Society to run into the State; and thus of keeping the action of the State constantly and wholesomely responsive to the play of social thought.[1]

In their developed form and full function, as has just been suggested, parties are imperfect, or at any rate inchoate, until the appearance of a cabinet system gives them a salt and solid reality. Down to the end of the eighteenth century, when that system was hammered into being, parties were loose aggregations, or floating bodies of opinion, with no firmly fixed adhesion and no clearly seen objective. The addition of a cabinet system gave them a clear and valuable objective—the winning of political power and the actual conduct of government: it solidified their membership, and it encouraged and even required their definite organization. The general effects of the cabinet system on the nature and the development of parties have indeed been profound. But there are, of course, other factors besides the cabinet system which have affected, and in turn been affected by, the nature of the party system. One of these factors is the electorate. The wider the electorate, and the greater the mass of its numbers, the greater becomes the need for its organization, and the greater therefore the opportunity for the organizing

---

[1] In this paragraph the writer has used the argument and the language of a passage in his book on *Principles of Social and Political Theory*.

power of party. The expansion of the electorate since 1832 has accordingly been accompanied by an extension of party control and discipline. Another great factor besides the electorate is the elected Parliament; and this too has been increasingly affected by the power and discipline of party. A party-controlled electorate will tend to produce a party-controlled Parliament; and the tendency to a party-controlled Parliament will naturally be accentuated by the growing strength of the cabinet system and the growing power of cabinet ministers to manage the business, the legislation, and the general action of Parliament.

What has just been said may lead us to reflect that our system of Government, as it stands today, is a system of four factors—party, the electorate, Parliament, and cabinet. What is the relative strength of these factors, and what balance, if we can properly speak of balance, should be expected among them? It has often seemed to the writer that this system of four factors involves the reconciliation of two different and conflicting necessities. One necessity is that each of the factors should think highly of itself and its duty, and act as if everything hung on itself and upon its own decision. That is a condition of efficiency; but it may also lead, if it is not checked, to self-sufficiency and arrogance. The other necessity is that each factor should keep in touch and harmony with the rest, acknowledging that they too have the right and duty to do their work and to be left free to do it effectively. This latter is the sovereign necessity; but the first necessity is only too apt to make itself particularly felt. The electorate, feeling its own importance, may claim to impose an "imperative mandate"; Parliament, with a collective pride, may seek to institute a system of parliamentary autocracy for the duration of its term, installing and evicting cabinets at will; a cabinet may attempt to vindicate sovereignty for itself, and may use its majority and its Whips to drill and discipline Parliament; or finally, and this is a danger which in the contemporary world is particularly apparent, a victorious party or combination of parties may claim the last word for a party caucus and for its manipulating managers. But a just and proper system of parliamentary democracy depends not only on a general spirit of give and take in the mind of the people at large: it also depends on a similar spirit, a spirit of balance and accommodation, among the four factors by and through which it works—party, electorate, Parliament, and cabinet; and the greater the ardour of each factor, the more difficult it is to secure such a spirit.

The exaggeration of party is a matter which is closely connected with the number of parties in a country. Here there are three possibilities. One is the system of a single party, which the Communist States of Eastern Europe regard as the basis of a true or popular democracy, based upon the people and acting for the people. Another is the system of multiple parties, common in a number of the States of Western Europe; a system which has, or may claim to have, the advantage of producing a true reflection of the varied currents of social thought, but which has also the disadvantage of making government uneasy and dependent on fluctuating combinations between a number of different parties. A third is the system of two parties, or at any rate two main parties, which is the system generally followed in Anglo-Saxon countries. It may be said that both of the two first possibilities are favourable to the exaggeration of party. A single party prevents that discussion, and that choice, between political alternatives which is a necessary condition of a free electorate: it establishes the open tyranny of one party, whether of the Right or Left. A system of multiple parties may seem to give a large possibility of choice to the electorate; but its ultimate effect may be the secret tyranny of a cabal which unites the leaders of several parties in an interested coalition and controls behind the scenes both the representative body and the nominal government. Nor is that all. If a system of multiple parties is accompanied, as it often is, by the device of proportional representation, it accentuates the ardour of each party, and stimulates all to press for their full pound of flesh and to urge their claims to the uttermost. The third possibility—that of a system of two parties, or at any rate two main parties—also has its defects. It reduces the choice of the electorate to no more than two alternatives: it eliminates shades and nuances, and substitutes in their place two gross averages of opinion: it may even be said to reduce the level of politics to that of football or baseball, with two contending sides each madly cheered and supported by its different partisans. Can a nation ever be one when it splits itself into two?

But whatever may be urged against the system of two parties, there is much to be said in its favour. Life, after all, is largely a matter of choice between two alternatives: there are generally two rival schools in philosophy, two rival views of painting, two rival opinions about music; and why should there not also be two rival views of politics? We have also to reflect that a system of two rival political parties is far from meaning that every voter is attached to one or the other: it leaves room for the floating or unattached voter, who may now give his vote to one and now to another of the two, and can thus bring about those changes and alterations of government which are as valuable and refreshing as changes of the weather. In this respect the system of two parties is more conducive to freedom and change than either of the other systems; for a single party seeks permanently to ensure a total vote for its policy from the whole of the population, and a system of multiple parties tends to enlist every citizen in a permanent and unwavering allegiance to his particular party. In a word, the system of two parties leaves room for a margin of imprecision, or an area of incalculability, which is a safety-valve in the working of a democratic State.

There is also another thing to be said in favour of a system of two parties. It is a thing connected with the emergence and the growing influence of the cabinet system. A cabinet system inevitably produces a certain polarity in a nation, a tendency to develop in two opposite directions. When the cabinet swings into the centre, as it has increasingly done in our British development, there will always be those who are for the cabinet, and who form the Government side, and there will always be those who are against the cabinet, and who form the Opposition side. Whether or no there are only two parties, there will certainly be only two "sides". It is abstractly possible—indeed it is actually possible—that a "side" may contain more than one party, or at any rate more than one shade of opinion. That is true of both sides—the Left or progressive, and the Right or conservative. But the fact remains that on either side there will be a gravitational pull, or a centripetal force, which draws together the different parties or shades of opinion on the Left and the Right. Any party that seeks to escape this pull or deny this force will find itself left dancing aimlessly in the void. We may deprecate this pull or force; but if we do, we are deprecating the inevitable; and the part of wisdom is to make our account and to find some reconciliation with it. This is the task which today confronts the Liberal Party, reluctant to lose its ancient glory and to shed its independence, but none the less subject to an attraction which it cannot escape.

There is a sovereign merit still to be mentioned which belongs to the system of two parties. Each party or side, within itself, is permeated by a force of attraction; but each, in its relation to the other, is equally marked by a force of repulsion. The term Her Majesty's Opposition is one of the most significant and important in British politics. It signifies that a single nation, one in a common allegiance to a common way of life symbolized by its Queen, is none the less also two—two as well as one, and two at the same time that it is one. Her Majesty has her actual advisers, who form the cabinet: she has also her potential advisers, who form the anti-cabinet. The existence of such an anti-cabinet, or organized opposition to the acting cabinet, is the salt of the British system of parliamentary democracy. It supplies the constant criticism which is as necessary as constructive creation. It fans the flame of discussion and keeps it bright and clear. It gives the possibility of an alternative Government—an actual possibility, actually present and visible—to which the nation can look if it feels the need for a new hand at the helm. The general development of Her Majesty's Opposition, and the general recognition of its function (a recognition which has gone to the length of the parliamentary provision of a salary for its leader), are the clearest signs of the health of the British system of Government. But this development, and this recognition, are connected with, and are the results of, the growing tendency towards a clear two-party system. An organized and coherent opposition is only possible under such a system; and an organized and coherent opposition is a necessary condition of healthy democratic discussion and of a proper balance of all the factors and organs of democracy.

Apart from the question of their number, another matter which affects the character of parties is the nature of their composition. Ideally, the cleavage between parties should be vertical, and not horizontal: in other words, party divisions should not follow the strata of class or religious differentiation, but should rather cut down deep through those strata and leave on either side of the cleavage a similar cross-section of the nation. Each party will then seek, or at any rate tend, to represent a general view of the national interest, and neither will be committed to a single interest. It may seem, *a priori*, that a single party will include all interests; but in actual practice the single parties of the present century have been based on the interest of a class (the Fascist on the middle or lower-middle class, and the Communist on the proletariat or "toiling masses"), and they have sought to adjust the whole community to the pattern of this particular interest. A system of multiple parties obviously tends to the representation of particular classes or sects; it splits the community not only into Left and Right, but also into different classes, different confessions, and different particular interests. Even a system of two parties may be a system of "two nations", and may split the community into a party of the poor, or the comparatively poor, and a party of the well-to-do. This is not actually the case in Britain, and it need never be the case. The Conservative Party is an all-class party, though more in the composition of its voting mass than in that of its parliamentary representatives, and the Labour Party, though based in the main on the industrial masses, is also a party including members of the professions and other sections of the nation: indeed it is to the interest of both parties, as well as to that of the nation, that they should spread a wide net, for the wider it is, the more their appeal and the greater the number of votes which they are likely to gain. At the same time it must be admitted that the electoral map of Britain, when it registers the result of a general election, has one alarming feature: it shows a clustering of Labour in densely packed areas of urban industry, and a dispersion of the other side over the great rural space of the country. We seem to be drifting into a state of division between the town and the country mouse; and there is peril in that division.

Another question suggested to the mind by any reflection on party systems is the question of the place of doctrine in the life and action of parties. Should a party elaborate a body of doctrine, expressed in a programme, and should it seek to make its doctrine a fixed and permanent casing which encompasses and may cramp its life? Or should it rather be wedded to flexibility, and to ideas of progress and evolution; and should it accordingly abjure the expression of a creed, and be content to represent a general tendency and mental temper, with no precise definition in set terms and hard formulations? The question is one which vexes religious confessions as well as political parties; and in both cases there is more to be said for flexibility and evolution than for permanent expressions of doctrine and rigid sets of principle. A single party has a single doctrine or *Weltanschauung*, a single "general line" which all are expected to toe; a system of multiple parties, different as it may seem, may equally be a system of many hard-set doctrines, which harden themselves still more in their opposition and clash. It may be claimed as a merit for a two-party system that a party, seeking to increase the width of its appeal, progressively widens its scope and seeks to transcend old limitations and formulations. But it may also be said to be a demerit of such a system that a party seeks to deny or discredit the progress of the other, and attempts to limit and judge it by some form, or supposed form, of its past, so that the Conservative is condemned to be now what he was, or is supposed to have been, half a century ago, and the Labour candidate is equally condemned as still guilty of his past and outgrown extravagances, and as untaught and untrained by later experience. The chief enemy to the development of the temper and tendency of either party, under a system of two parties, is the refusal of the other party to acknowledge any development. On the other hand, when all is said that can be said in favour of development, the fact remains that there must be something of a hard inner core of steady principle in any party.

A problem in any system of parties is the problem of the proper management of a party in its own internal life. So far as it has a doctrine, and so far as it precipitates a programme, how should the doctrine or programme be formed? An obvious answer, which appears *prima facie* to be the democratic answer, is that the doctrine or programme should be formed from below, by the rank and file, in the general deliberations of a party conference, and should be accepted and obeyed by the party leaders as the ultimate and sovereign expression of the party's nature and policy. But the answer, although it is obvious and superficially attractive, does not go to the roots. The party conference is not the only nor the most responsible organ of party. The party members in Parliament also matter, and matter greatly: the party members in the cabinet (or the anti-cabinet, as the case may be) also matter, and matter even more; and the reason in both cases is the simple reason of the greater degree of their responsibility. Here we touch an old issue, which was raised more than eighty years ago in both the Liberal and the Conservative Parties, in the former by Mr. Joseph Chamberlain and in the latter by Lord Randolph Churchill. The issue was whether the party conference, or the manipulators of the party conference, should dictate to the party in Parliament and the party leaders in Parliament, or whether the opposite, or something near the opposite, should be regarded as the proper policy. The issue was then decided in the latter sense. A somewhat similar issue still vexes the modern Labour Party; but the logic of the parliamentary system, and of the cabinet system which stands at its core, is deciding the issue in the same sense in which it was decided by the other parties in the last quarter of the nineteenth century.

What has just been said of the problem of the proper management of party leads to a last reflection on a problem which is connected with it—the problem of the electoral mandate. Is the result of a general election, based on a programme or policy accepted by a majority of the electorate, a binding and sovereign instruction to the Parliament and cabinet which issues from the election, or may the Parliament and cabinet see and choose their way, according to the vicissitudes and alteration of circumstances? Much depends on the way in which the programme or policy has been constructed. If the party members in Parliament and cabinet have been largely concerned in the construction of a programme, they may feel themselves bound by their own past action, and they may thus wish to act in the future as they have themselves planned to act in the past. But that is not the whole of the matter. Whatever the electoral mandate, the freedom of Parliament remains; and Parliament, if it is composed of parties, is also something which transcends parties. Parliament must adjust its own free judgment to the march of events and to new conjunctures of circumstance; and while it must acknowledge the general instruction of the electorate, which is a general expectation that the majority of the persons elected will seek to carry into effect the programme on which they have been elected, it must also acknowledge that the future is something which cannot be wholly cased and entirely confined by the instruction of the past. But, above all, a parliamentary party majority must also acknowledge another thing. It must acknowledge that the execution of the programme on which it was elected is subject to the result of free discussion with the minority (who have also been elected, and who have also their just claims), and to the achievement of some sort of compromise based upon such discussion. The simple merit of two parties is just that they are two, and that either has always to acknowledge the presence and rights of the other. Neither of them is an absolute; and neither—not even the majority—can have an absolute mandate.

THE BRITISH PARTY SYSTEM

A SELECT BIBLIOGRAPHY

Compiled by SYDNEY D. BAILEY

THIS select bibliography is concerned with the evolution of the British party system and with the three political parties at present represented in the House of Commons. Most of the standard history books have some brief reference to parties and the party system, and the columns of *Hansard* itself form a primary source of information for the serious student.

The books selected deal with the history, fundamental philosophy, principles, and organization of the parties. Most but not all, of the books about the three parties are written by sympathizers with the party concerned. Certain types of publication have been excluded from the bibliography. These include books of an ephemeral character dealing with topical political issues. It has also been necessary to exclude political fiction and the biographies and memoirs of notable politicians. A small but representative list of Political Biographies will be found on pages 15 and 16 of *Parliament: A Reader's Guide* (published by the Cambridge University Press for the National Book League. 1s.).

It should be emphasized that the Hansard Society is completely non-party and independent, and is not to be associated with any views expressed in any book in the list.

Unless otherwise stated, the place of publication of each book is London.

I. GENERAL

ALINGTON, CYRIL ARGENTINE. *Twenty Years: Being a Study in the Development of the Party System between 1815-35.* Oxford University Press. 1921. 208 pp.

BELLOC, HILAIRE, *and* CECIL CHESTERTON. *The Party System.* 1911. Stephen Swift. 226 pp.

BURKE, EDMUND. *Thoughts on the Cause of Present Discontents.* First published 1770.

CAMBRAY, PHILIP GEORGE. *The Game of Politics: A Study of Principles of British Political Strategy.* Murray. 1932. 199 pp.

COOKE, GEORGE WINGROVE. *The History of Party from the Rise of the Whig and Tory Factions in the Reign of Charles II to the Reform Bill.* Cunningham. 1840. Three volumes.

DURANT, HENRY. *Political Opinion.* Allen & Unwin. 1949. 55 pp.

EMDEN, CECIL STUART. *The People and the Constitution.* Oxford: Clarendon Press. 1933. xii + 336 pp.

FARBMAN, MICHAEL. *Political Britain: Parties, Policies and Politicians.* Europa Publications. 1929. 193 pp.

MCCALLUM, RONALD BUCHANAN and ALISON READMAN. *The British General Election of 1945.* Oxford University Press. 1947. 328 pp.

MICHELS, ROBERT. *Political Parties: A Sociological Study of the Oligarchical Tendencies of Modern Democracy.* Translated from the Italian by Eden and Cedar Paul. Jarrolds. 1915. 416 pp.

NICHOLAS, HERBERT G., with an appendix by D. E. Butler. *The British General Election of 1950.* Macmillan. 1951. x + 354 pp.

NICOLSON, HAROLD. *The Independent Member of Parliament.* Hansard Society. 1946. 20 pp.

OSTROGORSKI, M. *Democracy and the Organization of Political Parties.* Translated from the French by Frederick Clarke. Macmillan. 1902. Two volumes.

PIKE, EDGAR ROYSTON. *Political Parties and Policies.* Third Edition. Pitman. 1950. 102 pp.

ROSS, JAMES FREDERICK STANLEY. *Parliamentary Representation.* Second enlarged edition. Eyre & Spottiswoode. 1948. 344 pp.

SAMUEL, HERBERT (*Viscount Samuel*). *The Party System and National Interests.* Hansard Society. 1946. 20 pp.

THOMAS, IVOR. *The Party System in Great Britain.* Phoenix House. In the press; ready 1952.

TREVELYAN, GEORGE MACAULAY. *The Two-party System in English Political History.* Oxford University Press. 1926. 28 pp. Reprinted in *An Autobiography and other Essays.* Longmans. 1949. 237 pp.

WALLAS, GRAHAM. *Human Nature in Politics.* Fourth Edition. Constable. 1948. xxii + 301 pp.

II. THE CONSERVATIVE PARTY

AMERY, LEOPOLD STENNETT. *Framework of the Future.* Oxford University Press. 1944. viii + 159 pp.

BENTINCK, *Lord* HENRY. *Tory Democracy.* Methuen. 1918. 139 pp.

BERRY, MICHAEL. *Party Choice: The Real Issue Between the Parties.* Eyre & Spottiswoode. 1948. 120 pp.

BIRCH, NIGEL. *The Conservative Party.* Collins. 1949. 50 pp. (Britain in Pictures No. 122).

BOYD-CARPENTER, JOHN. *The Conservative Case: Choice for Britain.* Wingate. 1950. 64 pp.

BRAINE, BERNARD. *Tory Democracy.* Falcon Press. 1948. 144 pp. (The Forum series).

BRYANT, ARTHUR. *The Spirit of Conservatism.* Ashridge: Bonar Law College. 1929. 175 pp.

BUTLER, GEORGE GEOFFREY GILBERT. *The Tory Tradition.* Murray. 1914.

CECIL, Lord HUGH RICHARD HEATHCOTE. *Conservatism, 1510-1911.* Oxford University Press. 1928. 256 pp. (Home University Library).

CLARKE, DAVID. *Conservatism, 1945-50.* Conservative Political Centre. 1950. 248 pp.

COHEN, PERCY (editor). *Campaign Guide: An Encyclopaedia of Politics.* Conservative Central Office. 1951. 419 pp.

COOK, E. THOMAS (*editor*). *Conservatism and the Future.* Heinemann. 1935. 319 pp.

FEILING, KEITH GRAHAME. *A History of the Tory Party, 1640-1714.* Oxford: Clarendon Press. 1924. 526 pp.

FEILING, KEITH GRAHAME. *The Second Tory Party, 1714-1832.* Reprint. Macmillan. 1951. viii + 452 pp.

FEILING, KEITH GRAHAME. *What is Conservatism?* Faber. 1930. 36 pp.

HAYTER, L. H. *An Outline of the History of the Conservative Party.* Taunton: Phoenix Press. 1925.

HEARNSHAW, FOSSEY JOHN COBB. *Conservatism in England: An Analytical, Historical and Political Survey.* Macmillan. 1933. xii + 322 pp.

HOGG, QUINTIN (now *Lord Hailsham*). *The Case for Conservatism.* Harmondsworth: Penguin. 1948. 314 pp. (Penguin No. 635).

HOLLIS, CHRISTOPHER. *Can Parliament Survive?* Hollis & Carter. 1949. 148 pp.

JONES, AUBREY. *The Pendulum of Politics.* Faber. 1946. 183 pp.

LLOYD, GEORGE AMBROSE (later *Lord Lloyd*), and EDWARD FREDERICK LINDLEY WOOD (now *Earl of Halifax*). *The Great Opportunity.* Murray. 1918. 110 pp.

NORTHAM, REGINALD. *Conservatism: The Only Way.* Gifford. 1939. xii + 276 pp.

Party Organization, The. Conservative and Unionist Central Office. 1950. 26 pp. (Organisation Series No. 1).

PERCY, Lord EUSTACE SUTHERLAND CAMPBELL. *The Unknown State.* Oxford University Press. 1944. 48 pp. (Riddell Memorial Lecture).

ST. JOHN, HENRY, Viscount Bolingbroke. *Letters on the Spirit of Patriotism and on the Idea of a Patriot King.* First published in 1749. New edition by the Oxford University Press in 1917. 172 pp.

SMITH, FREDERICK EDWIN (later *Earl of Birkenhead*). *Toryism.* Harper. 1903.

WALKER-SMITH, DEREK. *Coming this Way?* Sampson Low. 1948. 142 pp.

WHITE, R. J. *The Conservative Tradition.* Nicholas Kaye. 1950. 256 pp. (British Political Tradition, No. iv).

WILKINSON, WILLIAM JOHN. *Tory Democracy.* New York: Columbia University Press. 1925.

WOODS, MAURICE C. *A History of the Tory Party in the 17th and 18th Centuries, with a Sketch of its Development in the 19th Century.* Hodder & Stoughton. 1924.

III. THE LABOUR PARTY

ATTLEE, CLEMENT RICHARD. *The Labour Party in Perspective—and Twelve Years After.* Second Impression. Gollancz. 1949. 199 pp.

BAROU, NOAH. *British Trade Unions.* Third Edition. Gollancz. 1949. 271 pp.

BEER, MAX. *A History of British Socialism*. Reprint. Allen & Unwin. 1949. 451 pp.

BRADY, ROBERT ALEXANDER. *Crisis in Britain: Plans and Achievements of the Labour Government*. University of California Press. 1950. xii + 730 pp.

CITRINE, Sir WALTER (now *Lord Citrine*). *British Trade Unions*. Collins. 1942. 48 pp. (Britain in Pictures No. 45.)

COLE, GEORGE DOUGLAS HOWARD, *and* A. W. FILSON. *British Working-Class History, 1789–1875: Selected Documents*. Macmillan. 1951. 656 pp.

COLE, GEORGE DOUGLAS HOWARD. *A Century of Co-operation*. Manchester: Allen & Unwin. 1946. 428 pp.

COLE, GEORGE DOUGLAS HOWARD *and* RAYMOND WILLIAM POSTGATE. *The Common People, 1746–1946*. Fourth Edition. Methuen. 1949. 752 pp.

COLE, GEORGE DOUGLAS HOWARD. *A History of the Labour Party from 1914*. Routledge and Kegan Paul. 1948. 516 pp.

COLE, GEORGE DOUGLAS HOWARD. *British Working-Class Politics, 1832–1914*. Routledge. 1941. 320 pp.

COLE, MARGARET. *Makers of the Labour Movement*. Longmans Green. 1948. xv + 319 pp.

COLLINS, HENRY. *Trade Unions Today*. Frederick Muller. 1950. 141 pp. (Man and Society Series).

CROFT, HAROLD. *Party Organization*. Ninth Edition. Labour Party. 1950. 56 pp.

DALTON, HUGH. *Practical Socialism for Britain*. Routledge. 1937. ix + 401 pp.

DURBIN, EVAN FRANK MOTTRAM. *The Politics of Democratic Socialism: An Essay on Social Policy*. Routledge. 1940. 384 pp.

Facts and Figures for Socialists: Handbook. Labour Party. 1950. 454 pp.

HALL, WILLIAM GLENVIL. *The Labour Party*. Collins. 1949. 50 pp. (Britain in Pictures.)

HAMILTON, MARY AGNES. *The Labour Party To-day: What it is and How it Works*. Labour Book Service. 1939. 95 pp.

HEARNSHAW, FOSSEY JOHN COBB. *Survey of Socialism: Analytical, Historical, and Critical*. Macmillan. 1935. 485 pp.

HOBHOUSE, LEONARD TRELAWNY. *The Labour Movement*. Third Edition. Fisher Unwin. 1912.

HUMPHREY, A. W. *History of Labour Representation*. Constable. 1912. xxi + 199 pp.

HUTCHISON, KEITH. *Labour in Politics*. Labour Publishing Co. 1925. 127 pp.

JAY, DOUGLAS PATRICK THOMAS. *The Socialist Case*. Revised Edition. Faber. 1947. xx + 298 + 2 pp.

LASKI, HAROLD JOSEPH. *Trade Unions in the New Society*. Allen & Unwin. 1950. 182 pp.

MACHENRY, DEAN EUGENE. *The Labour Party in Transition, 1931–38*. Routledge. Toronto: Musson Book Co. 1938. 320 pp.

PARKER, JOHN. *Labour Marches On*. Harmondsworth: Penguin. 1948. 213 pp. (Penguin No. 628).

ROBSON, WILLIAM ALEXANDER (*Editor*). *Public Enterprise*. Allen & Unwin, for the Fabian Society. 1937. 416 pp.

SHAW, GEORGE BERNARD, and others. *Fabian Essays on Socialism.* Second Impression. Allen & Unwin. 1950 (Jubilee Edition). 246 pp.

TAWNEY, RICHARD HENRY. *The British Labour Movement.* Yale University Press. 1925.

TRACEY, HERBERT (*Editor*). *The British Labour Party: its history, growth, policy, and leaders.* Caxton Publishing Co. 1948. Three volumes.

ULAM, ADAM B. *Philosophical Foundations of English Socialism.* Harvard University Press. London: Oxford University Press. 1951. 173 pp. (Harvard Political Studies).

WEBB, SIDNEY, and BEATRICE WEBB (later *Lord and Lady Passfield*). *History of Trade Unionism.* Second Edition. Longmans Green. 1920. xviii + 784 pp.

WERTHEIMER, EGON. *Portrait of the Labour Party.* Putnam. 1929. 215 pp.

WILLIAMS, FRANCIS. *Fifty Years' March: The Rise of the Labour Party.* Odhams. 1950. 384 + 16 pp.

IV. THE LIBERAL PARTY

BEVERIDGE, *Sir* WILLIAM HENRY (now *Lord Beveridge*). *Why I am a Liberal.* Jenkins. 1945. 115 pp.

Constitution of the Liberal Party. Liberal Party Organization. 1949. 18 pp.

CRUIKSHANK, ROBERT JAMES. *The Liberal Party.* Collins. 1949. 50 pp. (Britain in Pictures No. 123).

DODDS, GEORGE ELLIOTT. *The Defence of Man.* Herbert Joseph. 1947. 160 pp. (The Liberal Library No. 3).

DODDS, GEORGE ELLIOTT. *Let's Try Liberalism.* Liberal Publications Department. 1945. 128 pp.

FOOT, ISAAC. *Liberty and the Liberal Heritage.* Gollancz. 1948. 34 pp. (The Ramsay Muir Memorial Lecture, 1947).

FYFE, HAMILTON. *The British Liberal Party: An Historical Sketch.* Allen & Unwin. 1928. 272 pp.

HOBHOUSE, LEONARD TRELAWNY. *Liberalism.* Oxford University Press. 1911. 254 pp. (Home University Library No. 21).

Liberal Candidates' and Speakers' Handbook. Liberal Party. 1950. 222 pp.

McFADYEAN, *Sir* ANDREW. *The Liberal Case.* Wingate. 1950. 64 pp. (Choice for Britain Series No. 3).

MUIR, RAMSAY. *The Faith of a Liberal.* Liberal Publications Department. 1933. 32 pp.

SAMUEL, HERBERT (now *Viscount Samuel*). *Liberalism: Its Principles and Proposals.* Richards. 1902. 414 pp.

SLESSER, *Sir* HENRY. *A History of the Liberal Party.* Hutchinson. 1944. 172 pp.

SMITH, REGINALD ARTHUR. *A Liberal Window on the World.* Herbert Joseph. 1947. 160 pp. (The Liberal Library No. 2).

INDEX

Aberdeen, *Lord* (see "Gordon, George Hamilton")
Acland, *Sir* Richard   66, 110
Acton, J. E. E. D., *Lord Acton* 81, 85
Adamson, William   38
Addington, Henry, *Viscount Sidmouth*   27
Anti-Corn Law League   33, 93, 105, 158
Asquith, Herbert Henry, *Earl of Oxford and Asquith*   37, 43, 47, 48, 61, 82, 83, 91
Attlee, Clement Richard   64, 65, 66, 122, 127, 130, 162, 205

Bagehot, Walter   x, 107
Baldwin, Stanley, *Earl Baldwin*   vi, 39-41, 47-48, 135, 161, 162, 164, 166
Balfour, A. J., *Earl of Balfour*   46, 98, 116, 163
Barker, *Sir* Ernest   x, 193-202
Bartlett, Vernon   110
Bentinck, *Lord* Henry   44, 45, 204
Benton, Joan   117
Bevan, Aneurin   68, 69, 129, 147, 148, 151
Beveridge Plan   66, 91
Bevin, Ernest   65, 67
Billing, Noel Pemberton   109
Bing, Geoffrey   137
Birch, Nigel   116, 120, 130, 204
Birrell, Augustine   82
Blackburn, Raymond   111
Bonar Law, Andrew (see "Law, Andrew Bonar")
Booth, Charles   36
Boyd-Orr, John, *Lord Boyd-Orr*   110
Bright, John   93, 106
Brooke, Henry   135
Brown, W. J.   110
Bryce, James, *Viscount Bryce*   v, 133
Burdett, *Sir* Francis   93
Burke, Edmund   vii, viii, ix, x, 20, 27, 39, 203
Burn, W. L.   18-25
Burns, John   36, 82

Butler, R. A.   118, 143, 144, 145
Butt, Isaac   95

Campbell-Bannerman, *Sir* Henry   82, 157
Canning, Stratford, *Viscount Stratford de Redcliffe*   27, 28, 44, 45, 79
Carson, *Sir* Edward   83
Carteret, John, *Earl Granville*   101
Castlereagh, *Viscount* (see "Stewart, Robert")
Cavaliers   17
Cavendish, Spencer Compton, *Duke of Devonshire*   165
Cecil, Robert Arthur Talbot Gascoyne, *Marquess of Salisbury*   34, 44, 45, 46
Chamberlain, Joseph   31, 33, 39, 46, 60, 93, 94, 159, 177, 201
Chamberlain, Neville   47, 48, 65, 112, 162
Charles I   vii, 15, 42, 78, 103
Charles II   17, 42-43
Chartists   29, 31, 80, 93
Chatham, *Earl of* (see "Pitt, William, Earl of Chatham")
Chrimes, S. B.   1-12
Churchill, *Lord* Randolph   33, 98, 201
Churchill, Winston   xi, 39, 41, 47, 48, 65, 82, 102, 109, 112, 116, 121, 142, 144, 158, 162, 164
Civil War   vii, 12, 15-16, 42
Clarendon Code   78
Clarendon, *Lord* (see "Hyde, Edward")
Cobden, Richard   95, 96, 98, 107
Cochrane, Thomas, *Earl of Dundonald*   ix
Cole, G. D. H.   59-70, 149, 206
Common Wealth Party   66, 99
Communist Party   99
Conservative Party   30-58, 97, 115-121, 134-137, 157-166, 171, 174, 175, 176, 178, 179, 199, 201, 204-5
Cooper, Anthony Ashley, *Earl of Shaftesbury*   14, 78, 153

INDEX

Cooperative Movement 60, 128-129
Cripps, *Sir* Stafford 64, 65, 110
Croker, John Wilson 44
Cromwell, Oliver 14, 16
Cunningham, Patrick 110
Cunningham-Reid, A. S. 110
Curzon, George Nathaniel, *Marquess Curzon of Kedleston* 157, 159, 163, 165

Dalton, Hugh 65, 206
Davies, G. M. L. 109
Disraeli, Benjamin, *Earl of Beaconsfield* v, xi, 27, 28, 29, 31-32, 34, 44, 80, 96, 98, 156, 158, 164
Divine Right of Kings 13-18
Driberg, Tom 110, 128
Durham, *Lord* (see "Lambton, John George")

Eden, Anthony 116
Edward I 5-6
Edward II 6, 7
Edward III 7-9
Edward IV 10
Edward VI 11
Eldon, *Lord* (see "Scott, John")
Elizabeth I (Queen of England) 11-12
Elton, Godfrey, *Lord Elton* vii
Emden, Cecil S. 152-167, 204

Finance of the Parties 134-139
Foot, Dingle 85-91
Foot, Michael 128
Fothergill, Philip 139
Fox, Charles James 24, 26, 79, 86
Fox, W. J. 93
French Revolution 23, 26, 43, 79, 104

Gaitskell, Hugh 85
Gallacher, William 99
General Strike 63, 83
George I vii, viii, 78
George III 20, 21, 22, 24, 26
Gilbert, W. S. 30-31, 38
Gladstone, William Ewart 27, 28, 30-33, 34, 35, 44, 45, 80, 82, 83, 86, 96, 156, 158, 161, 165
Gordon, George Hamilton, *Earl of Aberdeen* 86, 96
Gorst, *Sir* John Eldon 98
Goulburn, Henry 96
Graham, *Sir* James Robert George 96

Graham-Little, *Sir* Ernest 110
Grand Remonstrance 15
Granville, Edgar L. 110
Greenwood, Arthur 65
Grey, Charles, *Earl Grey* 28
Grote, George 93

Haldane, Richard Burdon, *Viscount Haldane* 82
Hamilton, Mary Agnes 130-131, 132-133, 138, 140, 206, 208
Hardie, James Keir 36, 59, 60, 61, 85
Harris, H. Wilson 110
Hartington, *Lord* (see "Cavendish, Spencer Compton")
Harvey, T. Edmund 110
Hawgood, John A. 26-34
Henderson, Arthur 61, 62, 64, 82
Henry II 4
Henry III 4-5
Henry IV 7, 9
Henry V 9
Henry VI 9-10
Henry VII 10
Henry VIII 10-11
Herbert, *Sir* Alan 110-111
Herbert Sidney, *Lord Herbert of Lea* 96
Hoare, Samuel, *Viscount Templewood* 162
Hobbes, Thomas 13
Hobhouse, John Cam, *Lord Broughton de Gyfford* ix, 93
Holmes, *Sir* Leonard viii
Hopkinson, Austin 109, 110
Hore-Belisha, Leslie 110
Hume, Joseph 93
Huskisson, William 27, 28
Hyndman, H. M. 36
Hyde, Edward, *Earl of Clarendon* 14, 17

Independents 101-113
Irish Nationalists x, 31, 32, 33, 35, 61, 94-97

James I 78
James II 78, 103
Jenkinson, Robert Banks, *Earl of Liverpool* 27, 28, 43, 85
John (King of England) 4
John of Gaunt, *Duke of Lancaster* 6-7

Kendal, W. D. 110
King-Hall, Stephen ix, 101-113

Labour Party 31, 35, 59-76, 83, 97, 121-131, 136-139, 159, 163, 164-165, 169-171, 175, 176, 178, 184, 186, 199, 200, 201, 206-208
Lamb, William, *Viscount Melbourne* 28, 79, 155
Lambton, John George, *Earl of Durham* 93
Lancastrians 6-10
Lansbury, George 64, 123
Laski, Harold J. 121, 128, 146, 206
Law, Andrew Bonar 46, 47
Liberal Party 30-39, 60, 77-91, 97, 131-133, 139, 157-165, 174-175, 176, 177-178, 179, 201, 207-208
Liberal-Unionists 31, 33, 35, 39, 46, 82, 97
Liverpool, *Lord* (see "Jenkinson, Robert Banks")
Lloyd George, David, *Earl Lloyd George* 37-41, 47, 61-62, 82, 83, 85, 91
Lindsay, Kenneth 110
Lipson, D. L. 110
Local Government 177-192
Locke, John 78-79
Lords Appellant 9
Lords Ordainers 6

Macaulay, Thomas Babington, *Lord Macaulay* 86
MacDonald, James Ramsay 35, 36, 40, 41, 61, 62, 63, 82
Macdonald, *Sir* Murdoch 110
MacIntyre, Robert 99
McKenzie, Robert T. 114-139
Magna Carta, 1215 4
Maine, *Sir* Henry James Sumner 160
Mann, Tom 36
Marquis, Frederick James, *Lord Woolton* 135, 136, 144
Marx, Karl 36
Mary I 11
Maxwell Fyfe, *Sir* David 115, 117, 119, 134, 135, 136
Melbourne, *Lord* (see "Lamb, William")
Mikardo, Ian 149
Mill, John Stuart 31, 80
Molesworth, *Sir* William 93
Montfort, Simon de, *Earl of Leicester* 5

Morley, John, *Viscount Morley of Blackburn* 82, 85
Morris, William 36
Morrison, Herbert 65, 125, 149, 150, 151
Mosley, *Sir* Oswald 99, 110
Mulvey, Anthony 110

National Political Union 93
Newman, *Sir* Robert 110
New Party 99
Nicholas, Herbert G. 140-151, 204
Nicolson, Harold 102, 204
North, Frederick, *Earl of Guildford (Lord North)* 22, 26, 105, 154
Northcote, Stafford Henry, *Earl of Iddesleigh* 98

O'Connell, Daniel 94
Old Sarum viii*n*
Opposition ix, xi, xii, 12, 198
Organization of the Parties 114-133
Osborne Judgment 61
Ostrogorski, M. 114, 133, 204

Palmerston, *Lord* (see "Temple, Henry John")
Parnell, Charles Stewart 33, 95
Passfield, *Lord* (see "Webb, Sidney")
Peel, *Sir* Robert 25, 27, 28-29, 34, 80, 81, 85, 96, 106, 155, 165
Pemberton Billing, Noel (see "Billing, Noel Pemberton")
Penn, William 152
Petrie, *Sir* Charles 42-49
Phillips, Morgan 148-149
Pickthorn, Kenneth 49-58
Pitt, Thomas viii*n*, 108
Pitt, William 21, 26, 43, 105
Pitt, William, *Earl of Chatham* viii*n*, 21, 154
Primrose, Archibald Philip, *Earl of Rosebery* 33
Pritt, D. N. 128
Privy Council 10
Proportional Representation vi
Provisions of Oxford, 1258 5

Radicals 27, 31, 79, 81, 82, 92-94, 96, 97
Rathbone, Eleanor 110, 111
Redmond, John Edward 95

INDEX

Reform Acts 27, 31, 32, 79, 93, 94, 106, 155, 156
Religious questions 11, 13-18, 26, 78, 79, 94-97
Richard II 6-9
Richard III 10
Roebuck, John Arthur 95, 106
Rosebery, *Lord* (see "Primrose, Archibald Philip")
Ross, J. F. S. 168-176, 204
Russell, *Lord* John 29, 31, 80, 81, 85

St. John, Henry, *Viscount Bolingbroke* 20, 205
Saklatvala, Shapunji 99, 110, 112
Salisbury, *Lord* (see "Cecil, Robert Arthur Talbot Gascoyne")
Salter, *Sir* Arthur 110
Samuel, Herbert, *Viscount Samuel* x, 82, 84, 204, 207
Savile, *Sir* George 105
Schnadhorst, F. 177
Scott, John, *Earl of Eldon* 27
Scrymgeour, Edwin 109, 110
Shaw, George Bernard 36, 59, 207
Sidmouth, *Lord* (see "Addington, Henry")
Shaftesbury, *Lord* (see "Cooper, Anthony Ashley")
Simon, John, *Lord Simon* 83
Slesser, *Sir* Henry 77-84, 207
Smithers, *Sir* Waldron 143
Snowden, Philip 37, 61, 82
Somervell, D. C. x, xi, 35-41
Stewart, Robert, *Marquis of Londonderry* 27
Stokes, R. R. 102

Taff Vale Judgment 37, 60, 82

Tamworth Manifesto 28
Temple, Henry John, *Viscount Palmerston* viii, 29-31, 79, 80, 81, 106
Thomas, *Earl of Lancaster* 6
Thomas, J. H. 63
Tierney, George x
Tories viii, 18, 19-31, 42-44, 78 (and see "Conservative Party")
Trade Disputes Act, 1906 61
Trades Union Movement 35-37, 59, 126-127, 158
Triennial Act, 1641 15

Walpole, Horace viii
Walpole, Robert, *Earl of Orford* 79, 101
Warren, J. H. 177-192
Webb, Sidney, *Lord Passfield* 36, 59, 62, 146, 193, 207
Wellesley, Arthur, *Duke of Wellington* 28, 44, 116
Wellington, *Duke of* (see "Wellesley, Arthur")
Wentworth, Peter 78
Whalley, George Hammond 107
Whigs viii, 13, 18, 19-31, 45, 77-82, 96 (and see "Liberal Party")
Wilberforce, William 79, 105
William the Conqueror 3
William III 18, 78
Williams, Francis 70-76, 207
Williamson, Hugh Ross 13-18
Wolff, *Sir* Henry Drummond Charles 98
Woolton, *Lord* (see "Marquis, Frederick James")

Zinoviev Letter 63